ANTIQUE TRADER BOOKS
20th Century American Ceramics
Price Guide

Edited by
Susan N. Cox

An illustrated comprehensive price guide to all types of 20th century
American ceramics including dinnerwares, artwares and novelites

Antique Trader Books
P.O. Box 1050
Dubuque, IA 52004

STAFF

EDITORIAL
Managing Editor - Books/Price Guides .... Kyle Husfloen
Assistant Editor .... Elizabeth Stephan
Editorial Assistant .... Ruth Willis

ART & PRODUCTION
Art Director .... Jaro Šebek
Book Designer .... Darryl Keck
Design Assistant .... Lynn Bradshaw

ISBN 0-930625-42-0
Library of Congress Catalog Card No. 95-76096

To order additional copies of this book or
other publications listed above, contact:

Antique Trader Publications
P.O. Box 1050
Dubuque, Iowa 52004
1-800-334-7165

TABLE OF CONTENTS

ACKNOWLEDGMENTS

I feel fortunate to live in this era. It is an exciting time (probably more so than any other) when a large number of people are collectors seeking information about their collections. All of us are eager for any bits of information that we can gather from one another. There are more books and newsletters printed on collecting than at any other time in history. Researchers and historians, writers, columnists, photographers, and collectors make up a unique group of talented people who can and do help with the work and understanding that goes into a book.

Two events occurred that permanently sealed my future and led me into a wonderful life-long adventure. In the 1980s, after writing several books, I began publishing the *American Clay Exchange* (ACE) newsletter and opened a one hundred space mall in El Cajon, California. Even though it is impossible to see into the future, ACE has achieved the distinction of being a pioneer publication in the field of American pottery, china and porcelain— anything made of clay. I have met many talented artists, collectors, authors, show promoters and auctioneers who were willing to share what they knew about collecting. Many subscribers I had not talked to for some time were willing to help when they learned I was writing this guide. Forgetful of the time differences, they were never unkind when I called at one o'clock in the morning thinking it was only ten o'clock in the evening. Lucile Henzke, Ft. Worth, Texas, went out of her way to furnish photographs and data and then to repeat the process when all was lost through the post office. Al Nobel, Los Angeles, California is the show promoter for the yearly Pottery Show-Calif. in Glendale, California. It is through his show that I can visit with dedicated, well-known pottery collectors and am able to maintain a grasp on the ever-changing world of collecting.

ACE afforded me the privilege of meeting many artists and establishing longtime friendships with some of them. In 1979 I wrote my first book on Frankoma Pottery; then followed it with two more

Frankoma books. I could not have done that without the help of Joniece and her mother, Grace Lee Frank. They will always hold a special place in my heart. Howard and Ellen Pierce became dear friends whom Bob and I visited often. Sascha Brastoff was a telephone friend who enveloped me with his sense of humor and his flavor for life. Hedi Schoop, Polia Pillin, Dorr Bothwell and Kay Finch added their unique personalities to my life. Just recently, I have talked to Don Winton (Twin-Winton) and learned about his life.

When Main Street Antique Mall dealers heard I was writing this guide, many of them immediately came forward offering their merchandise for photographs, marks or whatever it took to make the book a success. Sandy Williams, Lakeside, California; Gloria Spencer, Phoenix, Arizona; and Tom and Sandra Williams, El Cajon, California were four such dealers. Linda Guffey, who has assisted many writers by supplying photos and information, offered her knowledge and permission to photograph items in her collection. The employees at the mall went beyond what was expected of them to help with questions about marks, colors, descriptions, and so on.

My daughter, Patricia McPherson, helped with the categories, gathered data, did research, and she and Brian Williams, a much-valued employee who has been with the mall since it opened in 1988, efficiently took charge of its operation.

How do I thank my husband, Bob, for giving so much of himself and giving up so much of me in order that I might have the freedom to do what I love best? I suppose it is impossible to adequately thank someone for such a gift.

Lastly, but certainly very important, is Kyle Husfloen, Managing Editor of Antique Trader Books. His patience, knowledge and understanding made all phases of this experience run smoother than it would have without his guidance. With the numerous hats he has to wear and all those pesky loose ends he ties up, Kyle's professionalism never once made me feel he had other, more important, things to do.

PHOTOGRAPHY CREDITS

Robert L. Cox
237 E. Main Street
El Cajon, California 92020

and

Laura L. DeMerchant
P.O. Box 9643
San Diego, California 92169

ON THE COVER: In the upper left is a Red Wing *Bob White* pattern large water pitcher; in the lower left is a Hull Pottery *Wildflower* pattern vase, model No. W-5-6½"; in the lower right is a Franciscan *Desert Rose* quarter pound butter dish.

BACK COVER: Top: a Hall China New York shape *Red Poppy* pattern teapot. Bottom: a Blue Ridge leaf-shaped celery tray in the *Summertime* pattern.

COVER DESIGN: Jaro Sebek

ABINGDON POTTERY COMPANY

The *Abingdon Sanitary Manufacturing Company, Abingdon, Illinois began business in 1908. As a china plumbing fixture company they were operating two plants with three tunnel kilns. In 1934 they began producing art pottery using a white vitreous porcelain. In 1935 Abingdon Sanitary was turning out over 800 pieces daily. Over the years, almost 150 colors were created. Hand decorating on selected items was introduced in 1942. By 1945 the name was changed to Abingdon Potteries, Inc. Two years later controlling stock was purchased by Briggs Manufacturing Company of Detroit, Michigan. Art pottery production ceased in 1950. After that date, the company returned to the production of sanitary products; the art ware was purchased by Haeger Pottery and the molds were sold to Pigeon Forge Pottery. Later, Western Stoneware used some of those molds.*

Abingdon created flowerpots, animals, figures, candleholders, vases, book ends, and lamps. However, it is Abingdon's cookie jars that attract the most attention today. "Little Old Lady," the first cookie jar, was produced

in 1939 followed by the "Fat Boy" in 1940. In 1942 hand-painted decorations were applied to those two jars as well as the 1941 "Hippo" and "Baby" cookie jars.

A blue underglaze mark, "ABINGDON U.S.A.", and also the letter "A" in a diamond were used on practically all the pieces. On some occasions paper labels were used.

Abingdon Shell Line Candleholder

Ashtray, elephant, No. 5. .... **$95.00**

Candleholder, double, Shell line, green, No. 507, 4" h. (ILLUS.) **16.00**

Cookie jar, Bo Peep, No. 694 .... **255.00**

Cookie jar, Choo Choo (ILLUS. top, next page) **165.00**

Cookie jar, Clock (Cookie Time), No. 653 .... **110.00**

Cookie jar, Daisy, No. 677 (ILLUS. center, next page) **55.00**

Cookie jar, Fat Boy, No. 495 ..... **350.00**

Cookie jar, Hippo, No. 549 .... **150.00**

Cookie jar, Humpty Dumpty, decorated, No. 663 .... **275.00**

Cookie jar, Humpty Dumpty, undecorated, No. 663 .... **210.00**

Cookie jar, Jack-in-the-Box, No. 611 .... **300.00**

Cookie jar, Three Bears, No. 969 .... **100.00**

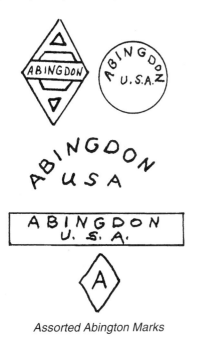

Assorted Abington Marks

Choo Choo Cookie Jar

Vase with Cattails

Daisy Cookie Jar

Model of a penguin, No. 573D,
5" h. **23.00**

Planter, Donkey, No. 669, 7½" h. ... **25.00**

Planter, Ram, No. 671, 4" h. **17.00**

Planter, ½" foot w/flared sides
rising to scroll ends, 10" w., 3" h.
(ILLUS. below)........................... **32.00**

Vase, 7" h., Swirl, No. 512............ **25.00**

Vase, 6¼" h., vertical ribs, three
hand-painted cattails, No. 152
(ILLUS.) **32.00**

Vase, 7" h., star shape, No. 463 .... **18.00**

Vase, wall, 6½" h., open book,
"Cook Book," No. 676D **23.00**

Cookie jar, Pumpkin,
No. 674 .... **450.00**

Figurine, Shepherdess w/Fawn,
No. 3906 .... **225.00**

Model of a goose, leaning, head
down, No. 99 .... **22.00**

Collecting tips: The darker glazes
such as black, brown, dark red, dark blue
and gunmetal are the hard-to-find colors.
For collectors who have patience, consider
an Abingdon Pottery collection of their figurines. Novices are generally not aware
that Abingdon made some beautiful

Planter with Scroll Ends

figurines such as the Fruit Girl, Scarf Dancer and Kneeling Lady which were created in the mid-1930s

Collectors' club: Contact Elaine Westover, 210 Knox Highway, Abingdon, Illinois 61410. Single membership $5, dual membership $6. includes quarterly newsletter.

Museums: Abingdon City Hall and the Abingdon Library, Abingdon, Illinois; club members, Walter and Martha Honigman have donated about 300 Abingdon pieces to the Knoxville Museum, Knoxville, Illinois.

Show and Sale: August yearly event held in Abingdon, Illinois

ALAMO POTTERY

Located in San Antonio, Texas, Alamo Pottery Inc., was in business about seven years from 1944 until 1951. Four entrepreneurs who had finished building the Panama Clay Products Company opened Alamo with the idea of making vitreous china bathroom fixtures. The principal owner was William H. Wallingford. Original molds for the bathroom fixtures proved useless so it was necessary to manufacture art pottery. They produced art pottery from mid-1945 until late 1946 when the manufacturing of bathroom fixtures replaced the art pottery department. In 1951, the Universal-Rundle Corporation purchased the company. Alamo Pottery was no longer in existence but because of the large amount of pottery remaining in San Antonio, sales continued for a few years.

A variety of large items such as urns, umbrella stands, sand jars and vases was produced. Utilitarian pitchers, bowls and ashtrays as well as hand-cast tableware resembling Fiesta colors were also created.

While not all Alamo Pottery is marked, especially the smaller items, most pieces have a backstamp. This backstamp is an outline of the Alamo and "Alamo Pottery Inc., Vitreous China, San Antonio, Texas" stamped in dark blue. In some instances this mark will be found stamped in black. Sometimes only small labels were used.

Alamo Marks

Ashtray, round w/three cigarette rests... **$15.00**

Flowerpot, round w/"waves" pattern flowing from bottom left to top right, 11" d., 12" h. **20.00**

Planter, oval, scalloped rim center at top on each side, white, 8" d., 2" h. (ILLUS.) **22.00**

Planter, swan, 6½" h. **34.00**

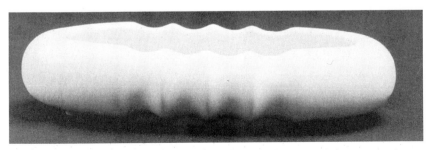

Alamo Oval Planter

Cone-shaped Vase

Vase with Flared Sides

Pitcher, hexagon, w/two
  hexagonal shaped insets,
  2 qt. **35.00**

Vase, 4" h., squatty bulbous body
  w/safety pin through it **26.00**

Vase, 5" h., cone-shaped folds
  rising to a scalloped rim, No.
  737 (ILLUS. above, left) **50.00**

Ruffled Edge Vase

Vase, 5 ¾" h., ruffled edge, rough
  texture, blue/green, black
  mark, No. 721 (ILLUS.) **55.00**

Vase, 6" h., wide angled handles,
  round body, man playing
  instrument w/tree nearby;
  reverse, grapes & vines motif..... **43.00**

Vase, 9" h., slightly flared rim,
  vertical ribs, white inside,
  turquoise outside **45.00**

Vase, 10" h., flared sides, blue
  outside, white inside (ILLUS.)..... **65.00**

  Collecting tips: Two men who worked
at Alamo Pottery left there to work for
Gilmer Pottery. They created similar Alamo
designs for the Gilmer company. It is
important to study the Alamo lines so as
not to confuse them with Gilmer. Until you
can determine the differences, buy only
marked pieces. Sometime in the mid-
1970s, Hall China Company purchased
Gilmer Pottery.

  Art pottery such as vases with interesting motifs and models of swans have a
higher monetary value than Alamo's general garden or utilitarian pieces.

AMERICAN ART CLAY COMPANY, INC.

*Indianapolis, Indiana is the home of the
American Art Clay Company, Inc. Begun in
1919 by Ted O. Philpott, the company still
operates at 4717 West Sixteenth Street.*

Today, they manufacture and distribute kilns, clays, glazes, wheels, molds, pottery and metal enameling supplies. However, it is the art pottery produced by this company in the 1930s that is gaining momentum with collectors. Among items created were lamp bases, sculptures and vases with a white vitreous body. The logo for this company is AMACO. Their marking system in the 1930s was unique and leaves no doubt as to the date an item was created.

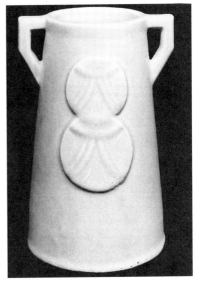

Handled Vase with Medallions

Date code

Ⓛ	**1931**
Ⓧ	**1932**
Ⓨ	**1933**
▣	**1934**
⦂⦂	**1935**
⑥	**1936**
⑦	**1937**

Marks and Date List

Vase, 6" h., two handles, large, round medallion slightly overlapping smaller medallion above it, Lorraine Lasly, finisher, No. 37 (ILLUS.) **$55.00**

Vase, 6" h., one inch foot w/bulbous body tapering gently to a flared rim, yellow & blue w/gold 'flecks' **40.00**

Vase, 7½" h., plain cylinder shape, maroon **45.00**

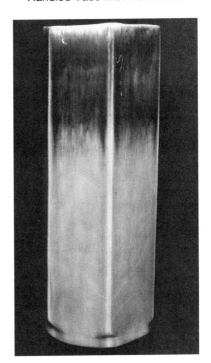

Six-sided Vase

Vase, 12" h., 4½" w., six-sided slender form w/dark brown streaky glaze at top above streaky blue-green glaze (ILLUS.) **55.00**

References: "Amaco Marking System" by Willard Heiss, *American Clay Exchange*, August 30, 1987.

AMERICAN BISQUE COMPANY

The American Bisque Company got its start in Williamstown, West Virginia in 1919 predominately producing Kewpie doll heads made famous by Rose O'Neill. By 1937, cookie jars were being made and are now eagerly sought by collectors. The company is most noted for its production of cookie jars, perhaps being second only to the McCoy Pottery Company. Very few American Bisque cookie jars will be found in a solid color. An airbrushing technique was used and most decorations were elaborately done.

Only a few cookie jars have paper labels; instead most will show "U.S.A." and possibly a number. However, one almost certain method to American Bisque identification is the wedges on the bottoms of their products.

Sequoia Ware was a trademark indicating that the items were sold in gift shops and Berkeley, another trademark, indicated those items were sold in chain stores. Both lines were introduced in the 1960s and had bright, modern colors with free-flowing shapes.

Collectors can find an incised mark that shows "A. B. Co." or "Design Patent/A.B. Co." The company closed in 1982.

American Bisque Company Marks

Bank, Chicken Feed, 4½" h. **$30.00**

Bank, Little Audrey, 8¼" h. **785.00**

Bank, Popeye, 7" h. **460.00**

Cookie jar, Barrel **35.00**

Cookie jar, Bear, girl **65.00**

Cookie jar, Bear, Teddy w/feet together **260.00**

Cookie jar, Bear w/cap **110.00**

Cookie jar, Bell w/words 'Ring for cookies' **50.00**

Cookie jar, Blackboard Clown .. **300.00**

Cookie jar, Blackboard Girl **345.00**

Cookie jar, Blackboard Hobo **300.00**

Cookie jar, Carousel **100.00**

Cookie jar, Casper the Friendly Ghost, 13½" h. **850.00**
(Caution: Reproduced jars measure 11½" h.)

Cookie jar, Cat in Basket **58.00**

Cookie jar, Cat w/tail handle **85.00**

Cookie jar, Cheerleaders, triangular shape, without flasher **225.00**

Cookie jar, Cheerleaders, triangular shape, w/flasher **330.00**

Cookie jar, Chef **200.00**

Cookie jar, Chick w/tam **55.00**

Cookie jar, Chick w/vest **80.00**

Cookie jar, Collegiate Owl **90.00**

Cookie jar, Cookie Time Clock **145.00**

Cookie jar, Cookie Truck, 11½" h. **80.00**

Cookie jar, Cowboy Boots **210.00**

Cookie jar, Davy Crockett in woods **980.00**

Cookie jar, Dino w/golf bag **1,500.00**
(Caution: This jar is being reproduced)

Cookie jar, Dog in Basket **80.00**

Cookie jar, Donkey Milk Wagon **85.00**

Cookie jar, Elephant w/Baseball Cap **145.00**

Cookie jar, Elephant w/Hands in Pockets **160.00**

Cookie jar, Elephant w/Sailor Hat **125.00**

Cookie jar, Feed sack **180.00**

Cookie jar, Fred Flintstone **1,400.00**

Cookie jar, Flintstone's Rubbles
House **1,000.00**

Cookie jar, Granny **150.00**

Cookie jar, Granny w/gold trim **175.00**

Cookie jar, Jack-in-the-box **265.00**

Cookie jar, Kids Watching TV
w/flasher, Sandman Cookies **395.00**

Cookie jar, Kittens on Beehive **55.00**

Cookie jar, Kittens w/yarn **125.00**

Cookie jar, Lamb w/paws in
pockets **175.00**

Cookie jar, Lantern **155.00**

Cookie jar, Majorette **450.00**

Cookie jar, Moon Rocket,
"Cookies Out Of This World" **290.00**
*(Caution: Do not confuse w/the
Spaceship cookie jar)*

Cookie jar, Pinky Lee **600.00**

Cookie jar, Poodle **100.00**

Cookie jar, Popeye **1,200.00**
(Caution: This jar is being reproduced)

*Rabbit In Basket Cookie Jar
(Front and Back)*

Cookie jar, Rabbit in Basket
(ILLUS.) **55.00**

Cookie jar, Rabbit in Hat (Magic
Bunny) **95.00**

Cookie jar, Recipe Jar,
hexagonal **135.00**

Cookie jar, Saddle without
blackboard **270.00**

Cookie jar, Sea Bag **190.00**

Cookie jar, Seal on Igloo **310.00**

Cookie jar, Spaceship
w/Spaceman, "Cookies out of
this world" **795.00**
*(Caution: Do not confuse w/Moon
Rocket cookie jar)*

Cookie jar, Toothache Dog **695.00**

Cookie jar, Treasure Chest, lid
slightly open **200.00**

Cookie jar, Umbrella Kids
(Sweethearts) **375.00**

Cookie jar, Water Bucket w/ladle
on lid **140.00**

Cookie jar, Wilma on
Telephone **1,400.00**

Lamp base, Baseball Boy sitting
atop baseball w/bat over
shoulder, 7½" h. **100.00**

Flower Painted Pitcher

Pitcher, milk, 6¼" h., cold painted
blue or red flowers
(ILLUS.) **28.00**

Donkey Planter

Lamb Figural Planter

Paddle Wheel Boat Planter

Swirl Teapot

Planter, figural, model of a
donkey in front of hay, "Bashful
Donkey," 4" l., 5¼" h. (ILLUS.
bottom, previous page).............. **13.00**

Planter, figural, model of a lamb,
yellow w/red bow around neck,
11½" l., 6" h., (ILLUS.)................ **33.00**

Planter, figural, model of a
paddle wheel boat,
9½" l., 4¼" h. (ILLUS.)................ **25.00**

Teapot, swirl, pale blue bottom,
white lid, 6" h. (ILLUS.).............. **35.00**

Collecting tips: Aside from American
Bisque cookie jars, other items produced by
this company are inexpensive. This is probably because buyers are wary since the
pieces are unmarked. Study them carefully
and learn the 'wedge' marks so that you can
readily ascertain if you have an American
Bisque piece. Now is the time to buy as
these products should increase substantially.

Suggested Reading: *American
Bisque, A Collector's Guide with Prices* by
Mary Jane Giacomini, Schiffer Publishing
Ltd., 1994

AMERICAN HAVILAND

*David Haviland was an importer of fine
English china and it was he who gave
Limoges, France the successful opportunity
of becoming a well-known ceramic center.
Theodore Haviland, David's son, continued
with the Haviland traditions of creating
fine china until his death in 1920. It was
Theodore's son, William David, who
bought out the French heirs and established
headquarters in the United States. Use care
not to confuse the china marked with the
single word 'Limoges' with that of
Haviland & Co., Limoges. The former was
made by a lesser known factory located in
Limoges, France.*

*From 1936 to 1958, Shenango Pottery
Company made china for Theodore Haviland
Company of France. Originally, the
backstamp was "Theodore Haviland, New
York." Later, "Made in America" was added.
Patterns included Apple Blossom, Avalon,
Cambridge, Gotham, Springtime and Wilton.*

Theodore Haviland Mark

Springtime Plate

Avalon Platter

Bowl, soup, Rosalinde patt. $22.00

Bowl, vegetable, 9¾" l., oval,
Apple Blossom patt. 38.00

Cup & saucer, Avalon patt........... 60.00

Cup & saucer, Gotham patt......... 45.00

Cup & saucer, Shelton patt. 58.00

Cup & saucer, Springtime patt. 65.00

Creamer & cov. sugar bowl,
Apple Blossom patt., pr. 45.00

Creamer & cov. sugar bowl,
Avalon patt., pr. 125.00

Creamer & cov. sugar bowl,
Regents Park Camellia patt., pr... 95.00

Creamer & cov. sugar bowl,
Rosalinde patt., pr. 95.00

Gravy boat, Gotham patt. 55.00

Plate, 8 ¾" d., Clifton patt............. 20.00

Plate, 10½" d., Apple Blossom
patt. 12.00

Plate, 10 ¾" d., Springtime patt.
(ILLUS.) 15.00

Platter, 11½" d., Springtime
patt. 35.00

Platter, 16½" l. Avalon patt.,
w/well at one end (ILLUS.) 85.00

References: "Haviland-Since 1842 It's Meant Quality" by Eleanor Hoppe, *Antiques USA* May-June 1981; "Haviland: China Supreme" by Ruth Beddie, *The Antique Trader Weekly,* March 26, 1980

AUTUMN LEAF
See Hall China Company

AMERICAN ART POTTERIES
See Morton Potteries

BATCHELDER, E. A.

Ernest Allen Batchelder began his press method tile production in 1910 in Pasadena, California. His goal was that no two tiles would be the same. Early tiles were brown with a blue glaze rubbed into the indentations of oak leaves and trees, birds and animals. Within two years larger quarters were needed for his expanding business so Batchelder moved to another site in Pasadena. Other changes took place: Frederick Brown became a partner and Emma and Charles Ingels were master mold makers. By 1916, with the business still growing rapidly, Batchelder took on another partner named Lucian Wilson and the operation was moved to Los Angeles, California. It was then that the Batchelder-Wilson Company began producing—in addition to glazed faience tiles—pavers, fountains, book ends, large garden-variety pots, corbels, moldings and facings for fireplaces. William Manker, hired in 1926, has been credited with many of the Batchelder-Wilson designs.

When the California construction craze was over and the effects of the Depression were felt, Batchelder-Wilson declared bankruptcy in 1932. Later, the stock and plant were sold to the Bauer Pottery Company.

In 1936 Batchelder started a business in Pasadena, calling it Batchelder Ceramics. Unlike the tile business, these Batchelder products were delicate, thin vases and bowls, many of which had Chinese forms. Interior glazes were, in many instances, different colors than the exterior. Even though the business was on a smaller scale than Batchelder's tile business, it was a success. Batchelder retired in 1951 and died in 1957.

G-256

Batchelder

Made in U.S.A.

64

EA Batchelder Pasadena

Various Marks

Book ends, figure of a Monk seated, knees bent, No. 256, 4½" h., pr. **$310.00**

Book ends, figures of a Dutch boy & Dutch girl, seated, No. 201, 4 ¾" h., pr. **295.00**

Bowl, 4" l., 5" h., octagonal sides, blue-grey **95.00**

Bowl, 9" d., round, grey interior, maroon exterior, No. 131 .... **75.00**

Bowl, 10" l., 2" h., oval, green **85.00**

Bowl, 11" d., 2" h., oval, grey interior, maroon exterior, No. 231 .... **100.00**

Bowl, 13½" d., yellow interior, light green exterior, No. 69 (ILLUS.) **215.00**

Model of a frog, sitting, round base, mouth open, 4" h. **125.00**

Pot, garden, peacocks under tree branches, 17" d., 14" h. **225.00**

Lion Walking Tile

Tile, lion walking, unglazed w/blue slip, 3 ¾" sq. (ILLUS.).... **125.00**

Tile, horse & rider, blue slip, 4" sq. **100.00**

Large Bathelder Bowl

Lavender Vase

Vase, 3½" h., 4¼" d., lavender exterior, aqua interior,¼" round foot w/paneled sides flaring slightly, marked "Kinneloa Kiln E. A. Batchelder," No. 44 (ILLUS.).. **245.00**

Vase, 7" h., square, straight sides, grey **65.00**

Vase, 10" h., pedestal base w/low baluster rising to a stick neck w/flared rim **145.00**

References: "Muckenthaler exhibits Batchelder works" by Doug Scott, *American Clay Exchange*, August 15, 1986; "Sincerity of Purpose: The Work of Ernest Batchelder" by Alice Stone, *American Clay Exchange*, November 1982

BAUER POTTERY

A talented entrepreneur, John Andrew Bauer, moved his Paducah, Kentucky stoneware business to Los Angeles, California in 1909. Bauer has been credited with the introduction of the mix-and-match variety of dinnerware in bright, eye-appealing colors. During Bauer Pottery's history many talented artists and business-minded people were hired. Among them were: Louis Ipsen, designer; Matt Carlton, a creative potter; Victor Houser, ceramic engineer; and designers and modelers, Fred Johnson, Ray Murray and Tracy Irwin.

John Bauer died in 1922 and his daughter, Eva, and her husband, Watson Bockman, took charge of the business. They, along with other partners and Bauer employees, have been credited with bringing the pottery into an age where it rivaled even the best of dinnerware producing companies. In the early 1950s, Herb Brusche, son-in-law of Watson and Eva Bockman, created the popular "Contempo" and "Al Fresco" lines. These items were marked with the Brusche name.

Victor Houser developed various opaque glazes in the 1930s which enabled Louis Ipsen to model a dinnerware line, the forerunner to their "Ring" pattern, which was introduced in 1932.

Cal-Art pottery was an early line (mid-1930s) which included in-mold marked flower bowls, vases, candlesticks, models of dogs, hippos and swans.

In the 1950s, Bauer Pottery, like so many companies during that decade, suffered financial losses and their problems were compounded by management disagreements and a strike. Bauer Pottery closed in 1962.

Assorted Bauer Marks

Oblong La Linda Butter Dish

Ashtray, model of a skillet w/two cigarette rests, orange glaze, inside bottom has "Bauer Pottery" w/oil jar outline **$80.00**

Ashtray with cigarette rests in each corner, 3" sq. **50.00**

Ashtrays, in metal holder, set of 4, 5 pcs. **260.00**

Bowl, flower, 8" d., 1½" h., green, Cal-Art line................................. **35.00**

Monterey Fruit Bowl

Bowl, fruit, 6" d., Monterey patt., turquoise (ILLUS.) **18.00**

Bowl, fruit, 6" d., Monterey patt., white **25.00**

Butter dish, oblong, La Linda patt., ivory (ILLUS.) **65.00**

Butter dish, round, Monterey Moderne patt., pink..................... **45.00**

Butter pat/ashtray, Ring patt., royal blue, 2" d.......................... **50.00**

Canister w/wooden lid, oval, strawberry decoration, 8" w., 8" h. **155.00**

Ring Pattern Casserole

Casserole, cov., Ring patt., orange/red, 9 ¾" d., 4" h., (ILLUS.) **65.00**

Churn, marked on front interior an "orange", J. A. Bauer Pottery Co., manufacturers Bockmon's Quality Pottery and Tile Los Angeles, 2 gal. **325.00**

Cookie jar, cov., swirl pattern w/"cookies" on lid, No. 823 .... **65.00**

Cookie jar, cov., Ring-Ware patt., yellow **210.00**

No. 97 Pickle Dish

Monterey Pattern Platter

Cup & saucer, El Chico line **60.00**

Model of a hippopotamus,
standing, open mouth, Cal-Art
line, satin matte white,
4½" l., 3¼" h. **175.00**

Model of a Scottie dog, seated,
Cal-Art line, satin matte white, ,
4½" l., 4" h. **200.00**

Model of a swan, open back,
Cal-Art line, white, 6½" l. **75.00**

Oil jar, turquoise, No. 129, 20" h.
(ILLUS. top following page) **825.00**

Pickle dish, yellow, No. 97,
6½" l. (ILLUS.) **45.00**

Platter, 12" l., oval, Monterey
patt., blue.................................... **35.00**

Platter, 18" l., Monterey patt.,
turquoise (ILLUS.) **75.00**

Salt & pepper shakers, salt
shaker, strawberry decoration,
"Salt thy food to please but not
to spoil" and the pepper,
"Pepper in excess stingeth thy
tongue," 6" h., pr........................ **85.00**

No. 129 Oil Jar

Cal-Art Vase

Vase, 8" h., Cal-Art line, No. 502, green (ILLUS.) **55.00**

Collecting tip: In 1986, a new company was producing earthenware using the name "Bauer." However, most items are marked with the word Bauer in script and in a color to match the decorated design color.

References: "Bauer Briefs" by Vicki Harman, *American Clay Exchange,* May 1982 and March 1983

BLUE & WHITE STONEWARE

Almost every American pottery company dabbled in producing some form of blue and white stoneware. To collect all the items with the varied embossed decorations would be an endless hobby. This Americana, made from the turn of the century until the mid-1930s, included pitchers, butter crocks, plates, rolling pins, soap dishes, salt crocks and many other items which were decorated in-mold with animals, flowers, children, fruits, birds and so on.

Brush-McCoy, Burley Winter, Roseville and Uhl are just a few companies who produced blue and white stoneware; however, only a few pieces will be found marked with a company name.

Companies such as dairies, banks, restaurants, and so forth commissioned stoneware companies to put their advertising on selected blue and white pieces to give to their customers. Today, these items are highly prized by collectors.

Since most of the items were utile they were used daily in many households and show some signs of age and normal wear. This should not detract from their value. However, it is wise to carefully consider if you want to buy pieces with large chips or hairlines. The scarcity of an item should help with this consideration.

Reproductions are plentiful in some items and patterns, particularly cow pitchers. This should not hinder a novice collector from purchasing blue and white stoneware. Reproductions are easily spotted as the glaze is a vivid blue and the items are lighter weight than the authentic pieces.

Baker, cov., Chain Link patt., downward curved handles, flat button finial, unglazed rims, 6" d., 5 ¾" h. w/lid **$145.00**

Barrel, cov., miniature, made by Uhl Pottery Co., Huntington, Indiana, 2" d., 4¼" h. (ILLUS. top next page) **80.00**

Bowl, 5" d., 2½" h., embossed Wedding Ring patt., dark blue trim **100.00**

Minature Barrel

Bowl, 6½" d., 3½" h., embossed
Flying Bird patt. **295.00**

Bowl, 7" d., 2½" h., Venetian
patt., made by Roseville Pottery
Co., Roseville, Ohio, (same as
Reverse Pyramids w/Reverse
Picket Fence) w/honeycomb
below pyramids (ILLUS.) **265.00**

Bowl, 7½" d., 5" h., embossed
Flying Bird patt. **225.00**

Bowl, 8" d., 4½" h., Chain Link
patt., hard to find size **110.00**

Bowl, 8" d., 4" h., embossed
Wedding Ring patt. **150.00**

Bowl, 9½" d., 5" h., embossed
Apricots w/Honeycomb patt...... **195.00**

Bowl, 9½" d., 4½" h., embossed
Gadroon Arches patt. **155.00**

Bowl, 9½" d., 5" h., embossed
Currants & Diamonds patt.
w/piecrust rim **150.00**

Bowl, 10" d., 5" h., embossed
Apricots w/Honeycomb patt...... **145.00**

Bowl, 10½" d., 5¼" h.,
embossed Reverse Pyramids
w/Reverse Picket Fence patt.,
Fence on rim collar, Pyramids
below rim collar, unglazed rim
& below collar, made by
Ruckels Stoneware Company,
Monmouth, Illinois
(ILLUS.) **200.00**

*Venetian Pattern
Bowl*

*Reverse Pyramids
with Reverse
Picket Fence bowl*

Butter Crock with Scalloped Medallions

Butter crock, original cover & bail, embossed Butterfly patt., w/four scalloped medallions, 4½" d., 3 ¾" h. (ILLUS.)............ **250.00**

Butter crock, original cover & bail, embossed Cows & Fence patt., 7¼" d., 5" h. **225.00**

Cookie jar, cov., embossed Flying Bird patt., 6 ¾" d., 9" h. ... **675.00**

Cuspidor with Buttterflies

Cuspidor, embossed Butterflies patt., 6" h. (ILLUS.).................. **210.00**

Grease jar, cov., round, embossed Flying Bird patt., 4½" h. **625.00**

Milk crock, embossed Daisy & Lattice patt., 10" d., 5" h. **210.00**

Milk crock, embossed Lovebirds patt., bail handle & wooden grip, 9" d., 5½" h. **155.00**

Mug, embossed Basketweave & Flower patt., 3" d., 5" h. **215.00**

Mug, embossed Flying Bird patt., 3" d., 4½" h. **225.00**

Windy City Mug

Mug, embossed Windy City patt. (Fannie Flagg), Robinson Clay Pottery Co., Akron, Ohio, no building cornerstones as are on the pitcher, branch handle, bottom shows "M. Friedman & Co. 237 Post St., San Francisco The biggest furniture house on the Pacific Coast," 5½" h. (ILLUS.) **225.00**

Pickle crock, cov., Blue Band patt. w/wire bail handle & wooden grip, lid w/flat button knob, 9" d., 12" h. **225.00**

Loop Pattern Pie Plate

Pie plate, Loop patt., plain
bottom, unglazed rim & under
collar, 8" d. (ILLUS.) **110.00**

Cattails Pitcher

Chain Link Pitcher

Pitcher, 5" h., Chain Link patt.,
solid dark blue (ILLUS.) **85.00**

Pitcher, 5 ¾" h., bulbous,
embossed Cattails patt.,
(ILLUS.) **165.00**

Pitcher, 7" h., 7" d., embossed
Grape Cluster on Trellis patt.,
light or dark blue exterior, Uhl
Pottery Co, Huntington,
Indiana..................................... **185.00**

Pitcher, 7 ¾" h., 6½" d.,
embossed Peacock patt. **475.00**

Pitcher, 8" h., 6" d., embossed
Grape Cluster in Shield patt. **235.00**

Pitcher, 8" h., 6" d., embossed
Grape w/Rickrack patt.,
Northstar Stoneware Co., Red
Wing, Minnesota....................... **175.00**

Leaping Deer Pitcher

Pitcher, 8" h., 6" d., embossed
Leaping Deer patt., deer on both
sides (ILLUS.)............................ **200.00**

Avenue of Trees Pitcher

Pitcher, 8" h., 7 ¾" d., embossed
Avenue of Trees patt., slightly
inward curve on base & rim, any
blue & white combination,
Brush-McCoy Pottery Co.
(ILLUS.) **210.00**

Pitcher, 8½" h., 5½" d.,
embossed Lovebirds patt. **425.00**

Cows Pattern Pitcher

Pitcher, 8½" h., 6" d., embossed
Cows patt. (ILLUS.) **275.00**

Pitcher, 8½" h., embossed Windy
City (Fannie Flagg) patt. (ILLUS.
front & reverse)......................... **455.00**

Fanny Flagg Pitcher (Front and Reverse)

Pitcher, 9" h., 5½" d., embossed
Iris patt., Brush-McCoy Pottery
Co. **225.00**

Pitcher, 9" h., 6" d., embossed
Flying Bird patt. **750.00**

Pitcher, 9" h., 6" d., embossed
Wild Rose patt., arc & diamond
band at bottom, two roses in
center, flower band at top, beaded
handle (ILLUS. next page).......... **225.00**

Pitcher, 9" h., 6" d., embossed
Windmill & Bush patt., Brush-
McCoy Pottery Co. **240.00**

Pitcher, 9" h., 6" d., embossed
Dutch Children w/Windmill patt.,
Brush-McCoy Pottery Co.
(ILLUS. next page) **235.00**

Wild Rose Pitcher

Cherries and Leaves Pitcher

Dutch Children Pitcher

Pitcher, 9" h., 6½" d., embossed Stag & Pine Trees patt. **300.00**

Pitcher, 9" h., 7" d., embossed Bluebirds patt. **260.00**

Pitcher, 9" h., 7" d., embossed Butterfly patt. **260.00**

Pitcher, 9" h., 7" d., embossed Native American Good Luck Sign patt. **265.00**

Pitcher, 9½" h., 5½" d., embossed Grape w/Leaf Band patt., blue & white or light or dark blue exterior, Uhl Pottery Co., Huntington, Indiana........... **185.00**

Pitcher, 9½" h., 6" d., embossed Cherries & Leaves patt. at top & bottom edges, plain center, Red Wing Union Stoneware Co., Red Wing, Minnesota **295.00**

Pitcher, 9½" h., 6" d., embossed Cherries & Leaves patt. at top & bottom edges, plain center w/advertising, Red Wing Union Stoneware Co., Red Wing, Minnesota (ILLUS.) **350.00**

Pitcher, 9½" h., 7½" d., embossed Grape Cluster on Trellis patt., light or dark blue exterior, Uhl Pottery Co., Huntingon, Indiana **225.00**

Plate, 8" d., embossed Rose patt., overall leaves & stems w/irregular scrolls and flower rim **125.00**

Salt box w/original cover, hanging-type, embossed Apricot patt., 5 ¾" d., 5" h. **215.00**

Salt box w/original cover, hanging-type, embossed Butterfly patt., 5 ¾" d., 5 ¾" h... **195.00**

Salt box w/original cover, hanging-type, embossed Daisy on Snowflakes patt., 6½" d., 6" h. (ILLUS. top next page) **225.00**

Daisy on Snowflake Salt Box

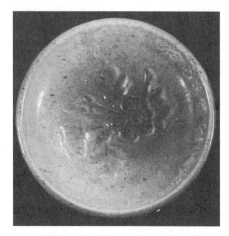

Embossed Flower Soap Dish

Soap dish, embossed Cat's
head, 3 ¾" d., ¾" h. (ILLUS.
bottom right) **155.00**

Soap dish, embossed Lion's
head, 3 ¾" d., ¾" h. (ILLUS.
bottom left) **155.00**

Soap dish, embossed Flower
Cluster w/Fishscale patt.,
4½" d., ¾" h. (ILLUS.).............. **135.00**

Tobacco jar w/original cover,
embossed Hunting patt., deer &
two elk on lid, recessed button
finial, two pound size, 6 ¾" d.,
4¾" h. (ILLUS.) **425.00**

Hunting Pattern Tobacco Jar

Embossed Cat and Lion Heads Soap Dishes

References: *Blue & White Stoneware* by Kathryn McNerney, Collector Books, 1981; *Blue and White Pottery* by Mary Joseph & Edith Harbin, Privately printed, 1973; "Blue and White Stoneware" by Susan N. Cox, *American Clay Exchange*, October 1983; Quartzsite...Not Just Rocks by Susan N. Cox, *American Clay Exchange*, March 1984.

BLUE RIDGE

Various Blue Ridge Marks

Clinchfield Pottery began in 1917 in Erwin, Tennessee. E. J. (Ted) Owen was its founder. It was so named because of the Carolina, Clinchfield and Ohio Railroad. Later, Clinchfield became known as Southern Potteries, Inc.

In the early 1920s, Charles W. Foreman purchased the plant and it was he who has been credited with revolutionizing the company's output when he developed the Blue Ridge dinnerware. It was an underglaze line hand-painted by women from the surrounding area. So popular was this ware that it came in a large assortment of shapes (approximately twelve basic ones) and over 2,000 different patterns. The colors are exciting and vivid. Floral arrangements, fruits of all kinds, animals and human figures are but a few of the charming aspects of this dinnerware. Childrens' pieces are whimsically creative with such characters as Humpty Dumpty, bunnies, mice, ducks, elephants and pigs. The Square Dance pattern is a popular line for today's Western memorabilia collectors. Production continued for this dinnerware until the plant closed in 1957.

Tulips Pattern Ashtray

Ashtray, advertising, two cigarette rests, Tulips patt., "Compliments of Southern Potteries, Inc., Erwin, Tenn." (ILLUS.) **$65.00**

Bonbon, flat shell shape, Chintz patt. **60.00**

Bonbon, flat shell shape, French Peasant patt. **110.00**

Bowl, 6" d., cereal, Sunbright patt. **9.00**

Bowl, 9" d., deep shell (ILLUS. top, next page) **55.00**

Cake lifter, Leaf patt. **30.00**

Cake plate, Pomona patt., 12¼" d. **50.00**

Candy box, cov., round Peacock patt., 6" d. **75.00**

Deep Shell Bowl

Celery dish, leaf-shaped, Rose
of Sharon patt. **55.00**

Celery dish, leaf-shaped, Swiss
Dancers patt. **60.00**

Cup & saucer, demitasse, Muriel
patt. (ILLUS. bottom right) **38.00**

Cup & saucer, demitasse, Spring
Bouquet patt. **35.00**

Cup & saucer, demitasse,
Sunfire patt. (ILLUS. left) **38.00**

Cup & saucer, Plume patt. **8.00**

Cup & saucer, Thistle patt. **9.00**

Mug, child's **40.00**

Pitcher, 5½" h., figural Chick,
Floral patt. (ILLUS.) **110.00**

Pitcher, 6¼" h., Pansy Trio patt.
(ILLUS. front & reverse, next page) ... **65.00**

Pitcher, 7½" h., Jane patt. **105.00**

Plate, 6" d., Belle Haven patt. **6.00**

Plate, 6" d., Briar Patch patt. **7.00**

Plate, 6" d., Heirloom patt. **6.00**

Chick Floral Pattern Pitcher

Plate, 6" d., Tropical patt. **6.00**

Plate, 6" d., Tulip Trio patt. **7.00**

Fruit Punch Pattern Plate

Plate, 6" sq., Fruit Punch patt.
(ILLUS.) **36.00**

Sunfire Cup & Saucer and Muriel Cup & Saucer

Pansy Trio Pattern (Front and Back)

Nove Rose Pattern Plate

Plate, 6" sq., Nove Rose patt.
(ILLUS. left, middle).................. **40.00**

Plate, 6" sq., Poinsettia patt.
(ILLUS. left, bottom) **35.00**

Plate, 6" sq., Violet patt. **40.00**

Plate, 7" d., Fruit Crunch patt. **16.00**

Wild Cherry Pattern

Plate, 7" d., Wild Cherry patt.
(ILLUS.) **10.00**

Plate, 9½" d., Christmas Tree
patt. **15.00**

Plate, 10" d., Chrysanthemum
patt. (ILLUS. top left, next page)... **15.00**

Poinsettia Pattern Plate

Chrysanthemum Pattern Plate

Mountain Ivy Pattern Plate

Plate, 10" d., Farmer Takes A
Wife patt. **25.00**

Plate, 10" d., French Peasant
patt. **55.00**

Plate, 10" d., Mountain Ivy patt.
(ILLUS. top, right) **12.00**

Plate, 10" d., Red Barn patt. **22.00**

Salt & pepper shakers, figural
chickens, model of hen &
rooster, hen 4" h., rooster
4 ¾" h., pr. **120.00**

Salt & pepper shakers, figural
mallards, model of male &
female, male 4" h., female
3½" h., pr. **200.00**

Salt & pepper shakers, marked
Charm House, 4" h., pr. **45.00**

Smoking set: cov. cigarette box
& four ashtrays; Violet patt.,
5 pcs. **145.00**

Snack plate w/cup, Square
Dance patt., novelty set,
2 pcs. **50.00**

Teapot, cov., demitasse,
Mountain Cherry patt. **98.00**

Teapot, cov., Delta Daisy patt.,
Snub-nose shape **115.00**

Teapot, cov., Sunflower patt.,
Piecrust shape........................... **95.00**

Tidbit tray, 3-tier, center handle,
Magnolia patt. **53.00**

Boot Vase with Flowers

Vase, model of a boot, any
pattern, 8" h. (ILLUS.)................. **95.00**

Vegetable bowl, open, oval,
French Peasant patt., 9" d. **69.00**

Collecting tips: See the section on
Technical Porcelain and Chinaware
Company (TEPCO) for a mark very similar
to one used by Blue Ridge. The French
Peasant pattern is highly collectible with
values reflecting that so start your collection with other patterns or shapes you like.
There is a great deal of printed information
on Blue Ridge so identifying, putting values
on various items and patterns and learning
about the history of the company is not difficult and will pay off in the long run.

References: *Dishes, What Else? Blue Ridge of Course!* privately printed 1983; *Southern Potteries, Inc. Blue Ridge Dinnerware, Revised 3rd Edition* by Betty Newbound, Collector Books 1989, values updated 1993

Collectors' Club: Blue Ridge Collectors' Club, Phyllis Ledford, 245 Seater Road, Erwin, Tennessee 37650-3295. Dues $5.00

Newsletter: National Blue Ridge Newsletter, Norma Lilly, 144 Highland Drive, Blountville, Tennessee 37617-5404

Museum: Unicoi Heritage Museum, Erwin, Tennessee

Bird Model Flower Holder

BORU, SORCHA

Born in San Francisco, California in 1906, Claire Stewart became known mostly for her sculpture work during the 1930s. She graduated from the University of California at Berkeley. She was a member of the Allied Arts Guild of Menlo Park, California and it was there, from 1932 until 1938, that she maintained a studio and sales shop.

Her professional name was Sorcha Boru and from 1938 until 1955 she and her husband, Ellsworth Stewart, had a ceramics business in San Carlos, California.

Besides sculpture, Boru created bowls, pitchers, salt and pepper shakers, figurines and wall pockets.

Production work was mostly incised 'S. B. C.' (Sorcha Boru Ceramics) although many pieces are being found with her full professional name incised underglaze and usually with a copyright symbol.

Sorcha Boru Mark

Figure of an angel holding small Christmas tree, white w/green tree, 6" h. **$110.00**

Flower holder, figural, model of a bird, white w/unglazed open mouth, flowers around base, full signature mark, 2½" l., 5" h. (ILLUS.) **65.00**

Pitcher, 4 ¾" h., 4" d., blended turquoise & white gloss, barrel shape w/applied handle, full signature **85.00**

Salt & pepper shakers, figural queen & king, initials mark, 5 ¾" h., pr. **100.00**

Wall pocket, round, pink w/darker pink applied roses, 4" d. **45.00**

BRASTOFF, SASCHA

Of all the potters starting their own businesses in the 1940s, there is no one who can hold the distinction as a Renaissance man with a personal crystal ball more than Sascha Brastoff. He seemed to know what the public wanted before they knew themselves. In 1953, Brastoff's friend, Nelson Rockefeller, built a pottery complex to house Sascha's various creations which, over the years, would encompass a multitude of styles and materials. He created a full line of hand-painted china with such names as Allegro, Night Song, Roman Coin and La Jolla. A pottery dinnerware line named Surf Ballet was done by dipping colors such as pink, blue or yellow into real gold or platinum, which created a 'marbleized swirl' effect. Artware items with patterns such as Star Steed, a leaping fantasy horse, and Rooftops, a series of houses where the roofs somehow seemed to be the prominent feature, were designed. Hard-to-find resin items are an example of Brastoff's diversified talents although it has been reported that these resin candles were manufactured by Continental Candle Company of Northridge, California. However, this has not seemed to cause a decline in the value of the pieces; the Sascha name meant success then just as it does today. Popular also is the line of enamels on copper created by Sascha. Brastoff even dabbled in textiles which are highly prized by collectors. A yard of cloth in good condition would command several hundred dollars.

Sascha's talents made it easy for him to flow gently, but with great flourish, from one decade to the next. In the late 1940s and early 1950s, Sascha created a series of Western motif cachepots which today cause great excitement when found. He designed a line of poodle decorated items during the late 1940s, almost a decade before the poodle craze of the 1950s. Smoking accessories were a popular necessity in the 1950s and Sascha was there with a line all his own.

In the very early years (1947-1952), pieces were signed "Sascha B." or with the full signature, "Sascha Brastoff." Later (after 1953 and before 1962), during the years of his factory-studio, pieces done by his employees showed 'Sascha B.' and, more often than not, also included the chanticleer backstamp. Because of health problems, Sascha left his company in 1963. After 1962, pieces were marked "Sascha B." and also included the 'R' in a circle trademark. It would be another ten years before the business closed.

Sascha Brastoff died on February 4, 1993.

Sascha Brastoff Marks

Ashtray, oblong, cigarette rests at each end, Model No. 08A, Citrus patt., 8" l. **$50.00**

Ashtray, rectangular w/six cigarette rests at one end, Rooftops patt., 7½" w., 10" l. **65.00**

Ashtray, Pagoda patt., 5" sq. **55.00**

Ashtray, gold w/black bottom, 5" sq. **60.00**

Ashtray, Mosaic patt., 5" sq. **50.00**

Ashtray, Star Steed patt., 5" sq. .. **65.00**

Bowl, 3½" d., 5" h., Surf Ballet patt., three small round feet, blue w/platinum **26.00**

Bowl, 6" d., 3½" h., Mosaic patt., glossy dark brown interior, marked on bottom w/chanticleer & "M21," Sascha B. production mark on outer side (ILLUS. top, next page) **65.00**

Bowl, 12" d., 4½" h., shell-shaped white matte w/gold & platinum glossy leaves in bottom of shell **95.00**

Cachepot, scalloped top, Rooftops patt., 4" h. **40.00**

Candleholder, blue resin, 4" d., 7¼" h. **35.00**

Cigarette box, cov., Star Steed patt., 5" l. **65.00**

Pipe-form Cigarette Holder

Cigarette holder, model of a pipe, Abstract patt., Model No. 080, 4¼" h. (ILLUS.) **55.00**

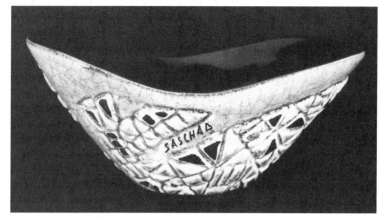

Mosiac Pattern Bowl

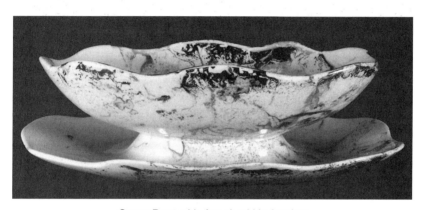

Gravy Boat with Attached Underplate

Cigarette holder, round w/straight sides, Abstract patt., blue & gold, 2½" h. **25.00**

Cigarette lighter, white w/pink, blue & purple flowers, 2" h. **26.00**

Creamer, Warwick patt. **25.00**

Cup & saucer, peacock design w/tan, gold, light blue & white over brown background, cup 3½" d., 3" h., saucer, 5½" d. **35.00**

Cup & saucer, Surf Ballet patt., dark green w/gold **45.00**

Gravy boat w/attached underplate, Surf Ballet patt., pink w/platinum, 9½" l., 2" h. (ILLUS.).. **28.00**

Model of a bear, seated w/legs straight, head slightly raised, arms across chest, dark green resin, 10½" h. **390.00**

Obelisk w/lid, horizontal stripes in brown, blue & tan over white background, full signature, 22" h. **610.00**

Pitcher, 6" h., 5½" d., bulbous, rim slightly raised forming angular spout, deep green background w/tan & rust fruits & leaves trimmed in green, gold & white **95.00**

Plate, 8" sq., Fruit patt. **60.00**

Plate, 10" d., Surf Ballet patt., white w/platinum **20.00**

Platter, 11" d., Winrock patt. **80.00**

Sugar bowl, cov., Surf Ballet patt., pink & gold, 4½" d., 3 ¾" h. **30.00**

Tankard, square-shaped, Rooftops patt., long handles, 5" h. **55.00**

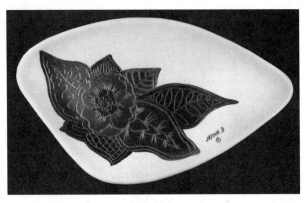

Angular Free-form Tray

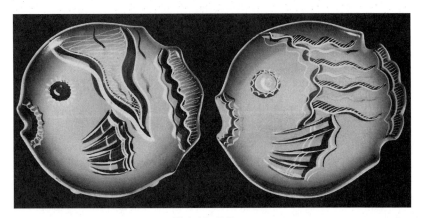

Fish Motif Trays

Tray, angular free-form shape, white background, platinum & gold flowers & leaves, Model No. F3, 9 ¾" l., 5½" w. (ILLUS.) **35.00**

Tray, fish motif, early 'Sascha B.' mark, 6½" d. (ILLUS. left) **75.00**

Tray, fish motif, early 'Sascha B.' mark, 8" d. (ILLUS, right.) **100.00**

Tray, shallow oval, Abstract patt., enamel on copper w/blue, black, yellow & green glazes, 4" l., 3½" w. (ILLUS. bottom, right) **28.00**

Vase, 10" h., figural, model of a high-buttoned shoe, Americana patt. **185.00**

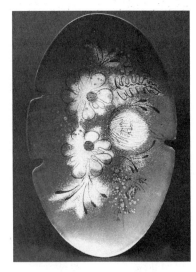

Abstract Pattern Tray

References: *Collectors Encyclopedia of Sascha Brastoff* by Steve Conti, A. DeWayne Bethany, Bill Seay, Collector Books 1995; Several personal conversations and correspondence between Sascha Brastoff and Susan N. Cox, 1983; "Sascha Brastoff, Innovator for all Times" by Susan N. Cox, *American Clay Exchange*, November 1983

BRAYTON LAGUNA POTTERY

One of the fastest growing collectibles in ceramics today is that produced by Durlin E. Brayton in Laguna Beach, California beginning in 1927. When he married Ellen (Webb) Webster Grieve she became his business partner and the venture proved highly successful. More than 125 people and about twenty designers were employed with the company. As with so many enterprises of the times, Brayton began to feel the effect of the mass importation of pottery products into the United States after World War II. Production ceased in 1968.

Hand-turned pieces were the first items created by Brayton and are growing in popularity. These would include a small number of vases, ashtrays and dinnerware items such as cups and saucers, pitchers, sugar bowls and creamers as well as plates in various sizes. The mark (ca. 1927-1930) would be the first one Brayton used. It shows 'Laguna Pottery' in Durlin Brayton's handwriting.

One of the most popular lines was the Children's series. These individual pieces were given first names which were included in a stamp mark (No. 4) that also showed the words 'Brayton Pottery.' Sometimes the stamp mark is faint so collectors should look carefully since the mark can attest to the authenticity of the item.

There were several other marks used during Brayton's history. Also, labels were used on occasion, sometimes in combination with a mark. On items too small for a full mark, designers occasionally would incise their initials. Both white clay and pink clay were used during Brayton's production.

(1)   ca. 1927-1930   Incised

(2)   1930-1937   Incised

(3)   1930-1937   Incised

(4)   1940s   Stamp

(5)   1940s   Stamp mark on Childrens' series

(6)   Stamp

(7)   Late 1940s-1950s   Incised

(8)   Late 1950s-1960s   Incised

(9)   Late 1950s-1960s   Incised

(10)   Late stamp mark

(11)   Stamp mark on Mammy cookie jar

Various Brayton Laguna Marks

Ashtray with Cigarette Rest

Honeycomb Texture Cookie Jar

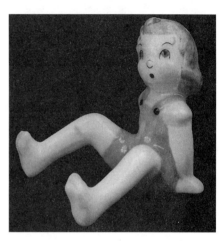

Children's Series "Ann" Figure

Ashtray, w/one cigarette rest, round, turquoise glaze, incised Mark 2, 4¼" d. (ILLUS.) **$19.00**

Book ends, figural, model of a seated clown, white w/red trim on hat and buttons, blue ruffled collar, wrists and ankles, black shoe soles, Mark 3, 4¾" l., 6" h., pr. **250.00**

Candleholder, figural, Blackamoor in seated position, colorful glazes w/lots of gold trim, designed by Ruth Peabody, 5" h. **85.00**

Candleholder, round, plain woodtone glaze, Model No. D-8, 4½" d., 3½" h. **16.00**

Cookie jar, cov., light brown matte body w/overall honeycomb texture, stick spatter dark brown straight tree branches w/five partridges around body in pale blue, yellow & orange; glossy white interior, pale blue lid, Model No. V-12, Mark 2, 7¼" h. (ILLUS. top, next column) **185.00**

Cookie jar, cov., figural black Mammy, bright blue dress, white apron w/yellow, black, green & blue trim, red bandana on head, yellow earrings, Mark 11 examples only (being reproduced), 12 ⅝" h. **1,450.00**

Creamer & open sugar bowl, round, eggplant glaze, Mark 2, 2½" h., pr. **27.00**

Figure, Children's series, "Ann," girl seated w/legs apart, knees bent, 4" h. (ILLUS.) **110.00**

Figure, Children's series, "Butch," boy standing w/present under each arm, short pants w/suspenders, 7½" h. (ILLUS., top left, next page) **70.00**

Figure, Children's series, "Dorothy," girl seated w/legs together & straight, hands by her sides, hair w/pigtails & tied w/ribbons, 4" h., (ILLUS. next page) **105.00**

Figure, Children's series, "Ellen," girl standing w/pigtails & a hat tied at neck, arms bent & palms forward, one leg slightly twisted, 7¼" h. **90.00**

Children's Series "Butch" Figure

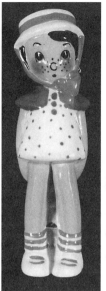

"Pat" Figure (Front & Reverse)

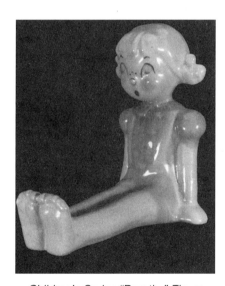

Children's Series "Dorothy" Figure

Figure, Children's series, "Ida,"
girl standing w/one arm
wrapped around full-sized doll,
both w/matching hats, 6 ¾" h. **65.00**

Figure, Children's series, "Millie,"
girl bent over w/legs apart, head
between legs, 3 ¾" h.
(scarce) **155.00**

Figure, Children's series, "Pat,"
girl standing, freckles on her
face, wearing a hat w/tie around
neck & short dress, holding full-
sized doll in back between her
legs, hard to find, 7" h. (ILLUS.
front & reverse).......................... **85.00**

Figure, Children's series,
"Petunia," African-American girl
standing w/basket of flowers,
wearing a pinafore, 6¼" h.
(ILLUS. next page, top right) **140.00**

*(Caution: This item, although
w/variations, has been found
marked "Occupied Japan.")*

Figure, Children's series,
"Sambo," African-American boy
standing w/chicken under one
arm, 7½" h. (ILLUS. next page,
top left) **155.00**

Figure, Gay Nineties lady holding
up her dress w/one hand,
umbrella in other hand, ruffled
flowing skirt, hat, high-top
shoes, ca. 1930, 9½" h............. **105.00**

Figure, "Tweedle Dee," character
from Alice in Wonderland,
non-Disney, 3" h. **28.00**

"Sambo" and "Petunia" Figures

Girl & Tree Figure Group

Figure group, girl & tree, girl
holding doll & standing in front
of tree; tree has two
strawberries on it, pink, blue,
green, yellow & brown glazes,
Mark 7 w/ST-20 underglaze,
8½" h. (ILLUS.) **45.00**

Figure group, "Bride & Groom,"
man seated, woman standing,
Mark 3, 8" h. **100.00**

Figures, dice players w/dice,
African-American boys on
hands & knees, pottery dice
show a "4" & a "3" & are
attached, 1" l., ½" h.; players are
4¾" l., 3½" h.., set of 3 .... **225.00**

Flower holder, figural, "Francis,"
girl standing & holding small
planter in front, blond hair
w/snood & flower, 8" h. **35.00**

Model of a bear, seated, green,
Mark 9, Model No. T-1, 3½" h. ... **18.00**

Model of a bonnet, large blue
bow forms base, white brim &
top back w/flowers, Mark 3,
4½" h. (ILLUS.) **55.00**

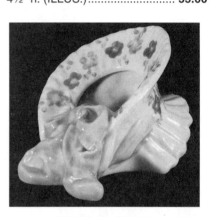

Model of a Bonnet

Model of a Duck

Model of a duck, textured bisque
body, glossy glazed green face,
Model No. 4138, 5½" l.,
5" h. (ILLUS.) **55.00**

Model of Elephant Standing

Model of a Swan

Model of an elephant standing,
trunk up, head turned slightly,
yellow vase in bent left arm,
right arm straight & holding
closed striped umbrella, black &
white shoes, blue vest w/black
buttons, checkered shirt w/black
buttons, yellow hat, unmarked
except "B" initial, 7¼" h.
(ILLUS.) **135.00**

Model of a peacock, pale blue &
white open feathers, light green
base, white body, Marks 5 & 6
combined, 5" l., 5" h....................**60.00**

Model of a swan, grey & white
glossy glaze, Mark 6, 6" l., 4½" h
(ILLUS.) **30.00**

Planter, figural, Dutch boy
pushing cart, boy w/brown hair
& trousers, turquoise hat, dark
yellow tie, pale yellow jacket,
white shirt w/turquoise trim,
black shoes; cart is white inside,
light brown exterior w/dark
brown trim on wheels, Mark 7,
11" l., 9" h. (ILLUS. bottom)........ **35.00**

Planter, figural, Dutch girl pushing
cart, girl w/yellow hair, blue
dress, white apron & hat, black
shoes, grey cart, Mark 7, 8" l.,
8" h. (ILLUS. top, next page)....... **18.00**

Dutch Boy Pushing Cart Planter

Dutch Girl Pushing Cart Planter

Oblong Planter with Fruit & Leaves

Planter, oblong w/fruit & leaves in relief, glossy turquoise w/dark pink fruit, Model No. F-12, Mark 2, 12" l., 4" h. (ILLUS.) **28.00**

Plate, 9" d., eggplant glaze, Mark 1 .... **40.00**

Salt & pepper shakers, figural clowns, white body, black shoes, blue ruffles on ankles, wrists & neck collar, red trim on buttons & hat, one hand behind back holding a flower, Mark 3, 6½" h., pr. (ILLUS. of one, right) **100.00**

Salt & pepper shakers, figural, model of a dog standing & dressed as a clown, white body, red trim on buttons & collar, unmarked, 5" h., pr. **65.00**

Clown Salt Shaker

Mexican Man Tile

Vase w/Man & Woman Planting Tree

Tile, decorated w/Mexican man taking siesta under tree w/cacti nearby, blue, green, white, Mark 2, 6½" sq. (ILLUS.) **95.00**

Vase, 3" h., 3¼" d., round w/straight, slightly flared sides, overall white body w/man & woman each planting a tree, h.p. blue, green & pink glazes on clothing & trees, Mark 10 (ILLUS.) **15.00**

Vase, 7" h. including 1¼" round foot, w/raised circles, Calasia patt., slightly bulbous body w/feather design flaring gently at rim, pale green, Model No. A-6 (ILLUS.) **55.00**

Wall plaque, figure of Blackamoor standing on black bowl-like base, wearing white pantaloons w/black waistband, lapels & trim, white turban on head w/painted-on medallion in green, red & blue glazes, gold shoes & square gold earrings, (also found w/long coat instead of pantaloons), arms bent & positioned at each side of turban so palms of hands & top of head form level base for separate bowl to sit on, unmarked, overall 22" h. w/separate bowl **175.00**

18" h. Blackamoor figure without separate bowl **130.00**

Bowl only, 4" h. **45.00**

Calasia Pattern Vase

Collecting tips: Brayton made a large assortment of various lines over the years. Today, these lines differ greatly in values. New collectors would be wise to study the Brayton lines before deciding which ones they like and can afford. The African-American products, Children's series and the earlier pieces are far more expensive than the later Provincial line or items with the No. 3 mark.

BROADMOOR POTTERY

Seven years (1933-1940) was the time Broadmoor Art Pottery and Tile Company operated in Colorado Springs and Denver, Colorado. Its first location was in Colorado Springs but in 1937 it was moved to Denver and operated there until 1940. Well-known artists, ceramists, designers, painters and sculptors—names such as J. B. Hunt, Cecil Jones Eric Hellman—worked at Broadmoor and their pieces are most sought after by collectors. Those names, and others, including P.H. Genter, turn up frequently when researching such companies as Newcomb Pottery, American Encaustic Tile Company, Catalina Island, Claycraft Tile Company, Fulper, Haeger and Rookwood.

Glazes will sometimes assist collectors in knowing whether an item was made in Colorado Springs or Denver. It is important to note that the stamp used on the Patent Pending trademark with two Egyptian potters inside a square and with one standing at a potter's wheel and the other at a tile pressing machine, was not used on Denver pieces. Use caution not to confuse this stamp mark with a sticker which is slightly different. While a nice addition to any piece, most stickers will not add any noticeable value to an item.

Various Broadmoor Marks

Squirrel Ashtray with Christmas Greetings

Ashtray, leaf-shaped, yellow, one cigarette rest, 3" l **$10.00**

Ashtray w/squirrel, round, advertising "Christmas Greetings, La Salle Hotel, Kansas City, Mo., Broadmoor Pottery Co., Denver, Colorado," stamp mark, green ashtray, white squirrel, 5" d., 2¼" h. (ILLUS.) **55.00**

Model of a squirrel, white, stamped "Broadmoor," 4" l., 2" h. **50.00**

Paperweight, model of Native American head, Oxblood Red, stamp mark "Denver, Colorado P. H. Genter" in script & in a square Egyptians at wheel & tile pressing machine, hard to find, 4" l., 2¼" h. (ILLUS. top, next page) **100.00**

Paperweight, model of a scarab, green, stamp mark w/"Denver, Colorado, Broadmoor Pottery P. H. Genter" in script & Egyptians

Oxblood Native Head Paperweight

Bulbous Honeycomb Planter

Scarab Model Paperweight

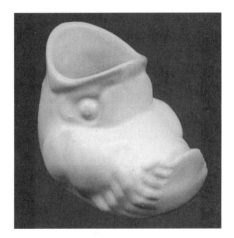

Bird Model Planter

at wheel & tile pressing machine
in a square, 3 ¾" l., 1¼" h.
(ILLUS.) **85.00**

Planter, three feet w/bulbous
honeycomb body & vertical tab
handles below slightly flaring
rim, black high gloss, 3" d.,
3" h. (ILLUS.)............................. **26.00**

Planter, model of a bird, head up
w/open mouth, white matte,
stamp mark "Broadmoor
Pottery, Denver, Colorado" &
sticker, 3¼" l., 2 ¾" h. (ILLUS.) **45.00**

Vase, 6" h., 5¼" l., model of a
cornucopia on rectangular base,
matte light blue, sticker (ILLUS.)... **55.00**

Cornucopia Vase Model

Vase, 6 ¾" h., ovoid footed body
w/loop handles, black high
gloss, "Broadmoor Pottery Co.,
Denver, Colorado" stamp mark
(ILLUS. top next page) **95.00**

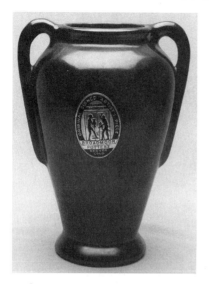

Ovoid Vase with Loop Handles

Haldeman worked about three years for that company. Molded pieces (numbers under 100), handmade pieces (200 numbers), figures, mostly animals and fowl (300 numbers), dancing girls (400 numbers), a continuation of handmade pieces (500-549), and molded pieces with roses added (550 and above numbers), were created. Since incised numbers are on many of the Caliente pieces, this system aids in their identification. Almost without exception, Caliente items have a solid bottom. A few dancing girls, especially the No. 401, have been reproduced. The reproductions have a hole in the bottom, are lighter weight and many have hand-painted flowers on the dresses.

Caliente used several marks over the years with the "Made in California" block lettered mark being the most commonly found. A mold number was included on many of the pieces. Paper labels were also used.

References: *Colorado Pottery* by Carol & Jim Carlton, Collector Books, 1994; "Cecil Jones and Broadmoor" by P. J. Shaw, *American Clay Exchange,* July 1986; "Broadmoor Pottery: A Tale of Two Cities" by W. C. Myers, *American Clay Exchange,* June 15, 1986; "Broadmoor Pottery" by Tom Turnquist, *American Art Pottery Journal,* July 1979

Caliente Pottery Marks

CALIENTE POTTERY

A *California sleeper has to be Caliente Pottery. Its satin feel and soft glazes make it one of the most well-made and appealing lines available in almost all areas of the United States. Yet, collectors not familiar with Caliente marks pass up wonderful pieces because they cannot tie the product to any particular company.*

In 1933, Virgil K. Haldeman opened his pottery in Burbank, California. He created the satin matte glazes and blended colors while his chief designer produced a variety of merchandise until 1941. In 1947, Haldeman moved the business to Calabasas, California and six years later the business closed. Mr. Haldeman died in 1979.

Early pieces have a strong Catalina Pottery influence, probably because Virgil

Basket, round, footed rim w/rope handle, green, Model No. 222, incised "Handmade Calif.," 7" l. (ILLUS. top, next page) **$23.00**

Bowl, 8" d., small round center foot rising to an irregular rim, applied leaves, one rose & one rosebud, light blue & white, Model No. 259 (ILLUS. middle, next page) **32.00**

Candleholder, model of a lily pad, pale green, 5" l., 2" h. **15.00**

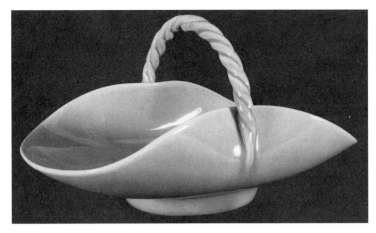

Model No. 222 Basket

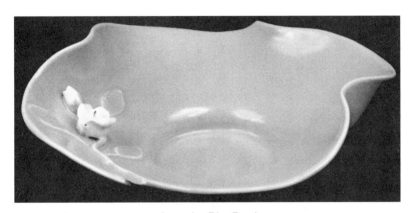

Irregular Rim Bowl

Figure of a Dancing Lady

Cotton dispenser, figural, model of a rabbit standing, long ears w/one bent forward, Model No. 308, 6½" h. **45.00**

Figure of a dancing lady, head tilted, back arched, left arm holding up edge of her dress, right arm across body touching left elbow, deep green glaze, script incised on white clay "Calif. 401," & Caliente sticker, 6 ¾" h. (ILLUS.) **65.00**

Figure of a dancing lady in bloomers, a scarf in each hand & draping to the floor, head bent & slightly tilted, face features indistinct, left hand resting on waist, Model No. 406, 6½" h. (hard to find) **70.00**

Figure of a dancing lady on base, right elbow pointed upward w/hand resting under chin, left leg bent back w/left hand holding up edge of her dress, right leg straight w/foot on tiptoes, ivory glaze, face features indistinct, weighs less than 4 ounces, Model No. 400, 4½" h................. **60.00**

Figure of Lady Standing

Figure of lady standing, holding lower section of long dress away from body exposing legs, head tilted slightly w/hat on her head, Model No. 405, impressed "Made in California" in block letters, 6¼" h. (ILLUS)... **38.00**

Floater dish, flat bottom w/elongated quatrefoil shape, green interior, ivory exterior,

Model No. 10-2, 13" l., 9½" w., 2" h. (ILLUS.)............................. **33.00**

Flower frog, model of a sailboat, white w/light blue, Model No. 73, 5" h. **30.00**

Model of a deer, standing, four legs separated & on an oval base, right front leg slightly bent, ivory glaze w/five tan brushed spots on body, Model No. 351, 5" h. **32.00**

Model of a duck, standing, wings up, webbed feet forward & together, Model No. 334, 4" h. **22.00**

Model of an Egret

Model of an egret, white, Model No. 369, 4 ¾" h. (ILLUS.) **36.00**

Model of a goose, head up, light green, Model No. 303, 4¼" h...... **18.00**

Model of a swan, floating position, ivory, Model No. 305, 3 ¾" l., 2" h. (ILLUS. w/floater dish)... **22.00**

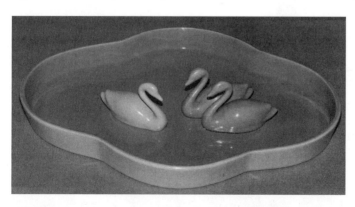

Floater dish with Swan Models

Model of Scottie Dog & Fire Hydrant

**Models of a Scottie dog & fire
hydrant,** dog standing w/left
rear leg raised, tail up, black
glaze, Model No. 311, 3½" h.;
hydrant, black glaze, Model No.
352, 3½" h., set of 2 (ILLUS.) **75.00**

Vase, 3½" h., 3¼" d., globular
shape, trefoil opening, applied
leaves on both sides of a single
rose **34.00**

Vase, 5 ¾" h., Art Deco design,
rectangular base w/two
buttresses on each side flaring
upward to a thin lip **35.00**

Vase, 6" h., ivy, spherical
w/closed rim, two applied roses
w/leaves, Model No. 560 .... **40.00**

Model No. 570 Vase

Vase, 8" h., flat front & back
w/curved sides, scalloped
rectangular opening, one
applied green rose & leaves
blending to gold top w/two
applied rosebuds, one rose &
one leaf, "Model No. 570" &
"Calif." etched into glazed
bottom (ILLUS. bottom left) **38.00**

Collecting tips: Look for the deeply
impressed mark, 'Made in California' in
block letters on small items such as animals and ladies. On larger pieces, such as
bowls and vases, look for the incised
'Calif.' or 'U S A' and a mold number.
Since there are usually no other markings,
many sellers are not aware the item is a
product of Caliente so the price is generally lower than its value. Applied flowers on
Caliente items should be in near mint condition, otherwise the value is greatly
decreased.

References: *Collectable Caliente
Pottery* by Wilbur Held, privately printed
1987; "Haldeman Pottery-Caliente Hunt" by
Wilbur Held, *American Clay Exchange,*
March 1984; "Caliente Follow-Up" by
Wilbur Held, *American Clay Exchange,*
October 1984

CALIFORNIA FIGURINE COMPANY
See Weil Ware

CAMARK POTTERY

The name "Camark" originated from its location. The first three letters of two words, "Camden" and "Arkansas" produced the name Camark. The pottery was founded in late 1926 by Samuel (Jack) Carnes who had married Gressie Umpstead whose wealthy family helped Carnes in founding the Camark Art and Tile Pottery. About 1927 John and Jeanne Lessell, along with Jeanne's daughter, Billie, came to work at Camark. John Lessell, as Art Director for Camark, has been credited with creating iridescent and lustre ware using Arkansas clays. Even with Jack's pottery talents, being an astute businessman, and the hiring of well-known ceramic artists, art pottery was produced only a few years. There were too many economic hardships associated with the late 1920s. The business was sold but Carnes stayed on to help with the transition. As Camark moved into the 1930s, drip glazes became popular and creation of simple commercial cast ware and utilitarian items were manufactured. At that time, the pottery began producing assorted novelty pieces, some decorated art ware and a variety of bowls, vases and planters. In 1962, the pottery was purchased by the Daniels family. After Mr. Daniels died in 1965, his wife, Mary, struggled to keep the pottery open. Mostly, the merchandise already produced was sold and not much new production occurred. In 1982 the pottery closed. However, in 1986, it was revived when the Ashcraft brothers, Mark and Gary, purchased the land, buildings, machinery, molds and inventory. As of this date, they have not produced any pieces and have stated that the old Camark molds will not be used.

CAMARK

CAMARK
HAND PAINTED
MADE IN USA

Camark Assorted Marks

Creamer & open sugar bowl on tray, creamer has small circle handle & lifts off tray, sugar bowl is attached to tray, maroon glaze, Camark sticker & mark on bottom "N-135 USA," finish 50, shape N135, 3" h., pr.......... **$27.00**

No. 436 Cup & Saucer

Cup & saucer, demitasse, any solid glaze, marked "436 USA," flower-shaped cup, 2½" h.; saucer w/flower petals rim, 4½" d., set (ILLUS.) **18.00**

Ewer, miniature, four horizontal rings from base to shoulder, pink glaze, 4 ¾" h. (ILLUS.)........ **20.00**

Salt & pepper shakers, model of an "S" & "P," any glaze, unmarked, 2¾" h., pr. (ILLUS.).... **15.00**

Sign, advertising, rectangular base w/State of Arkansas shape, light blue ground w/dark blue "Camark Pottery" letters, 6" h. **100.00**

Vase, 6" h., round scalloped base w/four short tulips rising from the base w/one taller tulip in the center, dark green **22.00**

Vase, 6½" h., round foot rising to short bulbous body & flaring to an irregular, fluted rim, dark blue high gloss **35.00**

*S & P Salt and Pepper
Shakers*

Camark Miniature Ewer

Tulip-Shaped Vase

Vase, 7½" h., round foot
rising to tulip-shaped bowl w/two
ornate large question mark-
shaped handles rising from foot
to above opening, green, sticker
& mark "505 USA" (ILLUS.) **40.00**

Vase, 8" h., bottle form, spherical
footed body tapering to a short
stick neck w/flared rim **38.00**

Collecting tips: Camark is one of a
few companies that produced wonderfully
eye-pleasing and lasting pottery that has
not yet realized its value potential. Prices
are inexpensive and items are plentiful; any

collector's dream. The only flaw in all this is
that dating Camark is difficult except for the
'La Camark' signature that was used only
on the rarer pieces produced by John
Lessell in 1927.

References: "A Salute to American
potters and their cats" by Marilyn Dipboye,
American Clay Exchange, May 15, 1987;
"Camark Metamorphosis" by Doris and
Burdell Hall, *American Clay Exchange,*
October 30, 1986; "Camark: A Legendary
Name in American Pottery" by Joseph D.
Alsbrook, *Arkansas Times Magazine,* City
Guide 1983 and reprinted in *American Clay
Exchange,* June 15, 1985

CATALINA ISLAND POTTERY

Also see: Gladding, McBean

About twenty-five miles off the coast of Los Angeles, California is Catalina Island which was owned by William Wrigley, Jr., heir to the Wrigley chewing gum operation. Wrigley opened Catalina Island Pottery in 1927 on Pebbly Beach located on the southeast shore of Catalina Island and adjacent to the city of Avalon.

The island was rich in natural resources ideally suited to pottery production. Today, Catalina Island is rich in preserving the history of the pottery plant. Strolling down the middle of a wide street or leisurely eating at an outdoor cafe, collectors can view multicolored tiles imbedded into planters, see tile plaques in vivid glazes depicting various birds or assorted landmarks, and generally bask in the pottery heritage of this quaint haven. A museum nearby keeps the island's pottery heritage alive and available for interested tourists and collectors.

During the early years (1927-1932) a brown clay body was used; the middle years (1932-1937) the body was a white clay and it sometimes included an overlay of brownware; and, during the Gladding McBean years, 1937-1941, a white clay body was used. Examples marked "Catalina Island" are more desirable and far more expensive than the items made at the Gladding McBean Company in Los Angeles, California.

Virgil Haldeman, later the founder of Caliente Pottery, became Calalina's ceramic engineer in 1930 creating beautiful, vibrant glazes. Not only does the color of the clay body aid in dating an item but just as important in determining age are the colors used. The early years included black, Catalina blue, Descanso green, Mandarin yellow, Toyon red, Monterey brown and white. Occasionally light blue, pale green, Old Rose and orchid were used in tile making.

By 1936, glazes were Colonial yellow, Coral Island, Mandarin yellow, Matte blue and Matte green, Pearly white, Powder blue, Toyon red and turquoise.

Catalina Island turned out varied pieces such as ashtrays, book ends, dinnerware, lamps, novelties and tiles. Occasionally they would create out-of-the-ordinary pieces such as handled wine servers with owl or penguin finials used as stoppers. These are not easy to find. Also, hand-painted plates, unique because the artists were given control over the designs and glazes used, are sought by collectors and can command more than eight or nine hundred dollars each depending on the amount of work involved, assorted glazes, themes, condition and so on.

$$C^{ATALI}N_A$$
$$MADE \ IN$$
$$U.S.A.$$
$$P_{OTTERY}$$

$$C^{ATAL}I_{NA}$$
$$C 801$$
$$P_{OTTERY}$$

Catalina Island Pottery Marks

Ashtray, individual, inverted three-tier, round w/a single cigarette rest extending outward, No. 508 .... **$22.00**

Candelabra, three-tier, Pearly white, Model No. 382, impressed mark, 12" l., 4 ¾" h. (ILLUS. top, next page) **235.00**

Candleholder, round w/fingerhold, blue, Model No. 377, 5" l., 2" h. **75.00**

Coaster, round, Catalina blue, Pearly white glaze, 3½" d. **30.00**

Pitcher, 6" h., open syrup w/handle **100.00**

Pitcher, 8" h., Grecian style, turquoise................................. **150.00**

Plate, 8½" d., salad w/rope edge design **35.00**

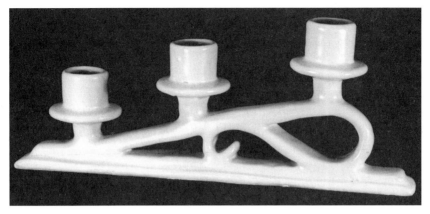

Three-tier Candelabra No. 382

Seahorse Plate

Plate, 10¼" d., glazed w/brown seahorse, sky blue center background, wide yellow rim (ILLUS.) **650.00**

Plate, 10½" d., dinner, round without decoration, Mandarin yellow glaze............................... **25.00**

Platter, 11" l., Powder blue glaze **75.00**

Tile, Spanish motif, turquoise, 6" sq. **150.00**

Tray, round w/rolled edge, green, brown clay marked "Catalina Island," 11" d. **125.00**

Vase, 6½" h., oblong scroll foot w/round body, Pearly white exterior, Powder blue interior, No. 604 .... **235.00**

Vase, 7" h., flat w/sawtooth edge on each side, turquoise, No. 601 .... **170.00**

Wall pocket, seashell design, turquoise, Model No. 376, 8" l. **150.00**

References: *Catalina Island Pottery, Collectors Guide* by Steven & Aisha Hoefs, privately printed 1993; *Suggestions in Catalina Pottery,* line drawings, Delleen Enge, privately printed 1987; "Catalina Island and Catalina Pottery" by Delleen Enge, *American Clay Exchange,* May 1983; *Catalina Pottery: The Early Years 1927-1937* by A. W. Fridley, privately printed 1977; "Catalina Tile, Brick and Pottery" *California Arts & Architecture Magazine,* November 1929

CERAMIC ARTS STUDIO

Ceramic Arts Studio of Madison, Wisconsin began in 1941 when Lawrence Rabbitt and Reuben Sand decided to open a studio pottery. Less than a year later, they met Betty Harrington and hired her as their designer. She had held a full time position at the State Agriculture Department but during the years 1942-46, Ceramic Arts Studio was booming and Betty had been asked to design exclusive pieces for Montgomery Ward. Based on those factors, Harrington felt secure enough to quit her position at the State Department. If items were designed by Betty Harrington (she created close to 500 pieces in just a few years), collectors can find a "B. H." stamped in black on them. The lines offered by Ceramic Arts Studio were varied and numerous. Figurines of children and adults, salt and pepper shakers, art wares, banks, vases and wall plaques were a few of the items produced. Not only were singles

created but also pairs and threesomes such as a Sultan and two of his harem.

In the 1950s when Ceramic Arts Studio was trying desparately to compete with the imports, new designers were hired. Betty introduced "African Man & Woman" in her terra cotta clay. She also created wood and wire accessories. Ullie Rebus created "Lightning & Thunder," "Waldo & Sassy," a Hippo ashtray and as many as fifteen or twenty more items. Ruth Planter created "Sonny & Honey." However, none of their efforts could save the struggling company and it closed in 1955.

A 5¼" plate with the wording 'Paul Bunyan of Wisconsin' was produced in large quantities in solid colors before Betty Harrington was associated with the company. Apart from its historical value, the plate is not too interesting and has little collector value. They are not hard to find.

This mark can be found with or without the copyright symbol. The initials of Betty Harrington can also be found with this mark. The name of the item such as "Tuffy" may also be included in the stamp mark.

Figurine, Balinese Dancer, woman, 9½" h. (ILLUS. top, next page) **$68.00**

Figurine, Spring Sue, 4 ¾" h. (ILLUS. top right, next page) **45.00**

Figurines, shelf-sitters, Farmer boy & Farmer girl, boy 4 ¾" h., girl 4½" h., pr. (ILLUS. bottom, next page) **65.00**

Balinese Dancer Figurine

Spring Sue Figurine

Farmer Boy and Girl Figurines

*Fluffy and Persian
Cat Models*

Model of a cat, shelf-sitter,
  stamp- marked, "Ceramic Arts
  Studio Madison, Wis., Fluffy,"
  white, 4 ¾" h. (ILLUS. right) **55.00**

Model of a Persian cat, white,
  5½" h., (ILLUS. left) **55.00**

Model of a Tuffy Cat

Model of a cat, shelf-sitter, stamp-
  marked, "Ceramic Arts Studio
  Madison, Wis., Tuffy," black,
  6 ¾" h. (ILLUS.) **65.00**

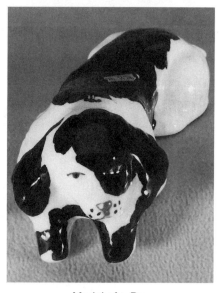

Model of a Dog

Model of a dog, lying down, two
  front feet hang over shelf, white
  dog w/black spots, sticker,
  4 ¾" l., 1¼" h.
  (ILLUS.) **65.00**

Planter, bamboo-form w/Chinese
  boy sitting on top, one foot bent
  at the knee, 3" l., 5" h. (ILLUS.
  top, next page) **38.00**

Bamboo Planter with Chinese Boy

Salt & pepper shakers, figurals
of an elf & a toadstool group, elf
seated w/knees bent to chest,
black trousers, blue & pink
accent glazes, toadstool group
has one tall toadstool in center

w/three small toadstools on one
side & a small toadstool on the
other side, same blue & pink
colors, elf fits underneath
toadstool, elf 2¼" h; stamp-
marked & also has "BH" initials,
toadstool, 2½" h., pr. **55.00**

Salt & pepper shakers, figural
Wee Dutch girl & boy, white
clothes, blue accessories,
yellow hair, girl 2 ¾" h., boy
3" h., pr. (ILLUS.)....................... **35.00**

Salt & pepper shakers, figural
Wee Scotch boy & girl w/kilts,
black jacket & shoes, yellow &
orange accents on clothes &
hats, 3½" h., pr. **45.00**

Vase, 6 ¾" h., 3" d., triple bud,
bamboo-form cylinders
(ILLUS. top, next page) **25.00**

Wall plaque, pierced to hang,
figural Zor, 9" h. (ILLUS. bottom,
next page) **50.00**

Separate metal palette
(ILLUS. bottom, next page) **55.00**

Wee Dutch boy and girl Salt & Pepper Shakers

Bamboo Cylinder Vase

Harlequin & Columbine Wall Plaques

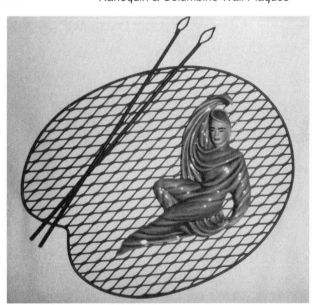

*Zor Figural Plaque and
Separate Metal Palette*

Wall plaques, figurals Harlequin
  & Columbine, man 9" h., woman
  8½" h., pr. (ILLUS.).................. **135.00**

  References: *Ceramic Arts Studio* by
Mike Schneider, Schiffer Books 1994;
Video Series One and Two (1986) with
updated price guides by B. A. Wellman;
"Ceramic Arts Studio - The Early Years" by
B. A. Wellman, *Depression Glass Daze,*
January 1987; "Ceramic Arts Studio—The
Middle Years" by B. A. Wellman, *Depression
Glass Daze,* February 1987; *"Ceramic Arts
Studio of Madison, Wisconsin"* by Dr. M. W.
Lerner, *The Antique Trader Weekly,*
September 19, 1984

CLAYSMITHS, THE
See Will-George

CLEMINSON CLAY

Betty Cleminson began her home-based business, Cleminson Clay, in Monterey Park, California in 1941. Within two years it was necessary to move to larger facilities in El Monte, California and the name was changed to "The California Cleminsons." Betty's husband, George, who was a school teacher, took care of sales, managing the money, supplies and constructing the factory.

Originally, Mrs. Cleminson concentrated on creating butter dishes, canisters, cookie jars—mostly kitchen-related items. After the move, and with up to 150 employees, she was able to expand her lines with giftware such as vases, wall plaques, cups and saucers, cleanser shakers and a full line of tableware called Distlefink. The incised, stylized "BC" mark was the first mark used; the California Cleminson mark can be found with or without the boy and girl on each side. As with so many companies of the times, the Cleminsons could not produce a competitive product and the company went out of business in 1963.

Cleminson Clay Marks

Ashtray, model of a fish, two cigarette rests at bottom edge, hole for eye, light & dark ocean blue interior w/pale grey exterior, second mark without boy & girl, ca. 1950, 7½" d., 2 ¾" h. **$28.00**

Butter dish, cov., figural, model of a Distlefink sitting on an oblong base, bird's head turned toward back, brown glossy glaze w/dark brown & rust accents, 7½" l., 5 ¾" h. (ILLUS. bottom right) **45.00**

Grouping of Distlefink Pieces

"The World Is Our Oyster" dish

Cleanser shaker, figure of a woman standing, yellow hair, pink scarf over head, pink & white dress w/grey trim, five holes in top of head, 6½" h......... **22.00**

Mug, cov., man's face w/hangover expression, model of water bag forms cover, irregular-shaped mug & rim, reverse of mug w/lettering, "Morning after" & inside bottom of mug lettering, "Never again," white mug w/blue, dark pink, green & black accents, grey water bag bottom w/black rim & yellow top, second mark without boy & girl, 4½" d., 5" h. **35.00**

Oyster dish, easel shape w/"The World Is Our Oyster" & picture of the world & an oyster, white ground w/red, blue, black & pink glazes, 6½" d. (ILLUS.) **25.00**

Pie bird, figural, model of a bird, white body decorated in pink, green & blue, first mark, ca. 1941, 4½" h. **28.00**

Pitcher, 10½" h., figural, model of a Distlefink, beak forms spout, tail is handle, white body w/brown &

green accents (ILLUS. previous page, bottom left) **35.00**

Plate, 5¼" d., assorted glazed flowers, grey scalloped rim, two holes for hanging (ILLUS. next page, top left) **15.00**

Plate, 5¼" d., small flowers & leaves around one large flower in center, two holes for hanging, (ILLUS. next page, top right) **15.00**

Plate, 6½" d., pale blue ground w/white & black silhouettes, woman sitting at spinning wheel, two holes for hanging (ILLUS. next page, middle left) **18.00**

Plate, 6½" d., pale blue ground w/white & black silhouettes, woman standing & churning butter, 6½" d. (ILLUS. middle right, next page) **18.00**

Plate, 7" d., scalloped pale blue edge, pink & purple flowers, green leaves, light & dark pink butterflies, two holes for hanging, second mark without boy & girl **22.00**

Plate, 7" d., two holes for hanging, scalloped rim, white to muted blue ground w/blue, white rose & pink flowers (ILLUS. bottom next page) **24.00**

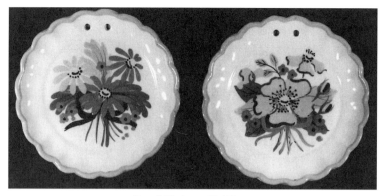

Small Plates with Flowers

Cleminson Silhouette Plates

Scalloped Plate with Flowers

Razor blade holder, model of a man's face w/hand holding razor, slot in top for used blades, solid unglazed bottom w/stamped mark, 3¼" d., 3¼" h. **20.00**

Recipe holder, small footed oblong base rising to scalloped sides & rim, hearts & flowers motif, words in brown & black show "Recipe holder," 4" l., 3" h. **28.00**

Ring holder, model of a hand, large flower covers wrist, 3½" h. **40.00**

Salt & pepper shakers, model of the Distlefink, 6¼" h., pr. (ILLUS. top page 51, top) **23.00**

Scoop Wall Pocket

Two Flower Wall Plaque

Soup mug, juvenile, straight sides w/one round knob on each side at rim, Native American boy & his dog playing & encircled by a white ring, pale pink body w/green, brown & white glazes for dog & boy, second mark w/boy & girl on each side, 4" d., 4¼" h. **40.00**

String holder, model of a house w/lettering "Friends from afar and nearabout will find our latchstring always out," string comes out through a portion of the door, string holder is also a wall plaque, 6½" h. **65.00**

Tea bag holder, model of a teapot w/words, "Let me hold the bag," yellow, blue & black glazes over white body, teapot open handle can be used for hanging, stamped mark, 4¼" h..... **10.00**

Wall plaque, h.p. girl w/green, white & brown dress holding bouquet of flowers, butterflies, two holes at top for hanging, first mark, ca. 1941, 3½" d., 4 ¾" h..... **15.00**

Wall plaque, two flowers, three buds & leaves in center, w/dark blue rim, two holes for hanging, second mark w/boy & girl on each side, 6½" sq. (ILLUS.)........ **20.00**

Wall pocket, model of a kettle w/three feet, black body w/white heart decorated w/words, "The kitchen is the heart of the home," bail handle, 4½" d., 4¼" h............ **28.00**

Wall pocket, model of a scoop, white body w/blue & red flowers & green leaves, second mark without boy & girl on each side, also has "hand painted" & a copyright symbol, 9" l. (ILLUS.) **35.00**

Wall pocket, model of a teapot, pale green body w/dark green lid, heart-shaped motif w/words, "Kitchen bright & a singing kettle make home the place you want to settle," bail handle w/round wood center decorated w/painted flowers, 9" d., 6" h. **30.00**

COORS PORCELAIN COMPANY

John J. Herold of Owens and Roseville potteries has been credited with developing the oxblood red line of Roseville called Rozane Mongol. In 1908, having the talent and the desire to have his own pottery, Herold moved to Colorado, linked up with the Adolph Coors family and opened Herold Pottery Company in Golden, Colorado. While Herold stayed for only two years, the name of the company would not change until 1920 when it became the Coors Porcelain Company.

Because of Colorado's prohibition vote, Coors became one of the largest producers of malted milk products. These items— including ceramic, glass and tin containers—were made from about 1917 until the mid-1950s.

After World War I, Coors expanded their ceramics operation. Homer Laughlin China Company had their Fiesta and Taylor, Smith and Taylor had their LuRay line. Collectors have commented how much Coors Rosebud and Coors Rockmount resemble Laughlin's Fiesta ware and that Coors Mello-tone reminds them of T. S. & T.'s LuRay. When you see what you believe to be Laughlin's 'Open Window' decal, look again because the item may be a Coors product with the same decal. During the decalcomania era, many companies used the same decals but with different blanks which, besides a company mark, would help determine which company produced the item. Coors used the Chrysanthemum, Floree, Tulip and Open Window decals.

Rosebud, a Coors product, is one of the most popular lines being collected today. There are several variations for the Rosebud and leaves but, generally, collectors are pleased to collect any Rosebud whether they be Double Leaf, Garland, Budded Triple, or another variation. Glazes are green, orange, rose, white (ivory), yellow, or blue. Today the ivory glaze is a hard-to-find color.

During the 1930s and 1940s Mello-tone and Rockmount dinnerware was manufactured. Mello-tone came in pastels of azure blue, canary yellow, coral pink and spring green. Rockmount was available in blue, green, orange, yellow, rose or ivory.

Until complete catalogs or identifying numbers or names can be determined, Carol and Jim Carlton, in their Colorado Pottery book, have given each one a name using Colorado towns. Since this will be a valuable aid in communicating with other collectors, the listings below show the "pattern" names in quotation marks.

Vases will be found today with a Colorado State Fair stamp and a date. This mark does not greatly increase the value of an item.

Coors Ceramic Division is still operating today. They produce porcelain items used in chemical laboratories.

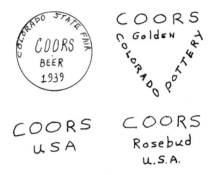

Assorted Coors Marks

Bowl, cereal 6" d., Rosebud patt. **$7.00**

Cake knife, Tulip decal, 10" l. **70.00**

Mixing bowl, Rosebud patt., green, 6" d., (no handle) **25.00**

Mixing bowl, Rosebud patt., orange, 10" d. (no handle) **85.00**

Pie plate, Rosebud patt., green, 10¼" l. **40.00**

Plate, 7¼" d., Rosebud patt.......... **10.00**

Platter, 13½" l., w/tab handles, Rosebud patt., blue (ILLUS. top, next page.) **35.00**

Platter, 15" l., Mello-tone patt....... **45.00**

Rosebud Pattern Platter

Elongated Egg Salt Shaker

"Beehive" Pattern Vase

Salt & pepper shakers, base tapers to an elongated egg on end shape w/green hops at the base & a shaft of golden barley, 5½" h., pr. (ILLUS. of one).......... **25.00**

Vase, 6" h., "Beehive" patt., spherical footed body tapering slightly w/a molded square loop handle on each side, small horizontal rings cover body, matte green exterior, white interior (ILLUS.) **50.00**

Vase, 6" h., "Boulder" patt., ovoid body, tapering to a short, flared neck w/a molded ring handle on each side, matte tan exterior, turquoise interior (ILLUS. top, next page) **50.00**

Boulder Pattern Vase

Vase, 10" h., Empire patt., upright
rectangle w/two pinnacles on
each side, matte blue **95.00**

Water server w/stopper,
Rosebud patt., blue,
3 pt. **120.00**

Collecting tip: A company located in
Inglewood, California marked their pottery
"Coorsite." Use caution not to buy Coorsite
if you are wanting Coors art pottery of
Colorado. There is no connection between
the two companies.

References: *Colorado Pottery
Identification and Values* by Carol & Jim
Carlton, Collector Books 1994; *Coors
Rosebud Pottery 1st Edition* by Robert
Schneider, Busche, Waugh, Henry
Publications, 1984; "Coors Art Pottery
Pictorial" by Abigail Foster, *American Clay
Exchange,* April 1983; "Coors: More Than
Just Beer" by John M. Hightower, Jr., The
Antique Trader Weekly, July 27, 1976

COWAN POTTERY

To own a Cowan lady has long been the
dream of many collectors, even those who do
not consider Cowan Pottery on their list of
must collect.

Reginald Guy Cowan's grandfather was
the chief decorator for Onondaga Pottery in
Syracuse, New York. When Guy was eighteen
years old, he enrolled at the New York State
School of Clayworking and Ceramics. From
about 1912, Cowan had his own studio and
produced some art pottery and tiles. When
Guy Cowan enlisted during World War I,
production at the pottery stopped. It was
resumed in 1919 when Cowan reopened.
However, by 1921 he and his wife, Bertha
Bogue Cowan, moved to Rocky River, Ohio.

During the Cowan era, Guy Cowan
received many awards, one being the Mr. &
Mrs. Frank A. Logan Medal. The vase that
won this award was named the Logan vase
and is a popular one among collectors.

Cowan continued to win awards
throughout his career. Names in pottery such
as Arthur E. Baggs, Paul Bogatay, Waylande
Gregory, Elmer Novotny, Viktor
Schreckengost and Walter Sinz were his
companions and business associates.

In 1927 Cowan introduced Lakeware, a
less costly production created mostly for
florists. It was produced in red, olive green,
grey blue and green with blue.

Due to many factors, including the Great
Depression, Cowan pottery went into
bankruptcy in 1930 but it would be another
year before the company went out of business.
Due to a court order, the inventory that
remained was allowed to be sold and the
business closed in December 1931.

R. Guy Cowan then went to work for
Onondaga Pottery. He died in 1957.

From 1912-1917 Cowan hand signed items
as shown above. Sometimes he used his
initials and also COWAN POTTERY or LAKE-
WOOD WARE.

Most items with the marks shown above were
in a blue or black ink stamp. These marks
were used in the early 1920s.

Cowan Pottery Marks

Ashtray, footed, round shell
shape w/one cigarette rest,
shape No. 927F, 3 ¾" d............**$22.00**

Sunbonnet Girl Book End

Book ends, Sunbonnet girl on
base, white glaze, 7½" h., pr.
(ILLUS. of one) **475.00**

Bowl, 11" d., 3 ¾" h., footed oval
base rising to a flared body
w/two vertical ribs on each side
& three vertical ribs on each
end, ivory glaze on exterior
w/pale green interior (ILLUS.) **45.00**

Burlesque Dancer and Nubian Head

Bust, Nubian Head on pedestal,
signed "W. Gregory", 14 ¾" h.
(ILLUS. right) **1,400.00**

Candleholder, scalloped oval
base w/pink & white speckled
glaze, incised "RG Cowan" on
unglazed base, 4" d., 1¼" h........ **18.00**

Figure, Burlesque Dancer,
signed "Waylande Gregory,"
limited edition of 50, 17 ¾" h.,
(ILLUS. left) **1,650.00**

Figure of a lady dancer, standing
w/right knee bent & right foot
resting on left leg, right arm bent
at elbow w/hand resting on right

Footed Oval Bowl

buttock, left arm above head,
slightly bent at elbow & hand bent
at wrist w/palm facing forward,
shape No. 717, 15½" h............ **375.00**

Spanish Dancer Figure

Pierrot & Pierette Figures

Figure, Spanish Dancer, shape
No. 793, created by Elizabeth
Anderson, 8½" h. (ILLUS.) **450.00**

Figures, Pierrot & Pierette,
shape Nos. 791 & 792, 8¼" h.,
pr. (ILLUS.) **775.00**

Flower frog, figural nude lady,
Scarf Dancer, white high gloss,
shape No. 686, 7" h. **295.00**

Flower frog, figural nude dancer,
shape No. 680, 8½" h. **250.00**

Flower frog, figural lady on
flower petal base, upper body &
head bent back slightly, both
arms bent at elbows with left
hand bent at wrist & fingers
resting on shoulder, right hand
resting near hair, 9¼" h.
(ILLUS. bottom, next column)... **225.00**

Flower Frog Figural Lady

Flower frog, figural nude lady,
Swirl Dancer, shape No. 720..... **325.00**

Strawberry Jar with Saucer

Strawberry jar w/saucer, brown
glaze, shape SJ-1, 7½" h.
(ILLUS.) **100.00**

Scalloped Ovalfoot Vase

Vase, 6" h., scalloped oval foot
w/seahorse base & a heart
rising to a fan-shaped bowl
w/vertical ribs & scalloped rim,
mottled turquoise exterior, light
green interior (ILLUS.) **45.00**

References: *Cowan Pottery
Identification & Values* by Tim and Jamie
Saloff, Collector Books, 1994; "Brimfield
Collecting Paradise" by Ann Kerr, *American*

Clay Exchange, August 30, 1987; "Cowan:
Ohio Pottery of the Roaring Twenties" by
Grace C. Allison, *American Clay Exchange,*
March 15, 1985; "American Art Pottery Arts
& Crafts" by Dave Rago, *The Antique
Trader Weekly,* March 28, 1984; "Library In
Ohio Houses Museum of Cowan Pottery"
by Barb Mraz, *Tri-State Trader,* August 2,
1980; "Cowan Pottery," by Donald H.
Calkins, *The Antique Trader Weekly,*
November 30, 1977

Museums: Cleveland Museum of Art,
Ohio; Cowan Pottery Museum housed at
the Rocky River Public Library, Ohio; The
Western Reserve Historical Society,
Cleveland, Ohio.

CRESCENT CHINA COMPANY
See Leigh Potters, Inc.

CROOKSVILLE CHINA COMPANY

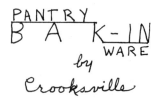

Crooksville Marks

*Ohio has been home to some of the more
highly collectible dinnerware of days past.
Crooksville, Ohio was the home of Crooksville
China Company beginning in 1902 and
continuing until 1959.*

*During those years, the company turned
out a large and varied line of dinnerware that
has proven to be of lasting quality and piqued
the interests of numerous collectors.*

*The dinnerware is a semiporcelain that
resembles vitrified china of high quality.
Probably more than any other dinnerware*

manufacturer, they used embossed blanks of fine scrolls, grapevines, bluebirds and fruits such as oranges and strawberries. As to their patterns, literally thousands of decals were used. They ranged from a delicate, simple rose, assorted fruits, black silhouettes of people and animals, black flowers, such as their Tulip pattern, and their Pantry Bak-In line which had its own decals. These were houses, flowers, windows with flowers in flower pots or a simple arrangement of leaves.

Farberware chrome-plated holders were used many times with the Crooksville products. Collectors will find them with candy or relish dishes, round sandwich trays, oblong bread trays, covered casseroles and other items.

Silhouette pattern can be found with marks such as Pantry Bak-In, Provincial Ware, or simply a Crooksville mark.

Use care not to confuse Crooksville's Silhouette with Hall's Silhouette. The most noticeable differences are that the Crooksville items have a dog sitting on the floor in a begging position while the Hall product is minus a dog; and the chairs of both people have shorter, slightly flared backs while the Hall chairs, are straight-backed and almost directly in line with the top of the peoples' heads. On close inspection, collectors will also see that Crooksville's items have distinct legs on the chairs while Hall's pieces appear in silhouette as if the chairs are solid.

Stinthal China is a mark of Crooksville but there does not seem to be any identification in the mark noting that it is a Crooksville product. One has to wonder why they did not want their name on it, since it is one of the thinnest, most delicate lines the company produced.

Candy dish, round, Silhouette patt., 6 ¾" d. **$12.50**

Candy dish, round, Silhouette patt. w/Farberware chrome-plated frame w/handle, 6 ¾" d. **24.50**

Creamer, Rust Bouquet patt., flower grouping w/dark shading in center.. **7.00**

Creamer & cov. sugar bowl, Birds blank, Indian Tree variation patt., pr. (ILLUS. front) **25.00**

Cup & saucer, Birds blank, Indian Tree variation patt., (ILLUS. front) **8.50**

Cup & saucer, Blue Blossoms patt., flowers in varying shades of blue.. **7.00**

Indian Tree Variation Pattern

Window Flower Pattern Platter

Petit Point House Pattern Salt & Pepper Shakers

Gravy boat, Spring Blossom patt., pale pink flowers w/green leaves, 6¼" l. **23.00**

Pie baker, Rust Bouquet patt., flower grouping w/dark shading in center, 10" d. **15.00**

Pie server, Hibiscus patt., red flower w/light & dark green leaves **16.00**

Plate, 7" d., Birds blank, Window Flowers patt., Pantry line **9.00**

Plate, 10" d., Birds blank, Indian Tree variation patt. (ILLUS. rear) .. **10.00**

Platter, 14" l., Fruits blank, Patt. No. 1136, Window Flowers patt., Pantry line (ILLUS.) **35.00**

Salt & pepper shakers, Petit Point House patt., red rim band, 4" h., pr. (ILLUS.) **27.00**

Sugar bowl, cov., Apple Blossom patt., 4½" h. **8.00**

DENVER WHITE POTTERY

Denver

Denver
White

enver

Denver White Pottery Marks

This pottery is perhaps the lesser known of any Western states potteries but that should change within the next few years. The work is aesthetically pleasing, well-marked and available with just a bit of perseverance.

Frederick and his son, Francis (Frank), opened F. J. White & Sons in Denver, Colorado in 1894. In 1907 when they began creating art pottery, the company name was changed to Denver Art Pottery. The company location changed several times, even a move of one year to Oklahoma City, from 1907 until 1921.

Three distinct periods are important to collectors. From 1894 until 1906 utilitarian items such as bowls, flowerpots, teapots and jugs were made. The mid period was from 1907 to 1919 when art pottery began and which ended with the death of Frederick in 1919. Those twelve years were also known as the "gray ware" period because the items were of unique semi-matt grainy appearing glazes in colors of blue, brown, green and orange with a yellow shading.

The last period from 1920 to 1960 brought about changes and four basic artware lines were produced: Monochrome glazes in a large amount of colors; Niloak-type Mission Ware with the swirls being narrower on the Denver pieces; Jasper-type ware most often with a band of white impressed reeding over the body; and decorated creations that mostly were done over the glaze.

When Frank White died in March 1960 the pottery closed.

Several marks were used during the more than sixty years the pottery operated. One mark is an incised "Denver" and might include the date of manufacture. In 1910, the mark "Denver White" and the 1910 date was used. The most common mark is an incised "Denver" with a "W" inside the "D." The hardest-to-find mark would be the incised "D" with a "W" inside it.

Mug, plain, Gray ware, impressed "Denver White 1910," 3⅝" h. **$35.00**

Plate, 9½" d., blue glaze w/slightly darker mottled blue **10.00**

Jasper Ware Vase

Vase, 4⅝" h., Jasper ware-type blue w/white overglaze decorations, marked "Denver" w/"W" inside the "D" (ILLUS.)....**130.00**

Vase, 5½" h., Jasper ware-type blue w/white impressed reeding decoration (ILLUS., top next page) **105.00**

Vase, 6" h., bulbous ovoid body tapering to a short neck w/flat rim in a swirl pattern **155.00**

Vase, 6" h., flaring slightly w/crimped rim, dark green glaze.. **100.00**

Jasper Ware Vase

References: *Colorado Pottery Identification & Values* by Carl & Jim Carlton, Collector Books, 1994; "The White Pottery" by Tom Turnquist, *American Clay Exchange*, June 1981; *Denver's White Pottery, Frederick & Francis White, A Legacy in Clay* by Thomas G. Turnquist, Homestead Press, 1980

DICKINSON
See WPA

DICKOTA POTTERY
See WPA

ECKHARDT, EDRIS
See WPA

FIESTA
See Homer Laughlin China Company

FLORENCE CERAMICS

Florence Ceramics Marks

Florence Ward began her successful enterprise in 1939. By 1946 she had moved her home workshop into a small plant in Pasadena, California. About three years later it was again necessary to move to larger facilities in the area. Semi-porcelain figurines, some with actual lace dipped in slip, were made. Figurines, such as fictional characters and historical couples, were the backbone of her business. To date, almost two hundred figurines have been documented. From about 1954 and until 1956, sculptor Betty D. Ford created what the company called 'stylized sculptures from the Florence wonderland of birds and animals.' Included were about a

half dozen assorted doves, several cats, foxes, dogs and rabbits. These items are hard to find and when one is lucky enough to obtain such a piece, normally some damage has occurred.

While practically every studio and production pottery suffered as imports came into this country, Florence Ceramics was not among them. This has to speak highly of the quality of Florence Ward's work and the amount of detail she and her employees, which numbered around fifty, put into each piece.

Several marks were used over the years with the most common being the circle with 'semi-porcelain' outside the circle. The name of the figurine was almost always included with a mark. A "Floraline" mark was used on floral containers and related items. The Floraline group has not been as much in demand as Florence Ceramics figurines. This will, no doubt, change somewhat when collectors realize that the Floraline mark is that of the Florence company. Even though the name Florence is occasionally included with the Floraline mark, more often than not the name Floraline is by itself. Since Floraline is a sturdy product and does not often bear the Florence mark, it has taken collectors some time to associate Floraline products with the same company that produced the delicate semi-porcelain statues.

There was also a script mark and a block-lettered mark as well as paper labels. So much interest has been generated by collectors during the past ten years that values for Mrs. Ward's statues have climbed rapidly during that time.

The company was sold to Scripto Corporation in 1964 and all operations of the company ceased in 1977.

Candlestick, feather effect overall in white w/gold trim, marked "Floraline by Florence Ceramics Pasadena, CA," Model No. R6, 6" h. **$25.00**

Angel Figure

Figure of an angel w/yellow hair, all-white except gold-trimmed rope sash, cuffs & collar on robe, arms bent across upper body, part of angel's wings showing, gold & brown Florence Ceramics ribbon sticker, 7" h. (ILLUS.) **110.00**

Figure of a choir boy, singing w/head slightly tilted back & holding song book, brown hair, black tie, trim at wrist & pants, white choir robe to waist, 5½" h.... **65.00**

Figure of a boy, "Mike," standing w/head thrown back & arms straight up & back, palms up, 6½" h. **130.00**

Figure of a boy, standing w/legs apart & right leg slightly bent, holding a package in right hand, white shoes, jacket & shirt, pale blue socks, pants & hat, brown hair, 6¼" h. **105.00**

Figure of a girl, "Joy," standing w/green hat, yellow dress w/white & green color, 6" h. **90.00**

Figure of GIrl Standing Planter

Figure of a girl standing in front of rectangular planter w/left arm resting on top of planter, blond hair, green & brown hat, white coat w/green buttons, green & brown gloves, 6" h. (ILLUS.)....... **35.00**

Figure of a girl standing w/feet slightly apart, sand pail in right hand & left arm bent at elbow, holding shovel to shoulder, black bathing suit w/yellow polka dots, matching scarf tied around her short blond hair w/bow at top, 7" h. **90.00**

Figure of a Grandmother sitting in chair reading, "Memories," white w/22k. gold trim **245.00**

Madonna Figure

Figure of a Madonna standing, head slightly bent, arms out from sides, all-white except brown hair, gold sash at waist, gold trim on sleeve edges & collar, halo white w/gold trim, Model No. F31, marked & round Florence sticker, also faint stamp mark "Dude Corral Loveland, Colorado," 10" h. (ILLUS.) **195.00**

Figure of a mermaid, "Jane" shelf-sitter-type w/arms at shoulders, elbows bent, Model No. M2, 7" h. **195.00**

Figure of a mermaid, "Rosie," reclining & upper body resting on one arm, other arm bent at elbow resting on waist w/hand under chin, 7" l. **185.00**

Figure of a woman, "Amber," peach high gloss long dress w/windswept skirt, left hand holding skirt, puffed sleeves, V neck, wide brim hat, right hand bent at elbow holding attached parasol behind right arm **195.00**

"Amber," without parasol **175.00**

Figure of a woman, "Amelia," standing w/left elbow bent & right hand at waist, red brocade floor-length dress w/low scalloped neckline & short sleeves, Model No. F204, 7½" h. **155.00**

Figure of a woman, "Clarissa," gloved left hand resting on shoulder, gold trim, 7½" h. **115.00**

"Clarissa" Figure

Figure of a woman, "Clarissa," left hand bare & extended in air, gold-trimmed muff & hat, maroon long dress w/white collar trimmed in gold, 7½" h. (ILLUS.) **105.00**

Figure of a woman, "Elaine," long pale grey coat, maroon hat tied under chin in large bow, maroon gloves, hands in gold muff, 5 ¾" h. (ILLUS. top, next page).... **85.00**

Figure of a woman, "Matilda," w/brown hair, light pink coat, green gloves, hat & trim on long dress, gold-trimmed purse & hat, "Matilda," incised underglaze on base, 6" d., w/base, 8" h. (ILLUS. next page) **165.00**

"Elaine" Figure

"Matilda" Figure

Figure of a woman, "Patrice,"
white Victorian long dress,
dipped lace, puffs at waist, right
arm resting at side, left hand
holding open fan & bent at elbow
w/fan resting against face, 6 ¾" h.
(ILLUS. top, next column) **125.00**

"Patrice" Figure

Figure of a woman, "Roberta,"
standing, one arm behind back,
one hand holding skirt, head
tilted, blond hair in an upsweep,
yellow floor-length dress, brown
gloves, 8 ¾" h........................... **145.00**

Model of a sitting cat, head
turned to side, porcelain bisque,
woodland brown w/black &
white accents, designed by
Betty Davenport Ford, Model
No. B-11, 14½" h. **295.00**

Model of a dove on a base,
flying position w/tail up, wings
back, head down, porcelain
bisque, brown w/white, designed
by Betty Davenport Ford, Model
No. B-6, 8" l., 11" h. **265.00**

Planter, black semi-matte, 4" d.
round pedestal rising to an oval
2" deep bowl w/alternating one
or two vertical lines at regular
intervals, in-relief mark
"Floraline USA 463,"
6" h. (ILLUS. top, next page) **30.00**

Wall plaque, rectangular
w/scalloped edges, in-relief full-
sized girl holding fan, beige
plaque w/green clothing, Model
No. P-3, 6½" l., 9" h. **120.00**

Semi-Matte Planter

Wall pocket, shell-shaped, pale pink w/muted grey high gloss, 9½" h. **125.00**

References: "Florence Ceramics Pictorial" by Susan N. Cox with photos by Jeanne Fredericks, *American Clay Exchange,* February 1988; "Florence Ceramics Pieces," staff written, *American Clay Exchange,* March 30, 1986; "Florence of Pasadena" by Grace C. Allison, *American Clay Exchange,* July 1984; Florence of Pasadena company catalog, 1954; The Florence Collectibles, An Era of Elegance by Doug Foland Schiffer Publishing Ltd., 1995.

FRANCISCAN

See Gladding, McBean & Company

FRANKOMA POTTERY

John Frank began a studio pottery in Norman, Oklahoma in 1933. A few hundred pieces were made and marked "Frank Potteries" or "Frank Pottery" with "a black indelible rubber stamp," according to John Frank. Those pieces included assorted bowls, vases, coffee mugs, pitchers and a few salt and pepper shakers.

By 1934, Mr. Frank had incorporated "Frankoma Potteries" and impressed the name also with a rubber stamp. That mark was used for two years but not everything was marked. From 1935 until November 11, 1938 the pot and leopard mark was impressed on many items. Mr. Frank and his family had moved to Sapulpa, Oklahoma in 1938 but a fire on November 11, 1938 destroyed everything including the pot and leopard mark. Today, although this mark is not scarce, it is the one collectors seek and cherish. Without a doubt, the "First Kiln Sapulpa 6-7-38" is the rarest Frankoma mark as it was used only one day on about fifty to seventy-five pieces.

A creamy beige clay, known as Ada clay and highly collectible, was used until 1953 when Frankoma changed to a red brick shale which was found in Sapulpa. Today, most clay has a pinkish-red cast.

Rutile glazes were created early in the pottery's history which give the items a two-tone color treatment. In 1970 the U. S. government closed the rutile mines in America and Frankoma had to buy it from Australia. This Australian rutile produced different results, especially with Frankoma's Woodland Moss glaze; the older, with a grey tint, being preferred by collectors.

John Frank died in 1973 and his daughter, Joniece Frank, who had been a ceramic designer at the plant, became president of the company. Again, in 1983 Frankoma was destroyed by fire. A new plant, office and showroom facilities were built on the property.

In 1991, Richard Bernstein purchased the pottery and the name was changed to Frankoma Industries. New lines have been added, glazes have been discontinued as have many of the Frankoma pottery items. Since 1992, it has been rumored that the new owners were going to discontinue the Prairie Green and Desert Gold glazes. As of this writing, this has not been done. Since this has been a consideration for several years, it will, no doubt, happen in the near future.

Collectors prefer the sculptures, limited editions, miniatures and early wares, especially those marked with the pot and leopard or with the name "Frank Pottery."

Advertising Dish

FRANK POTTERIES

FRANK POTTERY

FRANKOMA

FRANKOMA POTTERY

$\mathcal{F}$ $\mathcal{D}$ F

$\mathcal{N}F$ $JOHN$ $FRANK$

$\mathcal{N}FRANK$

Various Frankoma Marks

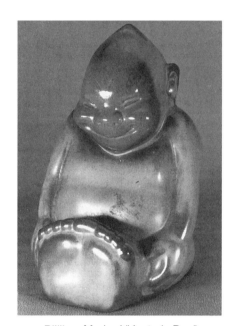

Billiken Marked "Jester's Day"

Advertising dish, "Golden Anniversary Oklahoma Natural Gas Company 1906-1956," Desert Gold, marked Frankoma, 6¼" d. (ILLUS. top, next column) **$75.00**

Baker, cov., Lazybones patt., tab handles on lid, Peach Glow glaze, Model No. 4V **28.00**

Bank, dog, brown satin glaze, Model No. 385, 1980-1982, 7½" h. **32.00**

Bank, mallard, yellow glaze, Model No. 382, 1980-1983, 4 ¾" h. **27.00**

Billiken, Prairie Green glaze, marked "Jester's Day, May 7-8, 1954 Host K. S. Boots Adams," 7" h. (ILLUS.) **90.00**

Bolo tie, model of an arrowhead, any glaze **35.00**

Book ends, model of a bucking bronco w/stepped base, Prairie Green glaze, Model No. 423, 5" l., 5¼" h., pr. (ILLUS. top, next page) **230.00**

Bucking Bronco Book Ends

Book ends, model of a charger horse, standing on a curved front base, head down & turned slightly to the side, White Sand glaze, Model No. 420, 6" h., pr. **175.00**

Book ends, model of a seahorse, ivory glaze, Model No. 426, pot & leopard mark, 5" h., pr. **725.00**

Bottle-vase, V-1, 1969, small round base rising to a bottle shape w/a long tapering neck, designed by John Frank, first in a limited edition series, 4,000 made, numbered, Prairie Green w/black base, 15" h. **115.00**

Bottle-vase, V-6, 1974, Celadon glaze w/round, black foot, designed by Grace Lee Frank Smith, sixth in a limited edition series, 4,000 made, numbered, 13" h. (ILLUS. next column).................................... **100.00**

Bottle-vase, V-8, 1976, white scalloped base w/thirteen stars, body of vase is Freedom Red w/thirteen stripes & a red stopper, designed by Joniece Frank, eighth in a limited edition series, 3,500 made, numbered, 13" h. **85.00**

Bowl, 6" d., 4" h., Jade Green glaze, pot & leopard mark, Model No. 35, ca. 1935-38 .... **95.00**

Limited Edition Bottle Vase

Bowl, 6" d., 4" h., Jade Green glaze, pot & leopard & Beauceant mark, Model No. 35, 1934 issue (ILLUS. next page) **185.00**

Bowl, 6" d., 4" h., Desert Gold, Sapulpa clay, Model No. 35 .... **23.00**

Candelabrum, holds five candles, ivory glaze, pot & leopard mark, Model No. 306, 11 ¾" l., 3" h. (ILLUS. next page) **160.00**

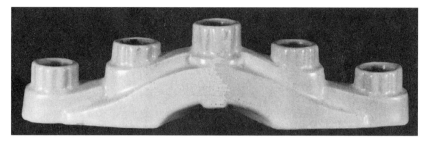

Candelabrum Model No. 306

Jade Green Bowl

Candelabrum, holds five candles, Prairie Green glaze, Model No. 306, 11 ¾" l., 3" h...... **70.00**

Christmas card, "Bird in Hand," by Grace Lee Frank Smith, bird at finger tips, palm of hand & star, White Sand glaze, 1975 (ILLUS.) **125.00**

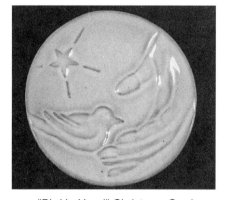

"Bird in Hand" Christmas Card

Christmas card, "Year of the Potter," two hands at potter's wheel & a star, White Sand glaze, 1975 .... **35.00**

Christmas card, "Three Frank Vases," Prairie Green, 1972 .... **55.00**

Christmas card, "Artist's Palette," shows 1978 V-10 bottle-vase, artist's palette w/three brushes & a star, White Sand glaze, 1978 .... **50.00**

Christmas card, "Baby Jesus," by Grace Lee Frank Smith, depicts Baby Jesus in a manger w/"19" on one side of manger & "78" on the other side, coffee glaze, 1978 .... **85.00**

Creamer & open sugar bowl, each w/round body w/handle, Red Bud glaze, Model No. 87A & 87B, 3¼" h., pr. (ILLUS. top, next page) **30.00**

Cup & saucer, Lazybones patt., Peach Glow glaze, Model Nos. 4C & 4E **10.00**

Cup & saucer, Mayan Aztec patt., Woodland Moss glaze, Model Nos. 7C & 7E **17.00**

Cup & saucer, Plainsman patt., Red Bud glaze, Model Nos. 5C & 5E... **15.00**

Cup & saucer, Wagon Wheel patt., Prairie Green glaze, Model Nos. 94C & 94E, cup, 5 oz., saucer, 5" d. **10.00**

Cup & saucer, Westwind patt., Peach Glow glaze, Model Nos. 6C & 6E **12.00**

Earrings, clip-on, rose glaze, pr. (ILLUS. right, next page) **28.00**

Earrings, screw-on, Prairie Green glaze, pr.......................... **25.00**

Open Sugar Bowl and Creamer

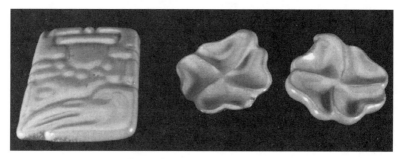

Rose Glaze Pin and Earrings

Figure of a Fan Dancer, Prairie
Green glaze, Model No. 113 .... **225.00**

Figure of a Torch Singer, black
glaze, Model No. 126, ca. 1934-
35,13½" h. (ILLUS. left) **1,400.00**

Donkey Flower Holder

Flower holder, miniature, model
of a donkey, 1942 only,
turquoise, Model No. 164
(ILLUS.) **115.00**

Figure of Torch Singer

Duck Model Flower Holder

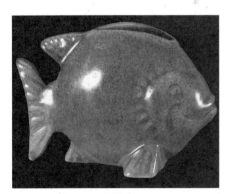

Fish Flower Holder

Flower holder, miniature, model
of a duck, 1942, Model No. 184,
Prairie Green, 3 ¾" h.
(ILLUS. top) **155.00**

Flower holder, miniature, model
of a fish, turquoise, Model No.
184, 3½" l., 2½" h. (ILLUS.)...... **155.00**

Jugs, three connected by brass
chain, solid glazes of rosetone,
jade & blue, Model No. 559,
1942 only, 2 ¾" h., set
(ILLUS. bottom) **125.00**

Bucking Bronco Model

Model of a bucking bronco, no
base, pot & leopard mark,
Model No. 121, 5¼" l., 4 ¾" h.
(ILLUS.) **205.00**

Model of a cocker spaniel dog,
reclining, Ada clay, Desert Gold
glaze, 1949, Model No. 144,
8½" l. **185.00**

Model of a deer group, bronze
green, Model No. 109, pot &
leopard mark, 9" l., 8¼" h.
(ILLUS. top, next page) **900.00**

Three Jugs Connected by Brass Chain

Model of Deer Group

Elephant Walking Model

Model of an elephant walking,
miniature, Red Bud glaze, 1951-
1957, Model No. 169, 2" h.
(ILLUS.) **95.00**

Model of a Pekinese dog,
seated in a 'begging' position
with front paws extended, ivory
glaze, pot & leopard mark,
Model No. 112, 7 ¾" h. **500.00**

Mug, Political, (Republican)
elephant, flame-red glaze
exterior, white interior,
Nixon-Agnew, 1969 .... **85.00**

Mug, Political, (Democrat)
donkey, Autumn Yellow glaze
exterior, white interior, 1975 .... **35.00**

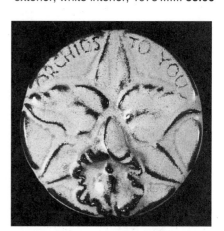

"Orchids to you" Paperweight

Paperweight, round w/orchid in
relief & "Orchids to you," Desert
Gold glaze, marked on reverse
"Nov. 14, 1964 Harold Whitley,
Tressa Whitley," 4" d. (ILLUS.)... **28.00**

Pin, Cacti, flowerpot shape
w/three ridges, slightly flared
sides w/clasp on back,
any glaze, ca. 1940s, 1½" h. **50.00**

Pin, rectangle w/Aztec patt., any
rose glaze (ILLUS. left
w/earrings)................................. **20.00**

Model No. 551 Pitcher

Pitcher, 3¼" h., Osage Brown
high gloss, Model No. 551,
production dates 1942-1961
(ILLUS.) **45.00**

Planter, model of the Alamo,
Desert Gold glaze, Sapulpa
clay, 6½" l. **20.00**

Planter, model of a cactus,
Sapulpa clay, Desert Gold
glaze, Model No. 1206, 10" l. **10.00**

Plate, 7" d., Wagon Wheel patt.,
Clay Blue glaze, Model No.
94G.. **12.00**

Plate, 7" d., Wildlife series, first
edition, Bob White Quail, 1000
created, Prairie Green glaze ... **175.00**

Plate, 7" d., Wildlife series,
seventh edition, Buffalo, 1000
created, Prairie Green glaze **90.00**

Plate, 8½" d., Bicentennial series,
1972, first edition, White Sand
glaze, "Provocations" w/staits'
spelling **130.00**

Plate, 8½" d., Bicentennial series,
1974, third edition, White Sand
glaze, "Battles for
Independence" **60.00**

Plate, 8½" d., Bicentennial series,
1976, fifth edition, White Sand
glaze, "Symbols of Freedom" **50.00**

Plate, 10" d., Mayan Aztec patt.,
Woodland Moss glaze, Model
No. 7F1...................................... **10.00**

Plate, 10" d., Westwind patt.,
Peach Glow glaze, Model No.
6F **10.00**

Platter, 13" d., Mayan Aztec patt.,
tab handles, Woodland Moss
glaze, Model No. 7Q.................. **14.00**

Salt & pepper shakers, model of
a bull seated, ivory glaze, Model
No. 166H, 2" h., pr...................... **75.00**

Salt & pepper shakers, model of
a Dutch shoe, holes show 'S' &
'P', Desert Gold glaze, Model
No. 915H, 4" l., pr. **28.00**

Sign, dealer display, "Frankoma"
on bottom front w/pacing
leopard above it, Prairie Green
glaze, 8½" l............................... **600.00**

Tepee Shaped Sign

Sign, dealer display, tepee-
shaped, Prairie Green glaze,
6½" h. (ILLUS.)........................ **525.00**

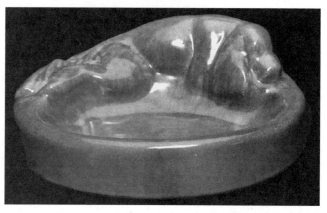

Tray with Recling Dog

Spoon holder w/hole for
hanging, Woodland Moss glaze,
Model No. 4Y, 6" l......................... **8.00**

Tray w/reclining dog, Ada clay,
turquoise glaze, Model No. 460,
7¼" l., 2½" h. (ILLUS. top)........ **155.00**

Same tray made in 1980, Model
No. 402...................................... **30.00**

Trivet, Lazybones patt., produced
1957 only, Red Bud glaze,
Model No. 4TR, 6" d. **75.00**

Trivet, Lazybones patt., produced
1957 only, Prairie Green glaze,
Model No. 4TR, 6" d. **52.00**

Trivet, Zodiac signs, 1971-1976,
Prairie Green glaze, Sapulpa
clay, Model No. ZTR, 6" sq......... **15.00**

Vase, 3½" h., Thunderbird, Model
No. 506, 1942 only, Prairie
Green glaze (ILLUS. lower left) ... **45.00**

Vase, 3¾" h., round ringed foot
rising to a spherical body,
heavily glazed Jade Green,
marked "Frank Potteries,
Norman, Oklahoma" **255.00**

Vase, 4" h., ringed footed body,
Prairie Green glaze, without
Model No., pot & leopard mark,
ca. 1933-35 .... **75.00**

Ringed Footed Vase

Model No. 506 Thunderbird Vase

Vase, 4" h., ringed footed body,
blue high gloss, incised rare
"First Kiln Sapulpa 67-7-38"
mark & impressed "Frankoma"
(ILLUS.) **375.00**

Pillow-shaped Vase

Vase, 9" h., pillow-shaped w/vertical ribs rising 1" from base & 1½" from rim, silver at rim & 1½" below rim w/silver overlay flowers & leaves between the vertical ribs, impressed "Frankoma" & "sterling" lettering on one flower leaf, 1942 (ILLUS.) **475.00**

Bulbous Ringed Body Vase

Vase, 10" h., bulbous ringed body tapering to a 3½" ringed neck w/slightly flared rim w/leaf handle on each side extending from mid-neck to shoulder, Ada clay, Red Bud glaze, Model No. 71 (ILLUS. lower left) **100.00**

Peter Pan Clay Wall Mask

Wall mask, Peter Pan, Ada clay, 6" h., (ILLUS.) **65.00**

Wall mask, Peter Pan, ivory glaze, 6" h. **110.00**

Wall pocket, model of an acorn, Sapulpa clay, Prairie Green, Model No. 190, 5½" h. **32.00**

Collecting tips: Since most Frankoma pieces are marked and include stock numbers as well, collectors have only to learn the glazes to be certain they are paying a fair value. This has proven to be a formidable task for many. To learn the basic colors, find items in limited edition pieces and study those glazes. For example, the 1968 political elephant mug was available only in White Sand glaze; the 1972 political elephant mug came only in Prairie Green glaze and the 1973 political elephant mug with Nixon-Agnew on it was available only in Desert Gold glaze. Those were the three basic Frankoma glazes.

Many collectors confuse these basic colors because they have quite a bit of 'brown' on the items also. Frankoma uses a rutile in most of their colors which causes a brown to show through. If you can forget the 'brown' then the remaining color is the actual glaze.

References: *Frankoma Pottery Value Guide & More, 1933 to Present* by Susan N. Cox, Page One Publications, 1994 & 1993; *The Collectors Guide to Frankoma Pottery, Book Two* by Susan N. Cox, Page One Publications, 1982; *The Collectors Guide to Frankoma Pottery* by Susan N. Cox, Privately printed, 1979.

Collectors' Club: Frankoma Family Collectors Association, Raymond F. Stoll, 4618 NW 34th Street, Oklahoma City, OK 73122-1330

FRAUNFELTER CHINA COMPANY

The Fraunfelter China Company began as the Ohio Pottery Company (1900-1923) of Zanesville, Ohio. During Ohio Pottery's twenty-three year history, they first made hotel ware, then hard-paste dinnerware and finally kitchenwares.

When C. D. Fraunfelter, along with other investors such as H. R. Geyer, H. A. Ernest and Hugh Hamilton, took over Ohio Pottery in 1915, they brought John Herold into the business. Herold had been trained in Carlsbad, Austria as a glass and china decorator and had worked at potteries such as Owens, Roseville and Weller. At the Roseville Pottery he was superintendent of the art department from 1900-1908 and, while there, developed the formula which was used to create the Oxblood red line known as Rozane Mongol. Having inhaled toxic fumes from the development of this line, Herold moved to Golden, Colorado and opened the Herold Pottery Company in 1910. By 1915, Herold had returned to Zanesville and joined the Fraunfelter Company. C. C. Fraunfelter also had worked at the Roseville Pottery Company for about fifteen years.

In 1923, C. D. Fraunfelter and his group, formed the Fraunfelter China Company and George E. Fraunfelter became secretary. It was also at this time that the group bought American China Products Company located in Chesterton, Indiana. Fraunfelter products

ran the gamut from delicate, flowered items to Art Deco pieces. The company introduced a new line known as 'Petroscan' ware which was the first hard paste porcelain cooking ware manufactured in the United States. Petroscan is glazed on the outside with a deep brown and white on the inside. This ware is ovenproof and fireproof, allowing the use of it over a direct flame. It was this type of porcelain that became the mainstay for the company's two locations until Mr. Fraunfelter died in 1925. It was then that the Indiana plant was closed.

As did many companies of the era, Fraunfelter sold large quantities of blanks to other companies so that they could decorate the items themselves. It is also possible to find Fraunfelter items in Farberware frames, another not so unusual event for those times.

Fraunfelter China Company, even though their past was filled with busy, affluent times, went into bankruptcy in 1931 and closed in 1939 when it was sold to the National Plumbing Supply Company.

Fraunfelter Marks

Casserole, cov., oval w/downward curved small handles, "Petroscan" mark, 7½" l., 4½" h. **$29.00**

Coffeepot, solid white semi-matte glaze w/silver trim on spout, handle & rim, decorative Farberware base frame, 8" h. **75.00**

Creamer, solid brown exterior w/white interior, vertical tab handle, 2½" h. (See Gladding, McBean for photo of identical product) **15.00**

Teapot Model No. 370

Creamer, sharply angled handle, orange & white body w/silver trim, 3 ¾" h. **15.00**

Griddle, Petroscan ware, round w/slightly scalloped edges, two brown loop handles, incised mark, 10" d. **38.00**

Sugar bowl, cov., sharply angled handle, orange & white body w/silver trim, 3½" h. **18.00**

Sugar bowl, no cover, solid brown exterior w/white interior, vertical tab handles, 2 ¾" h. (See Gladding, McBean for photo of identical product) **15.00**

Teapot, cov., apple-shaped body w/flat sides, lid slides into slots on the pot body, silver over bright orange, 7" h. **60.00**

Teapot, cov., deep green w/gold-trimmed handle, spout, knob on lid & heart-shaped decor w/small chains connecting the hearts, Fraunfelter mark on unglazed bottom, Model No. 370, 6½" h. (ILLUS.).................. **55.00**

Teapot, cov., triangular shape w/built-in squared handle, brownware, 6½" h....................... **40.00**

Vase, 6½" h., spherical footed body tapering to a short neck w/flared rim, pink luster ground w/pale pink roses on body **225.00**

Vase, 9" h., footed ovoid body tapering to a medium neck w/a flared rim, mauve w/shades of grey exterior & white interior **275.00**

   References: "Fraunfelter China Company" by Grace C. Allison, *American Clay Exchange,* April 30, 1985

FREEMAN-MCFARLIN POTTERIES

Gerald (Mac) McFarlin began McFarlin Potteries in El Monte, California in 1927. But it was not until the beginning of the 1950s when Maynard Anthony Freeman became a chief designer and partner with McFarlin that the business took off. Freeman created many earthenware sculpture pieces including animals, birds and human figures. If Freeman-McFarlin particularly liked a design, it was copyrighted and the copyright symbol was included in the mark.

Freeman's line (simply incised 'Anthony') was well-received by many major department stores across the country. Considering that numerous birds and animals were created and remained in production until the business was sold, they seem to be scarce in today's collecting market. Collectors will find that some of the items seem 'tinny' with a hollow ring to them so it is possible that many have been broken over the years. The production of ashtrays, compotes, candlesticks and vases seem more solidly made and, therefore, are more readily available.

Sometime after 1977, Freeman-McFarlin closed their El Monte operation which produced mainly bowls, ashtrays and vases, but had earlier, in 1968, opened a plant in San Marcos, California. It was this plant that produced all the other items in the line and also housed their administrative offices and warehouse. Even though International Multifoods purchased the business around 1972, it continued to produce and sell Freeman-McFarlin products throughout the 1970s. Hagen-Renaker bought the plant in 1980.

It is important for collectors to know that well-known artist, Kay Finch, sold her molds to Freeman-McFarlin after she closed her ceramics business in 1963. If collectors know the work and glazes created by Kay Finch and the work and glazes created by Freeman-McFarlin, little confusion should exist as to which company made the items. Later, Kay did create new pieces, mostly cats and dogs, for Freeman & McFarlin.

Freeman-McFarlin Marks

Ashtray, rectangular w/six cigarette rests, turquoise & beige glazes, incised "F-McF 201" & a Freeman-McFarlin Originals label, 9" l. (ILLUS.) **$15.00**

Ashtray, round w/four cigarette rests, woodtone & white crackle glaze, Freeman-McFarlin label, 7" d. **18.00**

Bowl, short bulbous body w/lobed sides & incurvate rim, high gloss red, marked "Anthony" in script underglaze, 10" d., 3½" h. (ILLUS. top, next page) **28.00**

Ashtray with Six Cigarette Rests

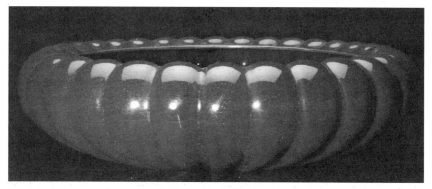

Bulbous Body Bowl

Figure of Mermaid

Figure of a mermaid holding shell-shaped soap dish, open back, pink tinge on unglazed bisque face & body, blond hair in a ponytail, some high gloss gold on mermaid's fish tail, marked "Freeman-McFarlin Potteries 1958 USA" and a copyright symbol, 8" h. (ILLUS.) **95.00**

Figure group of woman & horse, woman in riding clothes, standing with arms around neck of horse, oblong base, hand-applied black eyes on horse, goldleaf treatment, 11½" l., 10½" h. **68.00**

Model of an afghan, standing, back legs slightly apart, tail in upward position w/curve on end, head turned slightly, mouth open, Model No. 834, designed by Kay Finch & similar to her "Show Dog," Model No. 5082, 12½" l., 13½" h. **150.00**

Model of a cat, reclining, pale grey, marked "Anthony, Calif. U. S. A. 177" & a Freeman-McFarlin Potteries label, 11" l., 4½" h. (ILLUS. top, next page) ... **65.00**

Model of a falcon, standing on rock-shaped pedestal base, woodtone, beige & brown glazes, ca. 1974, 7½" l., 14" h. **80.00**

Model of a fox, sitting w/front legs straight & together between back legs, long mouth & nose, long ears, silverleaf finish, 10" h. **26.00**

Model of a kitten, reclining w/one eye shut, high gloss black fur w/grey on paws & ears, pink nose, "Freeman-McFarlin Originals" label, 5 ¾" l., 3¼" h. (ILLUS. middle, next page) **38.00**

Model of an orangutan, whimsical, sitting w/hands on top of head, wide round eyes, legs folded in front, marked "866" & label, stoneware finish, 9¼" h. **27.00**

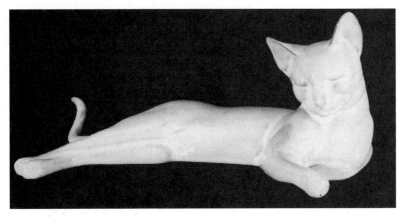

Model of Cat

Model of Kitten

Model of an owl, standing, porcelain white glaze finish, black eyes, Model No. 816, designed by Kay Finch & similar to her Model No. 189, 6" h.......... **25.00**

Planter, figural, model of a whale, tail up, stoneware finish, Model No. 408, 7" h.............................. **18.00**

Vase, 9" h., bottle-form w/body tapering to a medium stick neck w/flared rim, deep blue glaze, marked "Anthony"....................... **24.00**

Wall pocket, figural, model of a fish, pink body w/green fins & tail, black eye & eyelashes, label "McFarlin Potteries El Monte, Calif." & copyright symbol, 7½" h. (ILLUS.) **35.00**

Fish Wall Pocket

GEORGE (W.S.) POTTERY COMPANY

William Shaw George seems to have had his hand in several pottery establishments. He was involved with the East Palestine Pottery Company, Canonsburg Pottery Company, Wick China Company and the Continental China Company. Mr. George also owned a few potteries of his own.

Semi-porcelain dinnerware, hotel, and toilet wares were produced by W. S. George Pottery. Many decals and patterns were created with a large number of shapes to complement them. Shape names included Argosy (late 1920s), Bolero, Rainbow and Lido (1930s), Elmhurst (1939), Fleurette, Derwood and Times Square.

Patterns and decals were plentiful. One pattern popular with collectors is Shortcake which has several assorted sizes of red strawberries w/green leaf tops and the strawberries casting a shadow of grey, and includes a narrow rim border of a red glaze. Edwin M. Knowles also has a strawberry decal but it does not have the grey shadows. A not-so-popular pattern with buyers when it was produced was the Wampum decal (designed by Simon Slobodkin) on any shape. However, collectors today like this pattern probably because of its Native American theme and its simplicity. Any bird decal is popular with collectors and W. S. George Pottery had Bird and Bluebird decals which were usually found on the Derwood or Lido shape. In today's market, their Springtime, originally named Breakfast Nook was a decal of an open window with flowers and vines surrounding it, and their Mexican decals including Mexi-Gren that have a variety of brightly colored pots and bowls, and another (Mexi-Lido) with pots, a sombrero and a partial Spanish tile roof with green tree leaves and a small portion of an entry door showing are highly collectible. Then there is a Gracia decal which is the same as Mexi-Lido but without the partial roof and door. Gracia is also interesting to collectors.

Today collectors are finding that Rainbow and Petalware pieces are rivaling other solid color products created by Franciscan, LuRay and so on. The glazes were maroon, yellow, ivory, dark or light green, pink and blue. One line, Cavitt-Shaw, was not a success for the George Pottery. Mr. George's middle name was Shaw and it can be surmised that another family name was Cavitt, hence the Cavitt-Shaw Division.

W. S. George hoped to leave a pottery to each of his sons which is probably why he gave his production plants a number. However, only one son was interested.

Mr. George was a flamboyant man who died in 1925 but his family continued the operation until the late 1950s or early 1960s when the Royal China Company began using the facilities of the George Pottery.

George Marks

Creamer, Peach Blossom patt. **$4.00**

Cup & saucer, Bluebird patt.,
Derwood shape **15.00**

Cup & saucer, Blushing Rose
patt., any shape.......................... **10.00**

Cup & saucer, Breakfast Nook
patt., Lido shape..........................**13.00**

Cup & saucer, Gracia patt. **10.00**

Cup & saucer, Mexi-Lido patt. **11.00**

Cup & saucer, Peach Blossom
patt. **5.00**

Cup & saucer, Petit Point Rose
patt., Fleurette shape **9.00**

Cup & saucer, Rainbow patt.,
blue glaze **5.00**

Cup & saucer, Shortcake patt. **10.00**

Cup & saucer, Wampum patt.,
Ranchero shape **16.00**

Egg cup, Blushing Rose patt. **9.00**

Egg cup, Peach Blossom patt.,
Bolero shape **8.00**

Bird Pattern Plate

Shortcake Pattern Plate

Wampum Pattern

Egg cup, Petalware patt., yellow
glaze **5.00**

Egg cup, Roses patt. **8.00**

Gravy, Neville patt. **7.00**

Gravy w/underplate, Shortcake
patt. **20.00**

Gravy w/attached underplate,
Roses patt. **15.00**

Plate, 6½" d., Breakfast Nook
patt. **3.00**

Plate, 7" d., Gracia patt., Bolero
shape.. **7.00**

Plate, 9" d., Poppy patt., Rainbow
shape... **8.00**

Plate, 9" d., Bird patt., any shape **8.00**

Plate, 9" d., Petalware patt.,
maroon glaze............................... **6.00**

Plate, 10" d., Bird patt., Lido
shape (ILLUS.) **10.00**

Plate, 10" d., Shortcake patt.
(ILLUS.)....................................**10.00**

Plate, 10" d., Wampum patt.
(ILLUS.) **15.00**

Platter, 11", Poppy patt.,
Rainbow shape........................... **11.00**

Oval Platter with Center Decal

Platter, 11½", Petit Point Rose
patt., Fleurette shape **18.00**

Platter, 13½" l., oval, center decal
of man & woman of Colonial era
seated under trees, Derwood
shape (ILLUS.) **25.00**

Salt & pepper shakers,
Shortcake patt., 3 ¾" h., pr. **19.00**

Salt & pepper shakers, Blushing
Rose patt., 3½" h., pr................. **15.00**

Sugar bowl, cov. Petalware patt.,
light green.................................. **14.00**

Sugar bowl, cov., Wampum
patt., Ranchero shape **11.00**

References: "Collectible American
China—Part Six" by Jerry Barnett,
American Clay Exchange, March 30, 1985

GLADDING, MCBEAN
AND COMPANY

*Charles Gladding, Peter McBean and
George Chambers began the Gladding,
McBean Company in 1875 in Lincoln,
California. Originally they produced clay
drainage pipes, but in 1883 architectural
terra cotta was introduced and by 1926 the
company was one of the largest
manufacturers of clay products in the
western United States. Sometime later a line
of garden pottery was added. They soon
became the leading producers of tile in the
country.*

*In 1923 they purchased the Tropico
Pottery which had been in business since
1904 in Glendale, California.*

*Their line was expanded in 1934 to
include artware and dinnerware. At least
fifteen lines of art pottery were developed
between 1934 and 1942. The El Patio design
was made in twenty colors and over 100
shapes from 1934 until 1954 and the
Coronado line, introduced in 1936, also lasted
twenty years. It came in fifteen colors and
more than sixty shapes.*

*The first hand-painted Franciscan pattern
on the El Patio shape was introduced in 1937
and called Padua. It had six color
combinations and thirty-two shapes. Other
decorated dinnerware lines included Del Mar
and Mango in 1937; Hawthorne in 1938;
Apple in 1940; Wildflower in 1941; and the
highly collectible Desert Rose came out a year
later; and Ivy in 1948. These lines had border
designs embossed in the mold and were hand-*

tinted by decorators. The green trim on the edge of some Desert Rose lids was discontinued in 1947.

The Bountiful pattern is easily confused with the Fresh Fruit pattern of earlier years. Therefore, it is important to know the colors. Bountiful has golden peaches, pale red plums, purple grapes, lime green leaves and a blue tinted glaze which takes on the appearance of green.

The Ivy pattern is as it sounds; it has a green band (which was discontinued in 1968) along the edge, the larger ivy leaves are dark green while the smaller ones are a lighter green.

Forget-Me-Not is the only line with a basketweave design in the center of the plate. The flowers are light and dark blue with yellow centers, light and dark green leaves and stems. The dark green is also on the rim that has an irregular scalloped edge.

October pattern is aptly named because of its oak leaf pattern. The colors are orange, brown and tan, reminiscent of autumn.

Wildflower pattern is one of the hardest to find of all the Franciscan dinnerware lines. The California Poppy, Lupine, Mariposa Lily and Shooting Star are the flowers, with their respective colors, that make up this pattern.

Gladding, McBean purchased the Catalina line and molds in 1937 and continued production of Catalina rancho, a solid color satin matte and high gloss tableware until 1941. The company also produced an extensive line of artware vases and bowls with various glaze combinations that were marketed as Catalina Art Pottery. This artware included designs such as Angelino, Aurora, Avalon, Capistrano, Coronado, Encanto, Floral, Nautical, Polynesia, Reseda and Saguaro. Saguaro art ware was introduced in 1940 and lasted only two years because of World War II. There are at least twenty shapes and color combinations as well as ivory in Saguaro. After 1937 'Catalina Pottery' was used on some lines. (All items marked 'Catalina Pottery' were made in Glendale so use care not to confuse this mark with that of the Catalina Island mark.)

The oxblood glaze created by ceramic engineer Max Compton was used on Chinese-style shapes for Angelino ware from 1938-1942 and was produced in periwinkle blue, light bronze and satin ivory. Many of the Chinese shapes that used oxblood were in the Angelino design group.

A new vitrified body for hotel china was developed in 1939 and used the following year for Franciscan Fine China. The Masterpiece China line made from 1941-1979 featured over one hundred and sixty-five decorative patterns on nine basic shapes. Informal china called Discovery was made in a medium weight by a series of designers from 1958-1975. These artists included Harrison McIntosh, Rupert Deese, Henry Takemoto and Francis Chun.

The Tiempo line of dinnerware was introduced in 1949 in four colors: leaf, copper, stone and sprout. The flatware was square in shape and items such as cups and pitchers had oval handles with an indentation in the outer center of the handle for an easier grip. For 1949 this line could be considered futuristic, being billed in advetisements as "modern."

Many companies suffered great financial hardships when competition from well-made, inexpensive Japanese china was imported to the United States in the 1950s. Gladding, McBean was no exception and the company eventually stopped china production in 1979. However, earthenware products continued to be made. But, due to declining sales, Gladding, McBean sold its Franciscan plant in 1962 to Lock Joint Pipe Company which became Interpace Corporation in 1968.

New patterns continued to be developed in the 1960s and 1970s, including Tulip Time, Madeira, Pebble Beach and Hacienda, to name a few. Franciscan created Kaleidoscope, a plain design in solid color glazes. Wall, floor and decorative tiles were made until 1982.

Franciscan Ceramics was sold to Josiah Wedgwood and Sons, Ltd. of England in 1979. When production stopped in Los Angeles in 1984, a three day public auction was held on the forty-five acre site. Everything that was to be auctioned had a ten million dollar evaluation and when it was over, almost three hundred people had lost their jobs. Wares continue to be made in England.

A tremendous variety of marks was used during the years of production. For a short time Gladding, McBean stamped their wares *with the Tropico Pottery mark; but the majority of pieces were signed 'GMcB' in an oval. Later the mark was changed to 'Franciscan' with several variations.*

Gladding Marks

Ashtray, Apple patt., 4 ¾" sq. **$65.00**

Ashtray, Apple patt., 4½" l. **25.00**

Ashtray, Cafe Royal patt., 4 ¾" sq. **25.00**

Ashtray, Coronado artware, shell shape, 4" l. **22.00**

Ashtray, Ivy patt., leaf shape, 4½" l **20.00**

Ashtray, Poppy patt., 4¼" l. **55.00**

Ashtray, Wildflower patt., model of a Mariposa Lily, 3½" d. **65.00**

Ashtray, Wildflower patt., model of a Poppy, 3½" d. **60.00**

Bowl, 5¼" d., Forget-Me-Not patt. **14.00**

Bowl, 5¼" d., October patt. **15.00**

Bowl, 5½" d., 1¼" h., Ivy patt. **12.00**

Bowl, 6" d., 3½" h., mixing, Apple patt. **85.00**

Bowl, 7 d., Forget-Me-Not patt..... **15.00**

Bowl, 7 d., October patt. **16.00**

Bowl, 8" d., vegetable, Desert Rose patt. **35.00**

Bowl, 8½" d., 2½ " h., vegetable, Apple patt. **45.00**

Bowl, 9" d., 4 ¾" h., mixing, Apple patt. **125.00**

Bowl, 10 ¾" d., mixing w/handle & pour spout, vertical ribs & horizontal waves, marked "GMcB" in oval, beige high gloss, Cocinero patt. (ILLUS. below)...... **38.00**

Bowl, 10¾" l., 2¼" h., vegetable, divided, Apple patt. **45.00**

Bowl, 10¾" l., 2¼" h., vegetable, divided, Cafe Royal patt. **40.00**

Bowl, 11¼" d., salad, Ivy patt..... **110.00**

Bowl, 11¾" l., Capistrano artware, ivory satin exterior, turquoise interior......................... **25.00**

Bowl, 13" l., Coronado artware, footed, satin ivory glaze............. **35.00**

Butter dish, Cafe Royal patt., 7 ¾" l. **45.00**

Bowl with Handle

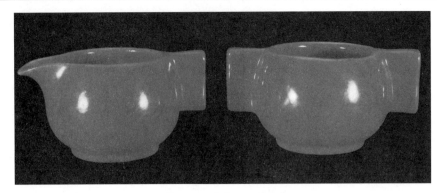

Creamer & Sugar Bowl

Butter dish, Forget-Me-Not patt.,
7½" l. **50.00**

Butter dish, Ivy patt., 8" l. **45.00**

Coaster, Apple patt., 3¾" d.,
1" h. **37.00**

Compote, footed, Ivy patt., 8" d.,
3¾" h. **80.00**

Creamer, Ivy patt., 4" h. **30.00**

Creamer, Wildflower patt.,
3¾" h. **65.00**

Creamer & open sugar bowl,
orange glaze, vertical tab
handle, Fraunfelter china made
an identical set, creamer
2¾" h., pr. (ILLUS.)
creamer **16.00**
sugar bowl **18.00**

Cup & saucer, Apple patt.,
2¾" h. **17.00**

Cup & saucer, Apple patt.,
3¾" h. **55.00**

Egg cup, Apple patt., 3 ¾" h. **26.00**

Figure of a Samoan woman on
round base, w/arms bent
holding child on her left
shoulder, designed by Dorr
Bothwell, ca. 1937, satin white
glaze, 13" h. (ILLUS. right) **85.00**

Flowerpot, Tropico artware,
round w/gently flaring sides,
blue high gloss, 6" h. **30.00**

Goblet, Desert Rose patt.,
6½" h. **95.00**

Figure of Samoan Woman

Gravy boat w/attached
underplate, Coronado patt. **30.00**

Gravy boat w/attached
underplate, Desert Rose patt.,
3½" h. **45.00**

Gravy boat w/attached
underplate, Poppy patt., 9" l.,
3½" h. **95.00**

Gravy boat w/unattached
underplate, Poppy patt.,
9" l., 3½" h., 2 pcs...................... **85.00**

Mug, straight sided, October
patt., 3½" h. **25.00**

Napkin ring, October patt.,
   1½" d. **38.00**
Pickle dish, Ivy patt., 10½" l. **40.00**
Pitcher, 8" h., Poppy patt. **200.00**

Apple Pattern Pitcher

Pitcher, 8 ¾" h., 2 qt. water,
   Apple patt. (ILLUS.) **90.00**
Plate, 6" d., Bountiful patt. **12.00**
Plate, 6¼" d., Poppy patt. **20.00**
Plate, 6½" d., Apple patt. **9.00**

Coronado Pattern Plate

Plate, 6½" d., Coronado patt.
   (ILLUS.) **9.00**

"Ambushed" Plate

Plate, 7" d., "Ambushed," fifth in a
   series of six, Charles M.
   Russell, American (1864-1926),
   limited edition of 2500, marked
   "Franciscan Masterpiece China
   Made in USA" in a curved oval
   similar to an early TV screen
   (ILLUS.) **50.00**
Plate, 8" d., Poppy patt. **32.00**
Plate, 10½" d., Apple patt. **15.00**

Desert Rose Pattern Plate

Plate, 10½" d., Desert Rose patt.
   (ILLUS.) **17.00**

Plate, 10½" d., El Patio patt.......... **14.00**

Plate, 10½" d., Forget-Me-Not
patt. **24.00**

Plate, 10½" d., October patt. **26.00**

Plate, 10½" d., Wildflower patt. **55.00**

Plate, 11" d., Apple patt............... **75.00**

Plate, 14" d., chop, El Patio patt. ... **30.00**

Platter, 12" l., October patt.......... **60.00**

Platter, 14" l., Wildflower patt. **115.00**

Platter, 19" l., Ivy patt. **250.00**

Salt & pepper shakers, Bountiful
patt., 3" h. pr. **29.00**

Salt & pepper shakers,
Coronado patt., 3" h., pr. **16.00**

Salt & pepper shakers, Desert
Rose patt., 2¼" h., pr.................. **25.00**

Salt & pepper shakers, Desert
Rose patt., 6¼" h., pr.................. **55.00**

Salt & pepper shakers, Ivy patt.,
2¾" h., pr. **25.00**

Sugar bowl, cov., Poppy patt.,
3¾" h. **90.00**

Sugar bowl, cov., Wildflower
patt., 4¼" h. **85.00**

Teapot, cov., Desert Rose patt.,
6½" h. **105.00**

Tile, Bountiful patt., 6" sq............. **60.00**

Tile with Bowl and Spoon

Tile, white w/red edge trim & center
w/open bowl & spoon decor,
marked "Gladding, McBean USA
trademark, U. S. Pat. No.
1628910," 6" sq.(ILLUS.)............... **20.00**

Tumbler, Apple patt., 3¼" h. **33.00**

Tumbler, Apple patt., 5¼" h. **25.00**

Tumbler, Wildflower patt., 5½" h. ... **80.00**

Vase, 5" h., model of a fish, white
satin glaze exterior, turquoise
interior **37.00**

Vase, 6" h., round foot rising to
bulbous body tapering to medium
neck w/flared rim, oxblood
exterior w/white interior.............. **200.00**

Vase, 6" h., bud, Cafe Royal
patt. **80.00**

Vase, 10½" h., scalloped base
w/rising flutes to a slightly flaring
body & rim, Coronado artware,
ivory glaze **100.00**

References: *Franciscan Embossed Hand Painted* by Delleen Enge, privately printed 1992; *Hot Tea* "From Our Readers" section, January 1986; *Franciscan Ware* by Delleen Enge, Collector Books 1981; "Capistrano Art Ware" by Delleen Enge, *American Clay Exchange* November 15, 1986; "Gladding, McBean—California's Renaissance Man" by Eloise V. Wilson, an in-depth study of Angelo Simone's restoration of buildings while an employee in the architectural department of Gladding, McBean and the uses of their materials, *American Clay Exchange,* October 1982; "Franciscan Dinnerware" by Lois Lehner, *Depression Glass Daze,* January 1981

Newsletter: Franciscan Newsletter, James Elliot, Editor; 8412 - 5th Avenue NE, Seattle, Washington 98115.

GLIDDEN POTTERY

In Alfred, New York in 1940, a young designer, Glidden Parker, Jr. established Glidden Pottery. Collectors today are beginning to take an avid interest in his work which has not yet reached the values that such unique and interesting creations will no doubt obtain within the next few years.

The stoneware body of Glidden pottery is enhanced by varying shapes, individually ground glazes and hand decorations. This personalized treatment expresses a feeling of fine art.

Even though Glidden Parker, having been trained at the New York State College of Ceramics at Alfred University, created many unusual art forms, collectors are finding his dinnerware and tableware of prime interest. Some collectors eagerly seek only the poodle motif while others prefer the feather or rooster designs. Then there are those who collect only the canape dishes, square-shaped and with varying decorations of butterflies, reindeer, sheep and other animals and characters.

Glidden's casseroles are unique in that the tab handles on lids fit into the tab handles on the bowls. Though not secure, the design was unique for the time and did create some safety for its contents.

While the composition of Glidden pieces is heavy, due to the stoneware body, and the bottoms are unglazed, many motifs are reminiscent of the work of Sascha Brastoff. For example, Glidden's sandstone boat ashtray, covered casserole and vase are similar to Brastoff's stripes, bands and rings that adorned many of his pieces. Occasionally, one might believe that some of the sugars with lids, creamers, or plates with their angled, bold designs are Russel Wright creations. This is not to say that any of the men copied the designs of others. It is merely a method by which collectors can be aware of the products of several artists, working in different media to create works borne of their own special talents.

By far, the majority of Glidden designs were created by Glidden Parker; however, Sergio Dello Strologo and George Fong Chow also designed several lines. Many of the patterns were sgraffito-type.

Glazes such as Gulfstream, Cayenne, Boston Spice, Celadon, Blackstone, Charcoal, Grey and Saffron (created by Sergio Strologo in 1956, were developed in the Glidden studios. Glidden Pottery closed in 1957.

Glidda
167

Glidden
103

Glidden Marks

Ashtray, three cigarette rests, Gulfstream blue, Model No. 4024, 8½" d. **$45.00**

Ashtray, Safex line, turquoise glaze, square w/two smaller decorated inner squares, 8½" **45.00**

Bowl, 7" d., Model No. 4011, 7" d. **50.00**

Bowl, 7" d., 2" h., turquoise glaze **20.00**

Canapé dish, clown motif, 5½" sq. (ILLUS.) **37.00**

Clown Motif Canapé dish

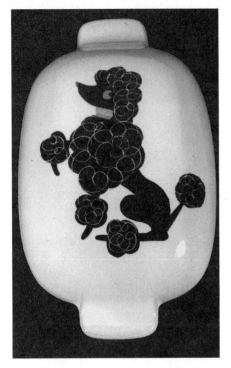

Poodle Pattern Casserole

Canapé dish, lion motif, 5½" sq. ... **30.00**

Canapé dish, rooster motif, 5½" sq. **25.00**

Canapé dish, tiger motif, 5½" sq. ... **30.00**

Canapé dish, tight rope walker
motif, 5½" sq............................. **35.00**

Canapé dish, trapeze artist motif,
5½" sq. **35.00**

Casserole, cov., poodle motif on
lid, marked "Glidden 163" on
unglazed bottom, 2 qt., 11¼" l.,
5½" h. (ILLUS.)........................ **105.00**

Casserole, cov., rooster motif on
lid, marked "Glidden 167" on
unglazed bottom,½ pt. size,
5½" l., 2 ¾" h. (ILLUS.).............. **50.00**

Plate, 7½" d., salad, Saffron
glaze, Model No. 465 .... **11.00**

Plate, 10¼" sq., Feather patt........ **15.00**

Tumbler, Feather patt., Model
No. 1127, 5½" h......................... **38.00**

References: "Glidden Pottery", by Jean
B. Lang, *The Antique Trader Weekly,*
January 6, 1982.

Rooster Motif Casserole "Glidden 167"

GONDER CERAMIC ART COMPANY

Gonder

E-1

GONDER
U.S.A.

Gonder Marks

Lawton Gonder had been associated with such companies as American Encaustic Tiling Company, Cherry Art Tile and Florence Pottery. Credited with influencing Gonder in his early years were his parents, who worked for Weller Pottery, and John Herold who worked at the Ohio Pottery Company. It was Herold who gave Lawton Gonder his early training when he worked for him during Gonder's teen years.

While Lawton Gonder was at American Encaustic Tiling Company, he worked in the research department and was associated with such talented men as Harry Lillibridge and Frederick Rhead. When American Encaustic Tiling built a plant in New Jersey in 1927, Gonder became its manager. He remained there until 1934 and was largely responsible for supervising the equipment installation for the Hermosa process. Called Hermosa tile, it was a trade name for a process developed by the Prouty family at Hermosa Beach, California. It was the initial process that allowed a bonding to tiles which was guaranteed to prevent crazing. The Hermosa Tile operation was sold to American Encaustic Tiling Company in 1926.

Gonder was also a consultant for Fraunfelter China and the Standard Tile Company from 1934-1936.

After the Florence plant was destroyed by fire in 1941, Gonder opened Gonder Ceramic Art Company in Zanesville, Ohio. It was there that he created animal and human figures, cookie jars, tiles and Oriental pottery.

He also made a line of dinnerware in the 1950s known as La Gonda which was thick, heavy and square-shaped.

Many collectors can see and feel RumRill characteristics in Gonder pottery. RumRill had been produced at Florence Pottery and speculation among historians, researchers and collectors indicates that some RumRill may have been made at the Gonder operation.

Gonder used his initials "LG" to create a new company named Elgee which was established to produce lamp bases. This company operated from 1946 until a fire destroyed it in 1954. Gonder moved the lamp business to the Gonder plant but all Gonder production ceased in 1957.

Swirl Bulbous Bottom Cookie Jar

Cookie jar, cov., swirl bulbous bottom w/horizontal rings from shoulder to lip, light blue high gloss, marked "Gonder P-24 U. S. A." underglaze, 7¼" h. (ILLUS.) **$38.00**

Creamer, beige ground w/dark brown spatterware treatment, 4½" h. **12.00**

Cup & saucer, square w/square-shaped handle on cup, yellow w/brown mottling, La Gonda patt., 3" h. set, ... **15.00**

Ewer, dark brown w/yellow mottling, incised "Gonder" underglaze, 6" h., (ILLUS. top, next page) **15.00**

Dark Brown Ewer

Closed-Handle Vase

Figure of an Oriental woman
standing on a round base, arms
clasped in front, green & pink
glaze, 8¼" h................................ **30.00**

Plate, 8" sq., pink w/white
mottling, La Gonda patt. **8.00**

Salt & pepper shakers, yellow
w/brown mottling, La Gonda
patt., pr. **13.00**

Sugar bowl, cov., beige ground
w/dark brown spatterware
treatment, 5 ¾" h. **15.00**

Tile, plain, brown w/dark brown
spatterware treatment, 6" sq. **15.00**

Vase, 6½" h., w/closed handles
above & below shoulder on
each side, yellow exterior w/pale
pink interior (ILLUS.) **20.00**

Vase, 8¼" h., upright cornucopia
on square base, pale blue
exterior w/pink interior **33.00**

Vase, 9" h., model of a feather
w/exaggerated detailing, pink
exterior w/brown interior **38.00**

Vase, 9" h., spherical 6" h. footed
body w/large trumpet neck, in-
relief question mark forms on
body... **35.00**

Vase, 9½" h., model of a swan on
rectangular base w/swan's head
low on front of body & neck bent
forming handle, pink & blue
mottling....................................... **50.00**

GRACETONE POTTERY

*John Frank, owner of Frankoma Pottery
Company, purchased Synar Ceramics of
Muskogee, Oklahoma in late 1958. Synar had
been using a white bodied clay with glazes
such as alligator, woodpine, white satin,
ebony, wintergreen and a black and white
straw combination.*

*It was late in 1959 that Mr. Frank
changed the name to Gracetone Pottery in
honor of his wife, Grace Lee. However, for a
short time, Mr. Frank continued to use Synar
catalogs, materials and the white body. Some*

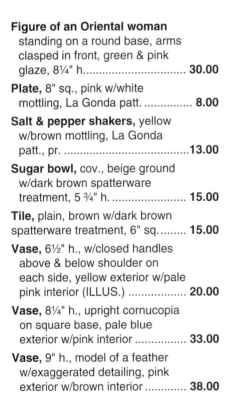

problems have existed in minor details. For example, Synar had two fawns, white clay bodies, one eight inches high and the other six inches high. One was Model No. 100 and the other was No. 101. Gracetone made the identical fawns, except with a red clay body and the mark, with Model Nos. 200 and 201.

It was only a few months, still in 1959, that Orbit dinnerware was introduced. It had Frankoma's red clay body and Mr. Frank was financially able to have new molds and glazes as well as Gracetone's own catalogs made.

Orbit originally came in two glazes: pink champagne or cinnamon (originally named cinnamon toast). Later, a blue-grey (called aquamarine by the Franks) was added. The line is unique as its form is of a circular nature, reminiscent of space orbit, and some of the circles are pierced. This piercing, even though Orbit is sturdy, causes some damage to the items.

After converting from the white clay body to Frankoma's red clay, Mr. Frank added many Frankoma pieces to the Gracetone line. For example, he had issued for the year 1963 the Willard Stone sculptures of the coyote (Frankoma's No. 102) and the mare & colt (Frankoma's No. 103). He would not reissue them until the sculpture catalog came out in 1972-73. These two items are still available in Frankoma's line. Also, the squirrel (Frankoma's No. 105) was in Graceton's catalog as No. 215, the coyote as No. 209 and the mare & colt as No. 210. While the catalog is undated, it had to be between 1959 and 1962.

John Frank had taken Mr. J. C. Taylor, an employee at Frankoma, with him to manage Gracetone. When Mr. Frank decided that Gracetone was not profitable and wanted to sell, Mr. Taylor offered to buy it. The deal took place on May 31, 1962. Mr. Taylor closed the business in early 1967.

In the years the Frank family owned Gracetone Pottery, approximately 700,000 pieces were made. This is a small number considering that all the Orbit dinnerware pieces and the art pieces are included in that figure.

Evidently, John Frank wanted to use some of Gracetone's molds to make Frankoma pieces but did not want to cause confusion between the two companies. Generally, if a Frankoma item has the letter "F" before a stock number, it most probably was a Gracetone product before it went into Frankoma's line.

GRACETONE

Gracetone Marks

Ashtray, Orbit patt., round, Model No. 2AT1, pink champagne glaze, 7" d................................. **$23.00**

Irregular Scalloped Rim Bowl

Bowl, 8¼" d., 1 ¾" h., round w/irregular scalloped rim, wintergreen glaze, Model No. 128 (ILLUS.) **20.00**

Christmas card, reverse "1960 Christmas Gracetone Pottery," aqua or pink champagne glaze, 3¼" h. (ILLUS. top, next page) ... **95.00**

Without Christmas & date, it was an ashtray, Model No. 2AT3... **15.00**

Christmas card, reverse "1960 Christmas Gracetone Pottery," matte black, 3¼" h.................... **135.00**

Christmas Card

Cup & saucer, Orbit patt., aqua glaze, Model Nos. 2C & 2E **12.00**

Gravy boat, Orbit patt., cinnamon glaze, Model No. 2S, 24 oz., 7" h. **35.00**

Model of Fawn No. 201

Model of a fawn, standing on round base, non-descript front & back legs, head bent, one ear touching front leg, satin white glaze, Model No. 201, incised "Gracetone," 6" h. (ILLUS.)......... **45.00**

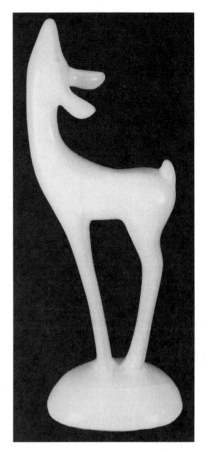

Model of Fawn No. 200

Model of a fawn, standing on round base, non-descript front & back legs, head up & back, satin white glaze, Model No. 200, incised "Gracetone," 7 ¾" h. (ILLUS.).......................... **55.00**

Model of a terrier dog, woodtone finish, Model No. 205, 5½" h. (ILLUS. top, next page) **200.00**

Planter, model of a horse, white high gloss body w/pink decorations, incised "Synar 524," 6½" h. (ILLUS. next page) ... **49.00**

Planter, Nautilus, pink champagne glaze, incised "Gracetone 307," 4¼" h. (ILLUS.) **28.00**

Model of Terrier Dog No. 205

Model of Horse Planter

Gracetone 307 Planter

Plate, 10" d., Orbit patt., pink champagne glaze, Model No. 2F... **10.00**

Platter, 17" d., Orbit patt., aqua glaze, Model No. 2P **28.00**

Salt & pepper shakers, Orbit patt., cinnamon glaze, Model No. 2H, 4¼" h., pr...................... **25.00**

Spoon rest, Orbit patt., aqua glaze, Model No. 2Y, 6½" l. **10.00**

References: "Orbit Dinnerware" by Susan N. Cox, *American Clay Exchange,* June 1983; *The Collectors Guide to Frankoma Pottery Book Two* by Susan N. Cox, Page One Publications 1982; Gracetone company catalogs and brochures

GRANTIER, CHARLES
See WPA

HAEGER POTTERY COMPANY

David Haeger began Haeger Pottery in 1871 in Dundee, Illinois. As with many companies of the time, it was created to produce bricks and tiles. It was not until Edmund, David's son, took charge of the operation in 1900 that art pottery was introduced four years later. With much foresight, Edmund built an entire operation for ceramics at the 1934 Chicago World's Fair.

As Haeger Pottery continued to grow, a small amount of dinnerware, children's dishes and tea sets was introduced in 1919.

Royal Arden Hickman, a talented designer who was born in 1893, worked for Joseph Estes, Edmund's son-in-law from 1938-1944. Hickman, known as "Hick," introduced a line of artwares and lamp bases. The letter and number "R-1" was assigned to the first piece designed by Hickman and thereafter his designs were in chronological order. This enables collectors to know that the lowest number was the first produced. In 1944, Royal Hickman left Haeger Potteries. He died in 1969.

In 1939 selected figurines that had been created at Haeger were used for lamp bases for the new Royal Haeger Lamp Company in Dundee. In 1969, this operation was moved to Macomb after Haeger bought the Western Stoneware plant.

Also, in 1939, artware for the florist trade was created when Haeger bought the Buckeye Pottery building in Macomb.

Eric Olsen, originally associated with Wedgwood and Spode, became responsible for designing most of the Haeger artware and lamps and was Haeger's chief designer in 1947. He remained with Haeger Potteries until 1972.

In 1971 Haeger put out a "Centennial Edition" catalog which featured two ceramic lines bearing a mold impressed "Sascha B" - "Esplanade" and "Roman Bronze." The glazes were in a gray, brown and green with a metallic overlay or in a white or gold. Other freelance artists were Ben Seibel, Helen Conover and Lawrence Peabody.

In March, 1978, Alexandra Haeger Estes, then Assistant Executive Vice President of Operations stated that, "Haeger's three factories employed approximately 500 people." She further commented that the "...clays were shipped in from Tennessee, Kentucky, Wisconsin, Florida, Georgia, South Carolina, New York and Canada." By 1981 (Haeger's 110th year), Alexandra Haeger Estes was President of Haeger Industries, Inc.

On several occasions Haeger Pottery assisted in the production of items for other companies. As an example, Frankoma Pottery of Oklahoma was commissioned to produce more than 200,000 Easter plates for the Oral Roberts Association in Tulsa. Frankoma could not produce them fast enough so they enlisted the help of Haeger and also the McCoy Pottery Company. The plates show "Frankoma" on the reverse but all of them were not made at that company. Haeger's plate is a plain white as opposed to Frankoma's white with a brown showing through; Haeger's plate is a seven inch diameter while Frankoma's is about a half-inch larger; and, probably the most helpful clue is that the inner rim (foot) on the reverse is a solid red clay from the Frankoma factory but a glazed white clay from Haeger. Haeger also fired on a tripod so if tripod marks are there, you can be assured it came from them.

Another example is the Haeger "Keebler Elf" cookie jar. Haeger created the original but Nelson McCoy later did it. The major difference is the little man was hand-painted by Haeger while the McCoy jar has a decal.

It is easy to predict that Royal Haeger will become a hot collectible within the next decade. The company was one of the most diversified businesses in terms of merchandise variety and the uniqueness of glazes used. Planters, statues, flower frogs, bowls, dinnerware, musical planters, decanters, lamps, mermaids and ashtrays are but a few items produced. The numerous glazes, generally known as "flambé" which blended two or more glazes, were named Cats Eye which resembled the whitish green of the cats eye gem; Blue of Sky, a dark blue with a blend of white producing a cloudy effect; and Chinese blue, a dark blue which might be found speckled with darker flecks. Many, many glazes with unusual names and treatments were a part of Haeger's marketing strategies.

Haeger used numerous labels over the years. They also incised pieces with "Haeger" sometimes within a diamond. In a letter dated 1978, Alexandra Haeger Estes wrote, "We find that to use a permanent mark on the bottom of our pieces is not feasible at times due to the design, as where possible, we do like to make an item from a 2-piece mold. If we imprint the bottom, it becomes necessary to make a 3-piece mold which in turn raises the price of the item considerably."

ROYAL HICKMAN
USA
459

Haeger Marks

Ashtray, octagonal shape, Esplanade line created by Sascha Brastoff, 6" d. **$35.00**

Ashtray, round w/one cigarette rest, "A Century of Progress 1933-34" souvenir, incised mark "Haeger" within a diamond, 4½" d. **20.00**

Bowl, 7 ¾" d., 3" h., three-footed w/tan & green flambé, Model No. 5, incised "Haeger" mark (ILLUS. below)............................ **30.00**

Box, octagonal w/lid, Esplanade line created by Sascha Brastoff, 5½" d. **55.00**

Candlestick, model of a plume, Model No. R295, 4" h. **10.00**

Cookie jar, cov. cobalt pedestal base w/wood lid knob, cobalt & pale blue shading, marked underglaze, "Royal Haeger R1730 U. S. A.," 9½" h. (ILLUS. first column, next page) **30.00**

Cookie jar, cov., "Keebler Elf" (see text) **85.00**

Creamer and open sugar bowl, square shape w/rounded corners, circle on each side of body, white matte, diamond-shaped dark green & gold sticker, creamer 4" l., 2½" h., pr. (ILLUS. top next page) **16.50**

Figure of a boy, "Little Brother" standing w/right leg turned slightly outward, arms folded at waist w/left arm holding handle of large basket, Model No. R1254, 11½" h............................ **22.00**

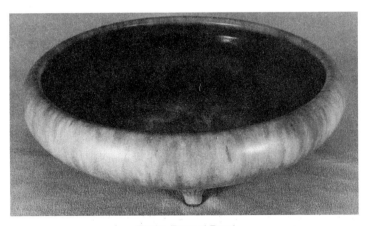

Three Footed Bowl

Open Sugar Bowl & Creamer

Pedestal Based Cookie Jar

Model of Dog No. 6009X

Figure of a Gypsy girl, long dress, basket at right elbow w/arm slightly bent, holding second basket w/left hand, arm outstretched, w/both baskets attached to dress, Model No. R1224, 16½" h............................. **65.00**

Lamp, TV, bucking bronco w/riding cowboy, cacti behind horse, Model No. 6105, 11½" l. **75.00**

Lamp w/planter, TV, model of a greyhound on a base, Model No. 6202, 13" l............................ **38.00**

Model of a dog, marked "Royal Haeger USA" & copyright symbol, autumn brown high gloss, Model No. 6009X, 4" h. (ILLUS.) **18.00**

Model of a horse on an oval base, walking position w/right leg bent & tail up, Royal Haeger gold & dark green sticker w/"Royal Haeger Pottery 75th Anniversary," 5¼" h. (ILLUS. top next page) **18.00**

Planter, model of a pig standing, bulbous body w/gold leaves & flowers, Model No. 454N, 10" l... **21.00**

Model of Horse

Oblonged Shape Vase Model No. R282

Model of Fish Vase

Cylindrical Shaped Vase

Plate, 7¼" d., Oral Roberts
Easter advertising (see text)....... **10.00**

Vase, 6" h., model of a fish, white
high gloss, green & silver
Haeger sticker (ILLUS.)............... **9.50**

Vase, 8" h., 10½" l., oblong-
shaped w/flared sides from top
of corner feet to rim, white 1¼" h.
oblong base, solid blue vase,
Model No. R282, marked "Royal
Haeger USA," (ILLUS. second
column)...................................... **20.00**

Vase, 9" h., cylindrical shape
w/ribbon tied above an irregular
base & rising to an uneven rim,
marked in-relief on unglazed
bottom "Royal Hickman USA
459," (ILLUS.)............................. **22.00**

Vase, 12" h., pillow-type,
Moonstone white glaze, Model
No. RG13 .... **12.00**

Vase, 16" h., three morning glory-
shaped holders rising from a
leaf base, Model No. R452......... **35.00**

Wall pocket, grapes form a cone shape w/grape leaves at rim & trailing down towards grapes, chartreuse & purple, Model No. R745 .... **15.00**

Wall pocket, model of a fish, Model No. R1627, 13" l. **18.00**

References: *Collector's Encyclopedia of Sascha Brastoff* by Steve Conti, A. DeWayne Bethany & Bill Seay, Collector Books 1995; *Collecting Royal Haeger* by Lee Garmon and Doris Frizzell, Collector Books 1989; Correspondence between Haeger Potteries and Susan N. Cox, 1980 through 1989; Haeger Potteries letter to Tran Turner, California, 1978; *Daily Courier News* December 7, 1971 insert Commemorative Edition 1871/1971 Haeger the Craftsmen for a Century; *Design for Living,* January 1967 "Ceramics in Action, Haeger Potteries"

HALDEMAN POTTERY
See Caliente Pottery

HALL CHINA COMPANY

When the East Liverpool Potteries Company went out of business in 1903, Robert Hall opened the Hall China Company. However, one year later he died and his son, Robert T. Hall, took over.

Originally, Hall Pottery created toilet sets, jugs and whiteware but by 1915 they had added a vitrified, fireproof cooking china. This china was advertised as sanitary with a leadless glaze and consisted mostly of coffeepots and teapots, sugars and creamers, custards, bean pots and casseroles. Also, they made large ice cream packing jars and steam table pots, insets and pans. Most of this ware came in white, green, brown or a combination of those colors. Hall guaranteed that these products could not craze, crack or absorb. The *Modern Hospital* journal ran an article in July 1915, explaining the difference between china and earthenware for cooking purposes with an emphasis on Hall's unique developments. After much success with this type of ware, it was used on the Gold Decorated teapot line in the early 1920s. Additional shapes and colors for teapots were added each year until circa 1948.

Hall developed many dinnerware and kitchenware lines from the 1930s through the 1950s. Decals and prints were readily and often used for decoration on these lines. Autumn Leaf, which was developed in 1933 for the Jewel Tea Company, began as a pattern for their kitchenware. By 1936 Hall was using this decal for its dinnerware line which became extensive over the years until it was discontinued in 1976. A few items were made again in 1978 as awards for their sales people. Most of these will have a 1978 dinnerware backstamp.

Hall's survived for many decades when other companies failed due to imports, so it is reasonable to understand the numerous and varied shapes, decals and patterns that were created. Hall China also made advertising items and lamps.

Hall China Company Marks

Ball jug, No. 3, Blue Bouquet
patt. **$75.00**

Bowl, 5½" d., fruit, Crocus patt....... **9.00**

Bowl, 5½" d., fruit, Silhouette
patt. **8.00**

Jewel Rainbow Bowl

Bowl, 5½" d., 3" h., small round
foot w/two rows of beading
above foot & flared rim w/one
row of beading near rim, marked
"Hall Radiant Ware," green high
gloss, from the Jewel Rainbow
Bowl Set, stackable size
(ILLUS.) **18.00**

Bowl, 6¼" d., Model No. 13,
brown glaze exterior w/white
glaze interior & white rim-
forming tab handles **7.00**

Bowl, 6½" d., "Hall Radiant
Ware," yellow high gloss, from

the Jewel Rainbow Bowl Set,
stackable size **19.00**

Bowl, 6 ¾" d., 3 ¾" h., oval
refrigerator w/lid, two rings near
foot & lid w/rings & recessed
oblong knob, marked "Made
exclusively for Westinghouse By
The Hall China Co., Made in
U.S.A." (ILLUS. below) **24.00**

Bowl, 7½" d., "Hall Radiant
Ware," deep blue high gloss,
from the Jewel Rainbow Bowl
Set, stackable size **26.00**

Bowl, 9¼" d., 3¼" h., round,
vegetable, Blue Bouquet decal
on two sides only consisting of
rosebud, blue band w/gold
lattice design, open roses in
pink & yellow, blue band w/gold
lattice design & rosebud,
marked in gold, "Hall's Superior
Quality Kitchenware, Made in
U.S.A." (ILLUS. top, next page).... **35.00**

Bowl, 9¼" d., round, vegetable,
Orange Poppy patt. **25.00**

Bowl, 9½" d., "Hall Radiant
Ware," red high gloss, from the
Jewel Rainbow Bowl set,
stackable size **28.00**

Casserole, cov., Orange Poppy
patt., 8" l., oval **45.00**

Oval Refrigerator Bowl

Round Vegetable Bowl

Casserole with Inverted Pie Dish Lid

**Casserole w/inverted pie dish
lid,** silver ring trim on casserole
lip, pie dish edge & below tab
handles, orange, red & purple
flowers w/light & dark green
leaves, marked in gold "Hall's
Superior Quality Kitchenware" in a
square w/"Made in U.S.A." below
the square, 6½" d., 4" h. (ILLUS.) . **38.00**

Coffeepot, cov., Autumn Leaf
design, four pieces, ca. 1945,
marked "Hall's Superior Quality
Kitchenware" w/a double circle
between Superior & Quality &
inside the circle "Tested and
Approved by Mary Dunbar Jewel
Homemakers Institute," 1942-
1945, 11" h., 4 pieces
(ILLUS. top, next column)......... **300.00**

Autumn Leaf Coffeepot

Coffeepot, cov., Blue Bouquet
patt., Terrace shape **70.00**

Creamer, Blue Bouquet patt.,
Boston shape **15.00**

Creamer, Orange Poppy patt.,
Great American shape **16.00**

Creamer, Serenade patt., Art
Deco shape **18.00**

Creamer, Tulip patt., modern **12.00**

Two Views of Cup; Mary & Three Lambs, Reverse with Cat Drinking

Creamer, white glaze w/pink rim trim & decal of Mary & three lambs; reverse has cat drinking from bowl, marked "Hall" in a square, copyright & trademark symbols, "Made in U.S.A.," 3½" h., (ILLUS.) **21.00**

Cup & saucer, Blue Bouquet patt. . **12.00**

Cup & saucer, Pastel Morning Glory patt. **12.00**

Cuspidor, Waldorf shape, bulbous base w/waisted center rising to a flared rim, green lustre color, Model No. 636, 7" d., 4¼" h. **30.00**

Custard cup, green glaze exterior, white glaze interior, Model No. 2, ca. 1916, 3⅜" d. **6.00**

Drip jar, cov., Yellow Rose patt., Radiance shape **25.00**

Gravy boat, Springtime patt. **21.00**

Marmite, cov., tab handles, solid pale blue glaze w/gold ring around rim of bowl, lid & knob, three gold flowers on lid, marked w/gold stamp on unglazed bottom, "Made exclusively for Forman Family, Inc. By The Hall China Co. U.S.A.," 6 ¾" d., 5" h., (ILLUS.) **37.00**

Hall China Marmite

Mug, Irish coffee, footed, high gloss yellow exterior w/white interior, marked "Hall" in a circle & "Made in U.S.A. 1273" outside the circle & an incised "B27," 6" h. (ILLUS. top, next page) **15.00**

Mug, Irish coffee, footed, 1985 advertising edition for the Tri-State Pottery Festival, decal depicts the Delta Queen steamboat, 6" h. **19.00**

Pickle dish, Sears' Monticello patt., 1941-1959, 9" l. **7.00**

Irish Coffee Mug

Pitcher, water, 5" h., straight-sided w/gold trim at rim & whiskey advertising "Seagram's VO Canadian" in gold w/"VO" in a square, finger grip handle, deep cobalt blue glaze **16.00**

Pitcher, water, 5¼" h., bulbous-shaped whiskey advertising, "Vat 69, The Scotch Stands Out," black high gloss exterior w/white high gloss interior, "Vat 69" also at top of recessed handle **19.00**

Pitcher, water, 8" h., angled handle, advertising on both sides, "Teacher's Highland Cream" & "WT&S" in a circle, sky blue, 6½" from base to shoulder, white high gloss spout section, angled handle also has two-tone blue & white glaze **24.00**

Plate, 6" d., Orange Poppy patt. **5.00**

Plate, 7" d., Wildfire patt. **7.00**

Plate, 7¼" d., Blue Bouquet patt. ... **9.00**

Plate, 9" d., Blue Bouquet patt. **14.00**

Plate, 10" d., Tulip patt. **22.00**

Platter, 11¼" l., oval, Blue Bouquet patt. **25.00**

Platter, 11¼" l., oval, Orange Poppy patt. **25.00**

Platter, 11¼" l., oval, Wildfire patt. **24.00**

Platter, 13¼" l., oval, Blue Bouquet patt. **28.00**

Platter, 13¼" l., oval, Silhouette patt. **30.00**

Platter, 15" l., Eva Zeisel design, Century Fern patt. **23.00**

Salt & pepper shakers, handled, Silhouette patt., 4½" h., pr. **55.00**

Salt & pepper shakers, handled, solid red glaze w/word "salt" & "pepper" in black glaze, 4 ¾" h., pr. (ILLUS. below) **45.00**

Handled Salt & Pepper Shaker

Star shape Teapot

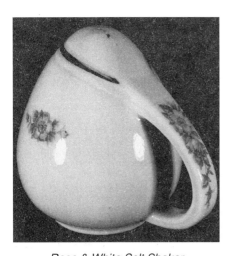

Rose & White Salt Shaker

Solid Pale Blue Teapot

Salt & pepper shakers, Rose White patt., holes form letters "S" & "P," pr. (ILLUS. of one)...... **29.00**

Salt & pepper shakers, Wildfire patt., Pert shape, pr.................... **55.00**

Sugar, cov., Orange Poppy patt., Great American shape **18.00**

Sugar, cov., Red Poppy patt., Art Deco shape **24.00**

Sugar, cov., Tulip patt., modern ... **20.00**

Sugar, individual, brown glaze exterior, white glaze interior, ca. 1915, 3 ¾" d., 2¼" h. **6.00**

Teapot, cov., Red Poppy, Aladdin shape........................... **95.00**

Teapot, cov., Orange Poppy patt., Donut shape **340.00**

Teapot, cov., solid pale blue high gloss w/white interior, complete w/dipper & spreader, Manhattan "French Drip Coffee Biggin," marked in black "Hall" in a circle & "Made in U.S.A." outside the circle, (ILLUS. above)................ **95.00**

Teapot, cov., Star shape, solid dark green w/gold ring trim at rim of pot & lid, gold stars motif, marked "Hall 9 7. 40. 6 cup Made in U.S.A." & also "Hall" incised, 5½" h. (ILLUS. top)........ **85.00**

Tea tile, Silhouette patt., 6" d. **100.00**

Collecting tips: Many novice collectors want to immediately begin collecting Autumn Leaf. However, it has become more expensive than most of Hall's other patterns. Also, since Harker, Crown, Paden City, Vernon and other pottery companies also used the Autumn Leaf decal, it would be to most collectors advantage to start with a Hall pattern other than Autumn Leaf. Study the company's products, availability and values before deciding on a pattern. Also, it would be helpful to learn the various shapes since those would also be a consideration in making decisions. If you decide on Autumn Leaf, consider joining clubs and obtaining books that focus primarily on that pattern.

References: *The Collector's Encyclopedia of Hall China, Second Edition,* by Margaret & Kenn Whitmyer, Collector Books, 1994; *The Jewel Tea Company, Its History and Products* by C., L. Miller, Schiffer Books, 1994, "China Souvenirs of East Liverpool, Ohio" by Grace C. Allison, *American Clay Exchange,* June 30, 1986; Hall's Vitrified Fire-Proof Cooking China, company catalog, 1915

Collectors' Club: National Autumn Leaf Collectors Club, Beverly Robbins, Secretary/Treasurer, 7346 Shamrock Drive, Indianapolis, IN 46217, $20. annual membership, newsletter six times a year; annual meeting July 11-13, 1996 at Colorado Springs, CO

Newsletters: Hall China Connection, P.O. Box 401, Pollock Pines, CA 95726; Hall China Encore, Kim Boss, editor, 317 North Pleasant Street, No. YP, Oberlin, OH 44074-1113

HARKER POTTERY COMPANY

The Harker Pottery was established in East Liverpool, Ohio, in 1840 by Benjamin Harker, Sr. However, Harker, Sr., was not a potter so he hired John Goodwin to train Harker's sons, Benjamin Jr., and George S., in the pottery trade.

It was the arrival of James Taylor in 1846 that made a change in Benjamin Harker's company. Harker and Taylor became partners and the company was named Harker, Taylor and Company. They called their three-story brick pottery Etruria from the Wedgwood English works but the union lasted only five years; Taylor left the pottery in 1851.

In the meantime, George S. Harker decided to start his own pottery and Mathew Thompson, a wealthy merchant, and Ezekiel Creighton joined him in the venture. Yellowware and Rockingham-glazed wares were produced. The name of this pottery was Harker, Thompson and Company. Benjamin Harker, Jr. decided to leave the Harker, Thompson and Company pottery in 1853. He and William Smith established a pottery which also produced yellowware and Rockingham wares. In 1855, business conditions were such that the partnership was dissolved and Benjamin Harker, Jr. returned to the original Etruria pottery.

Ben Jr. left to join in the Civil Ware effort and George S. died in 1864. These events left the pottery without leadership. David Boyce, George and Ben's brother-in-law, who was married to Jane, ran the pottery until George's sons were old enough to take over. It was Boyce who pulled Harker through difficult years and established a long relationship with the Harker family. David's son, Charles, is believed to have been instrumental in the success of the Harker Company; a grandson would become a Harker ceramics engineer; and another grandson eventually became president of Harker Pottery.

By 1877 Ben Jr., and his sons had established Wedgwood Pottery but sold it in 1881 to Wallace and Chetwynd.

Numerous ups and downs occurring with different partners (up until 1890 the pottery had at least eight partners) and the Harker brothers splitting their companies (seven name changes have been recorded) and then rejoining one another is an indication of the problems that beset this company. They are also reasons collectors are confused today about some of the Harker products.

Many Harker partners who left the company went on to establish East Liverpool potteries of their own. Thomas Croxall established the Croxall & Cartwright Pottery and John Goodwin opened the Goodwin Pottery Company.

In 1890 the pottery was incorporated as the Harker Pottery Company. By 1911 the company had acquired the former plant of the National China Company and in 1931 Harker purchased the closed pottery of Edwin M. Knowles in Chester, West Virginia. In 1972, Harker Pottery Company closed after it was purchased by the Jeannette Glass Company.

Harker's earliest products were yellowware and Rockingham-glazed wares produced from local clay. After 1900 whiteware was made from imported materials. The Etruria pottery manufactured toys, ceramic tiles, table tops and door knobs. George S. Harker and Company discontinued the production of Rockingham and yellowware and began manufacturing white ironstone. By 1880 they were producing tea sets, toilet, dinner and kitchenwares. About 1890, Harker Pottery began to manufacture semi-porcelain ware and discontinued ironstone. By 1931 the company was making vitreous dinnerware, toilet sets, hotel ware and advertising novelties. The plant eventually grew to be a large manufacturer of dinnerware and kitchenware, employing as many as three hundred people.

Perhaps their best-known line is Cameoware, decorated on solid glazes with white "cameos" in a silhouette fashion. It was George Bauer who introduced Harker Pottery to the intaglio method. It proved to be an expensive undertaking but one that was well-received by homemakers of the era. Blue and pink are more plentiful than yellow or teal. Blue is also more popular among collectors than the other colors. However, some other lines are almost as popular; HotOven, introduced in 1926 and Bakerite, which became available in 1935, are but two.

Carv-Kraft was the mark used exclusively for Harker's Montgomery Ward White Rose intaglio pattern. The Carv-Kraft name was used simply to avoid the word "Cameo" which was a patent belonging to Harker.

There were many patterns and shapes created by Harker over the years. To keep up with competition and public demand, Harker created such patterns as Deco Dahlia, Mallow, Cherry Blossom, Cock O'Morn, Coronet, Snow Leaf, Dainty Flower, Dogwood, Delft, Forever Yours and many more. Colonial Lady is a black "silhouette" w/black trim. The decals vary from a woman working at a flower trellis, to a tree with two people on horses or a tree nearby with two horses and two people sitting on the ground. Harker's purists collectors will not mix Homer Laughlin, W. S. George, or any of the other companies silhouette-type patterns or decals. Other collectors, however, feel mixing several companies' products adds to the beauty of the items.

Gadroon is a shape with rope rims or edges. Harker classified these into two groups: Chesterton and Royal Gadroon. Chesterton, which comes in solid glazes, is completely void of decoration except for the white rope adornment. Glazes include Bermuda Blue (a pale grey), Chocolate Brown, White, Yellow and Corinthian, a teal color. There are other glazes in Chesterton. Royal Gadroon was colorfully decorated or decals were used.

Since several writers have used various pattern names, the ones shown here are what have been found to be the most commonly used among collectors.

Harker Marks

Petit Point Bowl

Colonial Lady Custard Cups

Bowl, 7½" d., Cameoware, Dainty Flower patt., blue........... **$27.00**

Bowl, 10" d., 5½" h., Petit Point Rose patt. (ILLUS.).................... **16.00**

Bowl, 10" d., Red Apple II patt. **25.00**

Cake lifter, Amy patt. **15.00**

Creamer, Colonial Lady patt., spherical shape **10.00**

Cup & saucer, Colonial Lady patt., set....................................... **9.00**

Cup & saucer, Cameoware Provincial Tulip patt., blue, set ... **10.00**

Custard cup, Colonial Lady patt., 3¼" h. ea. (ILLUS.)...................... **4.00**

Custard cup, Red Apple II patt., 3¼" h. **6.00**

Lard jar, cov., Deco Dahlia patt., skyscraper shape, "LARD" printed in black, 5" h. **14.00**

Lard jar, cov., Mallow patt., skyscraper shape, "LARD" printed in black, 5" h. **19.00**

Mug, juvenile, Cameoware, part of Kiddo set, motif on one side is teetering elephant; a toy soldier on other side, pink ground w/white figures, white interior, marked "Cameo-Ware by Harker U.S.A. Pat pending," 3" h. (ILLUS. right & left top, next page) **30.00**

Pie baker, Deco Dahlia patt., 8" d. **18.00**

Pie server, Colonial Lady patt. **26.00**

Pie server, Deco Dahlia patt., 9" l. (ILLUS. next page) **20.00**

Pie server, Red Apple II patt........ **38.00**

Plate, 6" d., Colonial Lady patt. **6.00**

Plate, 6" d., Cameoware, Dainty Flower patt., Virginia shape, blue... **6.00**

Plate, 7" d., Red Apple II patt. on swirl, marked "BakeRite oven-tested, made in U.S.A." (ILLUS. next page) **7.00**

Cameoware Juvenile Mug (right & left)

Deco Dahlia Pattern Pie Server

Red Apple Plate

Plate, 7½" d., grill w/three divisions, Cameoware, juvenile, chicken, rabbit & bird w/boy in each section, blue **30.00**

Plate, 8" d., Colonial Lady patt. **8.00**

Plate, 9" d., Heritance line & shape, solid white, 16 panels on wide rim, mark shows circle of stars within a star & "Heritance Bone White Ironstone Ovenproof U.S.A." **6.00**

Plate, 9½" d., Red Apple II patt. on swirl shape, no scallops **9.00**

Plate, 9½" d., Red Apple II patt. w/scalloped edge........................ **15.00**

Plate, 12" d., Red Apple II patt. on modern age shape **28.00**

Platter, 8" d., Cameoware Provincial Tulip patt., celadon glaze **10.00**

Platter, 11½" l., Cameoware Cock O'Morn patt. **16.00**

Platter, 14" l., Red Apple II patt. on Virginia shape (straight top & bottom w/scallops at corners & tab-like embossed handles on sides) **28.00**

Columbia Pattern Rolling Pin

Petit Point Pattern Rolling Pin

Petit Point Rose Pattern Salt & Pepper Shakers

Rolling pin, Cactus patt.,
14½" l. **145.00**

Rolling pin, Calico Tulip
patt., 14½" l. **90.00**

Rolling pin, Columbia patt.,
14½" l. (ILLUS. top) **85.00**

Rolling pin, Mallow patt.,
14½" l. **115.00**

Rolling pin, Petit Point patt.,
14½" l. (ILLUS. middle) **95.00**

Salt & pepper shakers,
Cameoware, Dainty Flower
patt., skyscraper shape, blue,
4½" h., pr. **17.00**

Salt & pepper shakers,
Cameoware, Dainty Flower
patt., D-Ware shape,
pink, pr. **18.00**

Salt & pepper shakers,
Cameoware, Dainty Flower
patt., D-Ware shape, yellow,
4½" h., pr. **19.00**

Salt & pepper shakers, Deco
Dahlia patt., skyscraper shape,
4½" h., pr. **25.00**

Salt & pepper shakers, Petit
Point Rose patt., skyscraper
shape, 4½" h., pr. (ILLUS.) **23.00**

Scoop w/hole in handle for hanging, hard to find, any pattern. **45.00**

Spoon w/hole in handle for hanging, Mallow patt., 8" l. **23.00**

Sugar, cov., Colonial Lady patt., spherical shape **14.00**

Tile, hot, Red Apple II patt., octagonal, 6" d............................ **32.00**

References: *The Collector's Guide to Harker Pottery U.S.A.,* by Neva W. Colbert, Collector Books 1993; *The East Liverpool, Ohio, Pottery District: Identification of Manufacturers and Marks* by William C. Gates, Jr. and Dana E. Ormerod, The Society for Historical Archaeology, Volume 16, Nos. 1-2, 1982; "Collecting Harker China" by Rena London, *The National Glass, Pottery and Collectables Journal,* September 1980

HOLLYWOOD CERAMICS
See Maddux of California

HOMER LAUGHLIN CHINA COMPANY

After the Civil War, Homer Laughlin journeyed to East Liverpool, Ohio. A short-lived partnership with Nathaniel Simms was formed to manufacture stoneware. Homer and his brother, Shakespeare then opened a pottery in 1870 to sell yellowwares and Rockingham-glazed wares to the wholesale trade. Assisted by the town of East Liverpool, the Laughlin brothers constructed a pottery to manufacture whiteware. By 1874, the company was producing white ironstone excellent enough to win a premium at the 1876 Centennial Exhibition. It was also in 1876 that the pottery began manufacturing hotel ware. Even though the future looked promising for the company, Shakespeare left in 1877 and Homer continued the operation. In 1881, the Laughlin Company employed almost 150 people. Throughout the 1890s, the company also produced a semi-vitreous china and in 1896 the firm was incorporated as the Homer Laughlin China Company.

In 1898, Homer moved to Los Angeles, California and controlling interest went to the W. E. Wells family and was headed by Louis Aaron. In 1911, Marcus Aaron succeeded his father as president. William Wells died in 1931 and J. M. Wells took his position as general manager. In 1940, Marcus Lester Aaron became president and twenty years later J. M. Wells, Jr. was general manager. In 1989 M. L. Aaron retired and his son, Marcus Aaron II became president.

Many well-known people associated with china and pottery were employed by Homer Laughlin. For example, Dr. Albert Bleininger

Homer Laughlin China Company Marks

was a ceramic engineer beginning in 1920. He died in 1946. Frederick Hurten Rhead became the chief art designer in 1927. Rhead died in 1942. Harry Thiemecke was employed as a chemist by Homer Laughlin beginning in 1934. The name Don Schreckengost is a familiar one to collectors of almost any type of china. Mr. Schreckengost joined Homer Laughlin as art director in 1945.

Perhaps without realizing at the time it was happening, Homer Laughlin aided today's collectors in identifying many of what would otherwise be mysteries if it were not for their remarkable marking system. It is difficult with almost all potteries to know when an item was introduced and when it was discontinued. Laughlin left no doubt about this and the company, which had a multitude of manufacturing plants in different locations, also recorded where an item was made. Plant one was built in East Liverpool in 1873. It took more than twenty years, but plant two was constructed in 1899 and two years later plant three was built next to plant two. In 1907, Homer Laughlin opened a new plant (number four) in Newell, West Virginia and plant five was realized in 1914. In 1923, plant six was built, number seven was available in 1927 and number eight in 1929. Fortunately, for those willing to learn the various "codes" for Laughlin's marking system, identification of when and where a pattern or shape was created, will not be a mystery. (The books by Jo Cunningham, Lois Lehner and Gates, Jr. and Ormerod listed in the references section below have detailed information concerning the numerals and letters for Laughlin's marking system.)

Collectors cannot mention the name Homer Laughlin without having Fiesta (1936), Harlequin (ca. 1938), Virginia Rose (1929), Riviera (1938) or the earlier Wells Art Glaze come to mind. Laughlin created many excellent pieces of china in keeping with the times. Their Theme shape, created by Frederick Rhead, was made to commemorate the 1939 World's Fair. Rhead also was responsible for shapes such as Nautilus, Eggshell Georgian, Swing, Century, Brittany and others. Their Oven Serve line was introduced in 1933 and continued through the 1950s.

It was Don Schreckengost who created Cavalier, Debutante and Rhythm. Another line created by Mr. Schreckengost is Epicure which is beginning to have a large following. Typical Fifties colors were used such as Charcoal Gray, Dawn Pink, Turquoise Blue and Snow White.

Virginia Rose, created in 1929 and continuing until the 1970s for home use, was their most popular shape. While Harlequin and Fiesta have their own large group of collectors, Virginia Rose is one of the most often purchased Laughlin china shapes in today's market.

Usually when a line is reintroduced by a company, sales for both the old and new pieces decline. Such has not been the case with Fiesta. Introduced in 1935, Fiesta has continued to sell on the secondary market just as briskly as it did before its reintroduction on February 28, 1986. Perhaps that is because Fiesta glazes do not confuse even novice collectors. Originally bright solid colors in dark blue, ivory, light green, red and yellow were produced. Turquoise appeared in 1936. Red was discontinued for a few years due to the war. By 1951, dark blue, ivory and light green were no longer being made. Chartreuse, forest green, grey and rose replaced those that were no longer available. All six colors, including turquoise and yellow continued until 1959. It was then that red returned and chartreuse, dark green, grey and rose were dropped. The original Fiesta was discontinued by 1973.

After being off the market for thirteen years, Homer Laughlin brought back Fiesta. Names for glazes were apricot, black, cobalt, grey, rose, white and yellow. The plates and soup and salad bowls were a little larger than their older counterparts. A new covered casserole was included in the line and pieces such as the bud vases and candleholders were revived. All the revived accessory pieces are slightly smaller

Harlequin, introduced in ca. 1938, was a lighter weight than Fiesta. It was available in all the Fiesta colors except ivory and also had its own colors of spruce green, mauve blue and maroon. Harlequin was sold through the Woolworth stores and since that venture was so successful, Woolworth asked Laughlin to reissue Harlequin in 1979 for their 100th anniversary. The newer items seem to pose no threat to collectors of the older Harlequin because the serving pieces were restyled and only three of the original glazes were used.

Laughlin also manufactured a line of Harlequin animals during the early 1940s. They can be found as cats, donkeys, ducks, fish, lambs and penguins. Those seeking Harlequin animals will find them trimmed in gold with white overall glazes as well as some other harder-to-find colors. Dubbed "Mavericks" by collectors, it has become a term meaning that Homer Laughlin China Company did not do the glazing but, rather, an unrelated firm.

The Wells Art Glaze line came in Matt green, Peach, Rust and Melon Yellow. Laughlin's Vellum was so smooth that they advertised, "...soft mellow texture like the delicate surface of a bird's egg." It had an ivory glaze and became popular although not much of it seems to be available today.

Riviera was introduced in 1938 in five solid glazes on the Century shape. The glazes were blue, light green, red, yellow and ivory. It was sold exclusively by the Murphy Company.

The Century shape, having straight sides and scalloped corners, was a popular one for Homer Laughlin. Many different decals were used on this shape including the Mexicana, which is in demand today.

Ashtray, round w/four cigarette rests, 1939 Golden Gate International Exposition, 6¼" d... **$70.00**

Ashtray, round w/three cigarette rests, Fiesta, red, 5½" d. **48.00**

Bowl, 5" d., Fiesta, No. 1 size, red.. **85.00**

Bowl, 5½" d., Harlequin fruit, maroon **10.00**

Bowl, 5½" d., Riviera fruit, yellow **10.00**

Bowl, 6" d., Fiesta dessert, medium green **255.00**

Nautilus Shape Bowl

Bowl, 7" d., Nautilus shape, Amsterdam patt. w/trees, stream & bridge w/dog playing in stream, woman washing clothes in stream & woman on the bank, gold trim at rim, dark green band on the verge (ILLUS.) **10.00**

Bowl, 8" d., 3" h., Century shape, Mexicana patt. (ILLUS., below) .. **35.00**

Century Shape Mexicana Pattern Bowl

Marigold Shaped Casserole No. M207

Virginia Rose Cup & Saucer

Orange Custard Cup

Casserole, cov., Marigold shape, pattern No. M207 stamped inside the lid (ILLUS. top) **50.00**

Creamer, Virginia Rose shape **13.00**

Cup & saucer, Virginia Rose shape, set (ILLUS. middle) **10.00**

Custard cup, orange glaze, Oven Serve line, 2 ¾" h. (ILLUS. first column) **8.00**

Gravy boat, Cavalier shape, Lily the Valley patt. wide green band on foot & base, white, upper section & handle, silver trim, pink flowers & green leaves (ILLUS. top next page) **18.00**

Gravy boat, Virginia Rose shape... **20.00**

Gravy boat, Yellowstone shape, red line trim w/pink, yellow & rose flowers w/blue & green leaves (ILLUS. center next page) **24.00**

Cavalier Shaped Gravy Boat

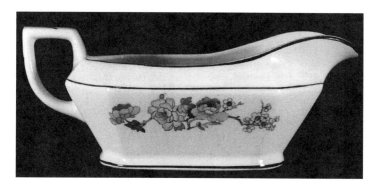

Yellowstone Shaped Gravy Boat

Kitchen Kraft Pie Plate

Pie plate, Kitchen Kraft w/pink, rose, yellow & blue flowers & black single band on rim, 9½" d. (ILLUS.) **30.00**

Pitcher, 4¼" h., (jug) Yellowstone shape, octagonal paneled cream glazed body w/pattern W127/30, orange & yellow flowers & green & black leaves, black rim & handle trim (ILLUS. top next page) **28.00**

Pitcher, 5" h., figural, bust of George Washington, marked, "First Edition for Collectors, New York's World's Fair, 1939" also can be found marked, "Joint Exhibition of Capital and Labor, American Potter, NY WF,1939," ivory glaze **55.00**

Yellowstone Shaped Pitcher

Plate, 6½" d., Epicure line, pink...... **6.00**

Plate, 7" d., Rhythm shape, Provincial patt. (ILLUS.) **8.00**

Plate, 7" d., Rhythm shape, wide pale blue rim, white center, gold design between the two colors, marked w/"Rhythm, Lifetime China, Semi-vitreous" & Laughlin's gold crown.................. **5.00**

Plate, 7" d., Riviera, light green...... **8.00**

Plate, 8" d., Epicure line, white....... **8.00**

Plate, 9" d., Fiesta, red................. **16.00**

Plate, 9" d., Fiesta, light green **8.00**

Plate, 9" d., Harlequin, yellow......... **7.00**

Plate, 9" sq., Century shape, pink flowers in each of the four corners w/silver design on verge rim, circle of flowers in center (ILLUS. top, next page) **10.00**

Plate, 9½" d., Century shape, Mexicana patt. **19.00**

Plate, 9½" d., Eggshell Nautilus shape, patt. No. N1690, gold banded rim separated by six flower sprays of one red & one blue flower & green leaves in each spray................................. **10.00**

Plate, 6" d., Fiesta, rose **7.00**

Plate, 6" d., Fiesta, chartreuse **6.00**

Plate, 6" d., Harlequin, spruce green **5.00**

Plate, 6" d., Riviera, red.................. **8.00**

Plate, 6" sq., salad, Cavalier shape, Berkshire pattern, teal band w/dubonnet & bronze colored flowers & leaves **10.00**

Rhythm Shape Plate

Century Shape Plate

Golden Gate International Plate

Plate, 9½" d., Empress shape,
  Bluebird patt. **17.00**

Plate, 9½" d., Virginia Rose
  shape... **10.00**

Plate, 10" d., Fiesta, cobalt........... **33.00**

Plate, 10" d., Fiesta, medium
  green **85.00**

Plate, 10" d., Fiesta, rose **35.00**

Plate, 10" d., Fiesta, yellow **25.00**

Plate, 10" d., Harlequin, red **23.00**

Plate, 10" d., Riviera, ivory **30.00**

Plate, 10" d., Virginia Rose
  shape... **12.00**

Plate, 10½" d., Empress shape,
  Bluebird patt. **18.00**

Plate, 10½" d., New York World's
  Fair, 1939 futuristic design,
  Frederick Rhead designer **275.00**

Plate, 10½" d., Golden Gate
  International Exposition, 1940,
  verge has a trailing of yellow
  flowers & green leaves, rim has
  pale blue background w/a bridge,
  buildings including pagodas,
  green trees, purple elephants,
  birds & the sun rising, green
  backstamp "Golden Gate

International Exposition
Copyrighted License 63C, Homer
Laughlin Co. Made in USA," also
made w/1939 date, either
date (ILLUS. top right) **100.00**

Platter, 11" l., Harlequin, ivory...... **20.00**

Platter, 11½" l., Oven Serve line,
  underside decoration only,
  green flowers & leaves in relief
  on the verge & tiny vertical
  ribbing around the rim (ILLUS.
  top, next page) **25.00**

Platter, 11½" l., Riveria, red **16.00**

Platter, 13" l., Harlequin, dark
  green **23.00**

Platter, 13" l., Virginia Rose
  shape... **28.00**

Platter, 15" l., Skytone shape,
  Marcia patt., blue w/silver
  trimmed rim, white flowers
  w/touch of pink & dark blue
  leaves (ILLUS. middle, next
  page) **25.00**

Platter, 15½" l., Eggshell Nautilus
  shape, pattern No. 1690
  (ILLUS. bottom, next page) **24.00**

Vase, bud, Fiesta, cobalt glaze,
  6¼" h. **70.00**

Oven Serve Platter

Skytone Platter

Eggshell Platter

Collecting tips: The Fiesta green glazes—a total of four—are somewhat confusing to collectors until they actually see all four tints at the same time. There was green, forest green, chartreuse and medium green. Medium green, the hardest to ascertain, and by far the most expensive green, has been referred to by some collectors as Christmas green.

References: *The Collector's Encyclopedia of Homer Laughlin China* by Joanne Jasper, Collector Books 1993, with prices updated, 1995; *The Collector's Encyclopedia of Fiesta, Seventh Edition* by Bob & Sharon Huxford, Collector Books 1992, with values updated, 1994; "The New Fiesta, A Progress Report" by BA Wellman, *American Clay Exchange,* August 30, 1987; "Homer Laughlin Company, The Early Years" by B. A. Wellman, *American Clay Exchange,* November 30, 1986; "Collectible American China, Part Five" by Jerry Barnett, *American Clay Exchange,* March 15, 1985; Homer Laughlin's Vellum by David Walker, *The Glaze,* May 1983; *The East Liverpool, Ohio, Pottery District: Identification of Manufacturers and Marks* by William C. Gates, Jr. and Dana E. Ormerod, The Society for Historical Archaeology, Volume 16, Nos. 1-2, 1982; *The Collector's Encyclopedia of American Dinnerware* by Jo Cunningham, Collector Books 1982; "Fiesta Fever" by S. Dan Anderson, *The National Journal,* January 1981; *Complete Book of American Kitchen and Dinner Wares* by Lois Lehner, Wallace Homestead 1980; "Mostly About Homer Laughlin's Mexican-Decaled Kitchen Kraft" by John Moses, *The Glaze,* March 1980

Collectors' Club: Fiesta Club of America, P. O. Box 15383, Loves Park, IL 61132-5383, membership fee includes quarterly newsletter

Newsletter: The Fiesta Collector's Quarterly, 19238 Dorchester Circle, Strongsville, OH 44136

Museum: Erie Art Museum, Erie, Pennsylvania has a section on the works of Frederick Rhead

HULL POTTERY

Hull Pottery Marks

Hull Pottery, one of the most collected and well-known of the turn-of-the-century companies, began in 1905 in Crooksville, Ohio. Prior to that, the Hull brothers, Addis Emmet and J. J., had been involved with the Star Stonery Company, Globe Pottery and the Acme Pottery Company which the brothers had acquired about 1907.

Hull Pottery, early in its long history, produced stoneware, florist ware, art pottery and tile until about 1935. They began the production of matte-glazed pastel artwares about that time.

The company was destroyed by flood and fire in 1950. Even though the factory was rebuilt and modern machinery installed, the company was not able to clone the formulas for their past glazes.

This began a new era for Hull Pottery. Gloss finishes, as opposed to matte finishes, were created in patterns and lines such as Ebb Tide, Classic, Blossom Flite, Marcrest and Parchment and Pine,

Hull's NuLine Bak-Serve produced in the late 1930s and early 1940s is popular with collectors today. There are three known embossed designs: "B" is a diamond quilted design, "C" is a fishscale pattern and "D" a drape and panel design. These letters are almost always included in the mark.

Hull made a Marcrest line in the late 1950s that should not be confused with the

dark brown Marcrest of the Western Stoneware Company. While Hull's product is completely different, the name sometimes confuses novice collectors. Hull's Marcrest items are high gloss kitchenware that grocery stores used as premiums. The Heritageware and House 'n Garden molds were used for Hull's Marcrest. Generally, on Marcrest ashtrays, the mark is raised; for other items the impressed mark is "Marcrest Oven Proof Quality Made in U.S.A." Heritageware came in pale colors such as pink, blue, green or yellow and also had a small amount of pale foam on its edges. Marcrest was also produced in white, blue, pink, green or yellow.

The company closed in 1985.

Tokay Pattern Basket

Basket, Poppy patt., No. 601,
9" h. **$780.00**

Basket, Tokay patt., 8" h.
(ILLUS. above) **70.00**

Bowl, 8" d., 4½" h., House 'n Garden line, Mirror Brown glaze w/ivory foam trim, pour spout, marked "8 Lip Oven Proof U.S.A." (ILLUS. top next page)... **18.00**

Bowl, 10" d., large mixing, Country Belle pattern, No. 6440 .... **27.00**

Bowl, 12" l., console, Iris pattern, No. 409 .... **300.00**

Casserole, cov., Sunglow patt., marked "51-7½ Oven Proof U.S.A." (ILLUS. middle next page) **55.00**

Cookie jar, Crescent Kitchenware line, ca. 1950s, bulbous body, slightly angled, chartreuse or strawberry body glaze w/dark green or maroon lid, No. B8, 9½" h. **75.00**

Cookie jar, Gingerbread Man, grey glaze **225.00**

Cookie jar, Heritageware, word "Cookies" in white glaze at shoulder, pale green, 9¼" h. **125.00**

Cookie jar, Kitchenware line, Debonair shape, lavender w/pink shading, narrow black band on body & black top of knob on handle, No. 0-8, ca. mid-1950s, 8 ¾" h. **70.00**

Cookie jar, NuLine Bak-Serve, drape & panel pattern, bulbous w/tab handles at shoulder, 2 quart capacity, No. D-20, 8" h. ... **95.00**

Cornucopia-vase, Parchment & Pine patt., No. S-2-5, 7 ¾" h. (ILLUS.) **55.00**

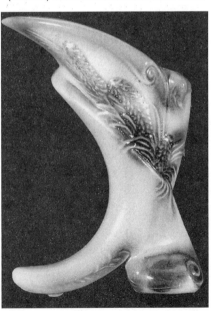

Cornucopia-Vase

Mirror Brown Glaze Bowl

Sunglow Pattern Casserole

Creamer, figural, model of Little Red Riding Hood, tab handle ... **280.00**

Custard cup, NuLine Bak-Serve, diamond & quilt pattern, No. B-14, 2 ¾" h................................ **8.00**

Ewer, Open Rose patt., No. 105, 7" h. (ILLUS.) **185.00**

Grease jar, cov., figural, model of Little Red Riding Hood, incised "Hull Ware USA," gold trim, 9" h. **1,650.00**

Mug, Marcrest patt., blue glaze, 3¼" h. **8.00**

Pitcher, 3 ¾" h., Early Art stoneware w/embossed flowers & scrolls, cobalt, maroon & turquoise splotching over cream ground (ILLUS. top, next page).... **38.00**

Open Rose Pattern Ewer

Early Art Stoneware Pitcher

House 'n Garden Pitcher

Early Utility Ware Pitcher

Stein, Early Utility stoneware w/Alpine scene, beige & brown, straight sides, No. 499, 6½" h. ... **30.00**

Sugar bowl, cov., figural, model of Little Red Riding Hood, "Pat Des No. 135889" **395.00**

Teapot, cov., figural, model of Little Red Riding Hood, incised "LRRH Pat Des. No 135889 USA," 8" h................................. **325.00**

Vase, 5¼" h., Wildflower patt., No. 52 .... **120.00**

Early Art Ware Vase

Pitcher, 4½" h., Early Utility ware, vertical ribs from base to bottom of handle, white thin horizontal line, wider dark brown line and a second thin white line directly below shoulder, marked "107" "H" in a circle & "36" below it (ILLUS.) **78.00**

Pitcher, 6" h., NuLine Bak-Serve, diamond & quilt pattern, one quart capacity, No. B-7 .... **85.00**

Pitcher, 7" h., House 'n Garden Rainbow serving ware, Tangerine glaze, two quart capacity, No. 925 (ILLUS. top, next column) **30.00**

Plaque, advertising "Little Red Riding Hood," 11¾" l., 6½" h. (ILLUS. top, next page) **3,900.00**

Vase, 5½" h., 4½" d., Early Art ware, 1920s, unmarked, cobalt & rose brushstroke pattern over pale blue w/a hint of green at rim, fake handles from shoulder to rim on each side (ILLUS.)....... **85.00**

Little Red Riding Hood Advertising Plaque

Vase, 6" h., Mardi Gras patt.,
ringed cylinder w/slightly flared
rim **45.00**

Vase, 6½" h., Pine Cone patt.,
No. 55 .... **165.00**

Vase, 6½" h., Rosella patt., No.
R-8, heart shape on base **120.00**

Vase, 6½" h., Thistle patt., No. 55
(ILLUS.) **100.00**

Royal Woodland Vase

Thistle Pattern Vase

Vase, 6½" h., Royal Woodland
patt., pale turquoise w/white
overall splotching, darker
handles & rim, marked "Hull W4-
6½ U.S.A." (ILLUS.) **38.00**

Vase, 8½" h., Wildflower patt.,
No. W-9 .... **75.00**

Woodland Gloss Pattern Wall Pocket

Woodland Pattern Vase

Vase, 8½" h., Woodland patt.,
Dawn Rose pastel, No. W16-8½
(ILLUS.) **185.00**

Vase, 9½" h., Wildflower patt.,
No. W-12 .... **110.00**

Vase, 10½" h., Poppy patt.,
No. 606 .... **465.00**

Vase, 12½" h., Bow-Knot patt.,
No. B-14 .... **1,110.00**

Wall pocket, model of a cup &
saucer, Sunglow patt., No. 80,
8½" h. **90.00**

Wall pocket, model of a pitcher,
Bow-Knot patt., No. B-26, 6" h... **235.00**

Wall pocket, model of a sad iron,
Sunglow patt., 6" h. **80.00**

Wall pocket, Woodland Gloss
patt., No. W-13, 7½" h.
(ILLUS.) **125.00**

Collecting tips: Now is the time to buy the dinnerware, kitchenware and high gloss lines made by Hull. Long-time collectors have been concentrating on the matte finished patterns, and with prices escalating, there is a new group of collectors buying other Hull products. With books and articles being printed on the newer pieces, now is the time to buy.

If you prefer the older items, the first thing to do is choose a pattern and buy the hard-to-find pieces in that pattern. The most popular patterns seem to be Poppy, Bow-Knot and the numbered Wildflower pieces. Little Red Riding Hood is top-of-the-line but is beginning to price itself out of the market.

References: *Collector's Guide to Hull Pottery: The Dinnerware Lines* by Barbara Loveless Gick-Burke, Collector Books 1993; *The Collectors Encyclopedia of Hull Pottery* by Brenda Roberts, Collector Books 1980, updated values 1993; "Little Red Riding Hood" by Lisa E. Van Hook, *American Clay Exchange,* March 1982; "Hull Pottery Cookie Collecting" by Brenda Roberts, *American Clay Exchange,* March 1981

Hull Pottery Association: Kimberly and Dan Pfaff, 466 Foreston Place, Webster Groves, Missouri 63119, membership $10 individual, $15 couples, includes monthly newsletter

Hull Convention: Crooksville, Ohio High School, July 13-14, 1996, contact Hull Pottery President, Clarence Crooks (614)982-2643 or Lowell Thompson (712) 328-2479

JOSEF ORIGINALS

Muriel Joseph George was the talented creator of the whimsical "Josef Originals" figurines. Known in the early 1940s as a jewelry designer, Muriel made items of lucite

and ceramic jewelry under the name "Muriel of California." During this time Muriel also enjoyed modeling clay figurines.

In 1946, Muriel and her husband Tom, now home from World War II, talked of opening their own pottery company. Working out of their garage, they produced their first commercial figure, "Pitty Sing," a small Chinese boy in a big coolie hat, sitting asleep, with a cat on his lap. Muriel's father took "Pitty Sing" to a department store, and with an order for two gross, Muriel went to work. It was this first commercial piece that determined the now infamous name, Josef Originals. The printer made an error in the spelling of Joseph, and with a too soon deadline, "Pitty Sing" and all his descendants, became "Josef Originals." Other figurines were shown and began to sell in a surprising volume.

If imitation is the greatest compliment, then Mrs. George should have been pleased with the flood of "Made in Japan" copies that began to appear on the market during the 1950s. In response to these inferior copies of her work, she produced new designs of unequaled excellence. Consumers wanted the Josef look, however, they did not want the price tag that accompanied the line. In 1959, with sales floundering at an all-time low, Muriel and Tom formed a partnership with George Good, a successful distributor of several California pottery lines. The production of "George Imports" was moved from California to Japan bringing labor costs to a new low. Muriel personally educated the workers at the Katayama Factory in Japan on her "design ways." Returning home, Muriel forwarded new designs to Japan with a final product shipped back to the United States for her approval. There were elegant Victorian ladies, Birthday girls, mice (Muriel is credited with over forty different ones), ostriches, monkeys and more. With production costs down and popular new designs selling, Josef was again a competitive ceramics line.

Retiring in 1981, Muriel continued to design for her former partner, and now company owner, George Good until 1985. Her daughter, Diane, joined in the creativity

from 1973-1986. In 1985, George Good sold the company to Applause, Inc. No new designs would be forthcoming under the Josef Originals name. Muriel Joseph George died in 1992.

From 1945 until 1959, Josef Originals were made in California. On the unglazed bottom is an incised script mark of "Josef" or "Josef Originals" and the encircled "C." Some pieces, mostly the animals, were too small for the incised mark. The figurines also carried a 5/8" oval sticker, black with a gold border and the lettering "Josef Originals" and under that "California." Post-1959, the "California" was replaced by a "curl" design and an additional half-inch oval sticker with "Japan" was added.

An interesting and helpful hint is that the pre-1980s (Muriel's retirement) girls were all made with black eyes and a glossy finish; most animals with a semi-gloss finish. Prices listed are for figurines in perfect condition; repaired or damaged pieces are not considered collectible.

Josef Original Marks

Candleholder, figural, model of a
reindeer sitting **$18.00**

Doll, half, blue dress, applied
pearl necklace, 4" h. **60.00**

Figure of a boy, "Poi," in
Hawaiian costume, 4¼" h. **60.00**

Figure of a girl, Birthstone
series, April, 3½" h. **25.00**

Figure of a girl carrying wrapped package, yellow dress, "Christmas Belle," Belle series, 3½" h. **40.00**

Figure of a girl, "Dolls of the Month," February, pink dress w/gold hearts, 3¼" h. **40.00**

Figure of Girl Holding Bear

Figure of a girl holding bear, Birthday No. 2, pink dress, 3" h. (ILLUS.) **25.00**

Figure of a girl, "Koi" in Hawaiian costume, 4¼" h **30.00**

Figure of a girl playing harp, "Robin," Musicale series, purple dress, 6" h. **75.00**

Figure of a girl sitting on sofa reading book, Gibson Girls series, yellow dress, 6½" h. **120.00**

Figure of a girl w/crown & wand, Birthday No. 9, blue dress, 4⅜" h. (ILLUS. top, next col.) **28.00**

Figure of a girl w/fancy dress & big ring, "The Engagement," Romance series, 8" h. **120.00**

Figure of a lady, "Wu Cha," yellow dress w/gold applied flower & fan, 10" h. **90.00**

Figure of Girl with Crown & Wand

Figure of a Native-American girl, "America" of Little Internationals series, 3 ¾" h. **45.00**

Figure of an Oriental boy, "Pitty Sing" w/big hat & cat, (hats & cats may be different colors), 4" h. **55.00**

Figure of a woman, "Mama" in green dress w/yellow hat, 7¼" h. **95.00**

Lipstick holder, figural girl w/bouffant skirt forming holes for lipstick tubes **30.00**

Model of a camel, 6 ¾" h............. **65.00**

Model of a dog, poodle, gloss white w/gray-black shading, 5½" l., 3" h. (ILLUS. top, next page) **25.00**

Model of an elephant holding fly swatter, brown w/pink accents, 2½" h. (ILLUS. next page) **20.00**

Model of an elephant rolling on back, head & trunk up, brown w/pink accents, 2" h. (ILLUS. next page) **18.00**

Model of a Poodle

Elephant Rolling on Back

Elephant Writing

Elephant with Fly Swatter

Model of an elephant writing w/green pencil on white paper that shows "I Love You," brown w/pink accents, oval Josef sticker 2½" l., 1½" h. (ILLUS.) **20.00**

Model of a mouse, brown w/peanut, 1¾" h. (ILLUS. next page) **20.00**

Model of a mouse, brown w/pink bow on tail, oval Josef sticker, 2" h. (ILLUS. next page) **20.00**

Model of a mouse, brown w/plate & spoon, wearing bib, "Nibbles," oval Josef sticker, 1½" h. (ILLUS. next page) **18.00**

Model of Mouse with Peanut

Mouse with Plate & Spoon

Model of Mouse with Oval Sticker

Mouse with Lipstick

Mouse with Telephone

Model of a mouse, brown w/red & black telephone, "Talky," w/oval Josef sticker, 2" h. (ILLUS.) **20.00**

Model of a mouse w/lipstick & compact, Mouse Village series, 3½" h. (ILLUS.) **18.00**

Model of an ostrich, baby, part of a family, ½" h. **60.00**

Model of an ostrich, mama, part of a family, 5" h. **35.00**

Model of Owls Salt & Pepper Shakers

Model of Skunk

Model of an skunk, black &
white semi-gloss w/round Josef
sticker, 4" l., 2½" h. (ILLUS.) **24.00**

Music box w/bride & groom,
"The Bridal March," **90.00**

Salt & pepper shakers, figural,
model of owls, brown bodies
w/black eyes, 3½" h., pr.
(ILLUS. top) **30.00**

Soap dish, "Your Soap Please"
w/figural girl (dress from waist
down forms dish to hold soap) **25.00**

Train, engine & four cars; engine,
black w/blue & pink applied
flowers & cars yellow & black
w/applied flowers, set **75.00**

References: *Josef Originals Charming
Figurines w/price guide* by Dee Harris and
Jim and Kaye Whitaker, Schiffer Books
1994

Club: Josef Collectors Club, Karen
Wagner, 13566 Z Street, Omaha,
Nebraska 68137

KAY FINCH CERAMICS

*Katherine Finch studied at Ward Belmont
College in Nashville, Tennessee and Scripps
College in Claremont, California. In 1930,
Katherine and her husband, Braden, whom
she had met at Ward Belmont moved to
Corona del Mar, California. As a hobbyist
potter, Katherine went back to Scripps
College to study with William Manker. A
little later Braden and Katherine took a
worldwide trip which convinced Katherine
that she should turn her interests primarily
to ceramics.*

In 1939, Kay Finch Ceramics opened with Braden leaving his job to assume the day-to-day operations of the business.

Animals, which were the mainstay of the operation, gave Kay a great deal of personal satisfaction. She created and painted many animals herself although she had trained over twenty-five decorators for the job. In the early 1940s, Kay created some charming pig figurines and banks which were well-received by the public. When she developed an interest in champion dog breeding, she seriously began a large line of ceramic dogs. These were incorporated into ashtrays, figurines in assorted sizes, wall plaques and pins. Even though animals far outnumber human figures, it is the animals that collectors prefer. The Finches' son, George, was the genius behind the production of bowls, bath accessories, ashtrays, planters and vases. Today, these items have a following of their own and other collectors are beginning to notice. Some collectors feel Kay's animal line is too expensive for them to begin a collection of these wonderful creations and are turning to other items made by Kay Finch Ceramics.

When Braden died in 1963, the business ceased. Kay then channeled her energies toward dog breeding shows.

In the mid-1970s, another California company, Freeman-McFarlin Potteries (who had previously purchased Finch's molds), hired Kay to create a set of dog figurines which Freeman-McFarlin manufactured in their glazes until about 1980.

Various methods of marking items can be found such as incised, impressed, ink-stamped and hand-painted. Kay Finch died on June 21, 1993 at the age of eighty-nine.

KFinch
Calif.

Kay Finch
CALIFORNIA

Kay Finch Marks

Figures of Peasant Boy and Peasant Girl

Bank, model of a Victorian house, red, pink, green & white, ca. prior 1946, 5½" h. **$85.00**

Bowl, 4" l., 2 ¾" h., shell shape, three feet, scalloped rim, ivory exterior, dark green interior, stamp mark "Kay Finch California," ca. 1946 .... **30.00**

Figure of a "Peasant Boy" on square base, head slightly bent, hands on hips, pink body, blue shoes, socks, vest, trim on shirt & hat, short pants just below knees, ca. prior 1946, 6 ¾" h. (ILLUS. right previous page) **75.00**

Figure of a "Peasant Girl" on square base, head slightly bent, pink body, blue shoes, apron, trim on sleeves & hat w/ribbon in back, short blond hair, (no pigtails) ca. prior 1946, 6 ¾" h. (ILLUS. left previous page)......... **70.00**

Figure of a lady standing, head down, Godey fashion attire, blue skirt w/purple dots around edge & flowers in front, pink w/dark pink flower at bottom in back, white cape w/rose neck closure & white muff w/rose, pink hat w/purple decoration, incised "K. Finch Calif," ca. prior 1946, 7¼" h. **85.00**

Figure of a man standing, slightly turned head, one arm behind him & other arm over waist holding bouquet of flowers, Godey fashion attire, mauve trousers w/purple stripe on each side, pink & purple hat, deep purple shoes, ca. prior 1946, 8" h. **85.00**

Figure of a Madonna kneeling, hands together on chest w/head bowed, blond hair, overall pink clay, blue & purple mantilla w/flowers over her head & shoulders, incised 'Kay Finch' & stamped in script 'Kay Finch' w/'California' in block letters, 1949, 6½" h. **125.00**

Model of a bird, perched on a branch w/two leaves in-relief at right foot, head turned to left, feathers out slightly & tail down, matte white, incised "Kay Finch", ca. early 1950s, 4" h........ **55.00**

Model of a camel, walking, ivory body w/grey & tan accents, ca. prior 1946, 5¼" l., 5" h. **130.00**

Model of a cat, standing, stylized w/sgraffito-type decorations, head turned slightly, brown glossy glaze, incised "K. Finch," ca. prior 1946, 5" l., 5" h. **100.00**

Model of a dog, poodle in playful pose, crouching on front legs, back legs almost straight, mouth open, light & dark grey w/gold trim, ca. 1952, 11" l., 7½" h. **350.00**

Model of a duck, "Peep," sitting, white high glaze body w/medium green tail & top of head, dark green front feet, bill, eyes & a few back feathers, marked "Kay Finch California," ca. prior 1946, 3 ¾" l., 3" h. **45.00**

Model of a hen, "Biddy," white body w/green accents, Model No. 176, ca. prior 1946, 5" l., 5½" h. **90.00**

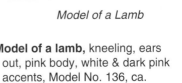

Model of a Lamb

Model of a lamb, kneeling, ears out, pink body, white & dark pink accents, Model No. 136, ca. prior 1946, 2½" l., 2¼" h. (ILLUS.) **35.00**

Model of a pig, "Winkie," tail & right ear up, right eye winking, left ear down, ca. prior 1946, 4" l., 3 ¾" h. **60.00**

Mug, bulbous w/wreath handle, white ground w/Santa face, red lips & hat w/green holly leaves, pink cheeks, black accents on beard & hat, stamp mark underglaze "Kay Finch California," 2 ¾" h. (ILLUS. below) **22.00**

Santa Face Mug

Egg-shaped Planter

Planter, egg w/irregular rim depicting 'broken' egg, mint matte green, 1950, 3¼" d., 4" h. (ILLUS.) **18.00**

Plate, 6½" d., Santa face, 1st edition, 1950, pale pink background, white beard, dark pink hat (ILLUS. top next col.) **95.00**

Santa Face Plate

Tray with Leaf

Powder jar, cov., cherry blossom in-relief on lid, sea green body, ca. 1946, 3½" d., 3" h. **45.00**

Tray, light pink w/pale green rim, dark green leaf in center, incised "K. Finch Calif." 1950, 3¼" l., (ILLUS.) **25.00**

Wall hanging, figural, model of a starfish w/flower decoration on center, five holes, dark green gloss, "Kay Finch Calif" incised in unglazed bottom (can be used as a flower arranger), 8" d. (ILLUS. top next page) **49.00**

Wall plaque, goldfish, light blue matte w/gold, 1957, 7¼" l., 6 ¾" h. **60.00**

Starfish Wall Hanging

Sconce Wall Plaque

Wall plaque, plain sconce-type
w/three scallop back, 7" l.,
6" h. (ILLUS.)............................. **45.00**

References: "Kay Finch Ceramics Identification" reprints of original catalog, Frances Finch Webb, 1992; "Examples of Kay Finch Ceramics" by Grace C. Allison, *American Clay Exchange*, November 15, 1987; "What's Hot? What's Not," *American Clay Exchange*, January 30, 1987

BRAD KEELER

In 1939 Brad Keeler's family used their residence garage in Glendale, California to open a small studio and Brad, at the age of twenty-six, created hand-decorated birds.

They were an immediate success so he leased some workspace at the American Pottery in Los Angeles. Evan Shaw, owner of American Pottery, liked the birds so much that he included them in his line. In 1946, Keeler opened his own company but Evan Shaw continued to help Keeler.

Brad Keeler's talents were as varied as the creations he produced. While not much has been written about him, except for his large assortment of bird designs, he created lobster dinnerware and Walt Disney figurines. He was president of the Art Potters Association, as well as a mold maker, sculptor and was adept at formulating glazes. Keeler, along with Andrew Malinovsky, Jr., developed a red glaze they named Ming Dragon Blood. It was used on many of Keeler's items, particularly his Chinese Modern household pieces which sometimes were combined with a glossy glaze black. Ming Dragon Blood was also used on Keeler's lobster line. It was a large line including serving bowls, oversized divided bowls with full lobsters' bodies making that division, chip and dip sets, soup bowls with lids and other serving pieces. The lobsters form the handles on the items and because of their natural shape and placement, they sometimes suffered damage.

Brad Keeler's bird line came in a variety of shapes, sizes and glazes. Many were soft, muted tones of greens, pinks, tans and beiges. Mold numbers start in the two digits and go upward into the hundreds. Collectors can find pheasants, swans, ducks, peacocks, herons and blue jays and Keeler's flamingos are sought by many collectors. Keeler made cats, dogs and fawns also in muted tones.

In 1952 at the age of thirty-nine, Brad Keeler had a fatal heart attack. At the time he was building a large factory in San Juan Capistrano and there was every reason to believe that his talents would outlast even the deadly imports playing havoc with so many California potteries.

Fortunately, most of the Brad Keeler Artwares products are marked. Some are in-mold "Brad Keeler" marks with model numbers and American Pottery labels; a Brad Keeler label; or the more uncommon copyright symbol with "B.B.K. Made in U.S.A." was stamped on small items or on outside designers' work. (Each designer used their initials to indicate they had decorated the piece.)

BRAD KEELER
MADE IN U.S.A.
87

IN-MOLD MARK

W   25

INCISED MARK

269
© CMK
MADE IN
U.S.A.

STAMP MARK

HAND DECORATED
Brad Keeler
ART WARES
LOS ANGELES CAL.

STICKER
ALL-GOLD COLOR

Brad Keeler Marks

Bowl, 6½" d., 4½" h., white bowl & lid w/Ming Dragon Blood lobster handle (ILLUS. bottom left) **$40.00**

Bowl, 8½" d., Ming Dragon Blood lobster handle on one side of rim, lime green bowl 30.00

Bowl, 15" l., divided, Ming Dragon Blood lobster creates the division, white bowl w/pale green 95.00

Figure of a cowboy on round base w/right hand on fence post, stamp mark "Brad Keeler," 7" h. (ILLUS. right top, next page) 42.00

Figure of a pioneer woman, stamp mark "Brad Keeler," 6 ¾" h., (ILLUS. left top, next page) 40.00

Fork, salad, solid white or solid lime green glaze, 9" l. 28.00

Model of a bird on pale green branch, incised, "Brad Keeler 720," 5½" h. 29.00

Model of a blue jay on round base, stamp mark "C.M.K. 269, Made in U.S.A." & copyright symbol, also has Brad Keeler sticker, 5" h. (ILLUS. next page)... **75.00**

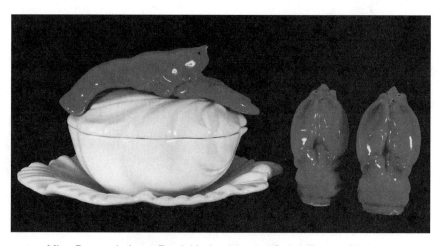

Ming Dragon Lobster Bowl, Underplate and Salt & Pepper Shakers

Figures of Pioneer Woman and Cowboy

Model of a Blue Jay

Model of a cockatoo, sitting on a tree branch, 8 ¾" h. **70.00**

Model of a cocker spaniel, sitting w/front paws in begging position, marked "Brad Keeler 735" **55.00**

Model of a doe, lying down w/head up, No. 878, 6" l., 4" h. **50.00**

Model of a duck, standing on a quatrefoil white base, brown body, yellow beak, 5" h. **60.00**

Model of a fawn, lying down w/head up, Model No. 879, 4" l., 3" h. **40.00**

Model of Flamingos

Model of a flamingo, standing on oval base, head erect, 9" h. (ILLUS. left) **100.00**

Model of a flamingo, standing on oval base, head bent, in-mold mark "Brad Keeler 3," 7½" h. (ILLUS. right).................. **75.00**

Model of a flamingo, standing on oval base, head bent slightly, wings up & back, stamp mark "Brad Keeler 47," 10¼" h. **80.00**

Model of a heron, incised "Brad Keeler 16", 9½" h........................ **78.00**

Model of a mallard on round base, wings up & back, white band on neck, green head & yellow beak, incised "Brad Keeler 25," 6½" l., 7½" h............. **85.00**

Model of a peacock, male, stamp mark, "Brad Keeler 717," 11" h. **140.00**

Model of a peacock, female, stamp mark, "Brad Keeler 715," 11" h. **135.00**

Model of a pheasant sitting on stump, stamp mark, "Brad Keeler 21," 7" h.......................... **70.00**

Model of a rooster, yellow, brown, green, rose & tan colors, stamped "935 Brad Keeler," 5½" h. **28.00**

Model of a sea gull on ocean wave, head down, wings up, in-mold mark "Brad Keeler 29," 10½" h. **145.00**

Plate, 8" l., underplate or salad dish, white glaze (ILLUS., previous page, left, below bowl)... **16.00**

Salt & pepper shakers, model of a lobster, Ming Dragon Blood glaze, stamp marked "Brad Keeler Made in U.S.A." 3¼" h., pr. (ILLUS. previous page, right, w/bowl) **29.00**

EDWIN M. KNOWLES CHINA COMPANY

The Edwin M. Knowles China Company opened in Newell, West Virginia in 1900 then moved to Chester, West Virginia. They were in business until 1963. This company should not be confused with Knowles, Taylor and Knowles. Collectors today feel each company's products have their own distinctive characteristics and are beginning to choose which they prefer. Edwin M. Knowles Company had a variety of dinnerware patterns that were popular in their time and still seem to be so today.

Mayflower, a Dutch motif pattern, shows a Dutch man and woman in the center with flowers around them. There is also another Dutch scene pattern with the man and woman holding one umbrella between them and the flowers are only on the sides of these two figures. Goldina, a color treatment is usually found on items with a yellow glaze. Knowles also used a variety of decals on many shapes. They produced large quantities of solid glazed dinnerware, Mexican motifs and items for the World's Fair of 1939.

36-1
Yorktown
SHAPE

EDWIN M. KNOWLES
CHINA CO.
MADE IN U.S.A.
39-11

Knowles Marks

Bowl, 8¼" d., vegetable, Golden Wedding patt., Accent shape, border of yellow roses & buds & green leaves accented in light brown, gold rim **$12.00**

Cookie jar, Sequoia patt., 7½" h. **65.00**

Cookie jar, Tulip patt., 8" h. **70.00**

Cookie jar, Tuliptime patt., 8" h. **75.00**

Creamer, Golden Wheat patt., Yorktown shape, sprays of wheat in natural colors, ivory semi-porcelain **4.00**

Creamer, Pink Pastel patt., vertical panels **4.00**

Cup & saucer, Tia Juana patt., Mexican w/sombrero sitting in doorway w/assorted pots hanging & sitting on shelves inside doorway, assortment of gourds on opposite side of item, set.. **6.50**

Custard cup, Magnolia patt., 4" h. **8.00**

Pie baker, Tulip patt., 8" d. **15.00**

Pitcher & bowl, white ground w/small pink roses overall, rims of pitcher & bowl & pitcher handle trimmed w/band of gold, pitcher, 10" h., bowl, 15½" d., set... **125.00**

Pitcher w/lid, 8½" h., Fruits patt. **45.00**

Plate, 6" d., bread & butter, Dutch man & woman w/umbrella, Goldina glaze **3.00**

Plate, 7" d., salad, Tia Juana II patt., same as Tia Juana except the gourds are missing **3.00**

Plate, 10" d., dinner, Deanna shape, deep blue **5.00**

Plate, 10" d., dinner, Dutch man & woman without umbrella, Mayflower shape **7.00**

Plate, 10" d., dinner, Golden Wheat patt., Yorktown shape **4.00**

Plate, 10" d., dinner, Ming Tree, Accent shape, blue & black **5.00**

Plate, 10" d., dinner, Tia Juana patt. **6.50**

Plate, 10 ¾" d., chop, 1939 World's Fair on Yorktown shape... **45.00**

Plate, 12 ¾" d., chop, Wheat patt., Yorktown shape (ILLUS. top, next page) **10.00**

Platter, 11½" d., Penthouse patt. of black trellises & red flowerpots w/assorted colored flowers, single pot w/flowers on trellis on opposite side, Yorktown shape (ILLUS. bottom, next page) **18.00**

Platter, 12" l., oval, Bench patt., brown bench w/Mexican pots on ground in front of bench & pots w/cacti sitting on the bench **15.00**

Yorktown Shaped Wheat Pattern Plate

Penthouse Pattern Platter

Salt & pepper shakers, ball
shape, Mango red glaze, pr........ **11.00**

Sugar, cov., Pink Pastels **6.50**

Sugar, cov., Golden Wheat patt.,
Yorktown shape........................... **5.50**

LEIGH POTTERS, INC.
CRESCENT POTTERY

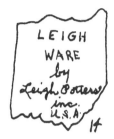

Leigh Potters, Inc. Marks

The Sebring family, well-known in the pottery and china fields, built a pottery in Alliance, Ohio in 1926. The company was named Crescent China and operated from 1920 until 1926 when the name was changed to Leigh Potters Inc. It was in operation until circa 1938.

Probably the most often found shape is "Ultra" which had straight edges except for the four corners which were rounded and had three points as shown in the illustrated wheat pattern plate. Leigh's Tulip pattern with its mustard, grey and rust tulips with a single black section in each tulip grouping makes a striking effect, one that is popular today.

Umbertone, usually marked as such, indicates the color of the body which is a creamy beige, and does not refer to a pattern name or a shape.

It has been reported that a Niles, Ohio company, also named Crescent, marked some of their pieces with a similar crescent moon shape.

Bowl, vegetable w/lid, 10" l., open
handles on each end, white
ground w/dark blue trim on rim
of lid, Martha Washington
shape.. **$24.00**

Candy dish w/Farberware frame
& handle, Ultra shape w/black,
maroon, green, & orange tulips,
6" d... **25.00**

Candy dish w/Farberware frame
& handle, Umbertone, orange
flowers w/black leaves & black
latticework around the verge,
6¼" d., 2½" h. (ILLUS.).............. **20.00**

*Faberware-framed
Candy Dish with
Orange Flowers*

Ultra Shape Plate

Creamer & cov. sugar, garden flowers in center, maroon & gold border, three pieces **15.00**

Cup & saucer, Ultra shape, Tulip patt., set....................................... **9.00**

Cup & saucer, ivory ground, gold rim on saucer, Ultra shape, Green Wheat patt., set **10.00**

Gravy boat, iris flowers in light & dark purple, orange & yellow, 7" l. **20.00**

Plate, 7" d., ivory ground, gold rim, Ultra shape, Green Wheat patt., (ILLUS.) **10.00**

Plate, 9" d., Clipper Ship patt. **9.00**

Plate, 9" d., Ultra shape, green & brown variation of Green Wheat patt. **9.00**

Salt & pepper shakers, one pink flower w/green leaves, Mayfair patt., 4" h., pr.............................. **6.00**

MADDUX OF CALIFORNIA

Maddux of California went into business in 1938. They sold a variety of figurines, planters, TV lamps, ashtrays, cookie jars, serving accessories and other items over the years. William Maddux originally owned the company and he also purchased Hollywood Ceramics and Valley Vista Pottery, both California companies. During this same period

Maddux sold the company to Louis and Dave Warsaw. In 1956, Morris Bogdanow bought Dave Warsaw's shares and later purchased the shares of Louis Warsaw, making Bogdanow the sole owner of Maddux. Maddux was affiliated with Sperry & Hutchinson (S&H Green Stamps), Top Value Stamps, Blue Chip Stamps and others, so their lines had to be diversified and large enough to support such well-known premium companies. Maddux went out of business in the early 1980s.

Maddux is well known for their bird line, especially flamingoes. However, collectors should not forget that Maddux created other items that are just as collectible. For example, there has been speculation as to the company that created the popular little brown pixies. Of course, other companies such as Gilner occasionally made pixies but they are the exceptions. The copyright credit goes to Maddux and they were manufactured by Hollywood Ceramics, the company that William Maddux had purchased in the late 1940s. The Maddux pixies have dimples on each cheek, brass rings on both ears and many of them have a copyright symbol on their bare backs or near their necks. Whether male or female, they are topless and clad only in loin cloths or garlands of flowers, many of which have been hand-applied in cold paint. Some of these features could apply to other companies but after handling pixies for awhile, the Maddux pixies will become apparent. Carl Romanelli, well-known sculptor for Metlox Potteries, also designed for other companies. Occasionally items can be found with the Maddux mark and the name Romanelli. At the present time values for this double mark do not make an item more or less costly.

Maddux Marks

Ashtray, round w/four cigarette rests, pale blue & turquoise squares over a light green glaze, 6" d................................... **$9.00**

Cookie jar, Humpty Dumpty, Model No. 2113, 11" h................ **95.00**

Cookie jar, squirrel w/yellow hat & jacket, green shirt, marked "Maddux of Calif. & Romanelli," Model No. 2110, 13" h................ **75.00**

White Glaze Cookie Jar

Cookie jar, white glaze w/purple grapes & green leaves, cluster of grapes on lid knob, Model No. B112, 9" h. (ILLUS.) **50.00**

Lamp, TV, model of a swan on water, white swan w/blue water base, Model No. 828, E21855 incised on back near light bulb, 12¼" h., (ILLUS. next page) **75.00**

Model of a cockatoo w/wings spread, round base trimmed w/open flower & buds, mid-1940s, 11" h. **55.00**

Model of an Oriental Pheasant on stump, head turned toward tail feathers, green, light brown, turquoise & yellow colors, 12" h. .. **60.00**

Model of Pixie Sitting on Tiger

Swan Lamp

Model of Pixie Kneeling on Canoe

Model of a pixie kneeling on a
canoe, paddle in hand;
chartreuse canoe, 7" l., pixie,
4" h. (ILLUS.) **28.00**

Model of a pixie sitting sideways
atop a tiger; tiger, 7½" l., pixie,
4" h. (ILLUS.) **34.00**

Model of a pixie, standing on
round base w/hands, garland of
flowers for bathing suit bottom
w/same flowers on base, 3½" h... **10.00**

Planter, model of a swan, black
glaze w/pink accents, green
eyes, Model No. 510, 7½" l.,
10" h., (ILLUS. top next page) **30.00**

Planter, oblong w/model of a
flamingo standing, legs on
planter, body & head above
planter, 6" h. **40.00**

Model of Swan Planter

Vase, 5" h., corset shape w/head & neck of flamingo on each side forming handles, bodies on the vase **45.00**

Vase, 15" h., model of a modernistic rooster, feet on oval base w/head & long neck on side of vase, wings & feathers form decoration on front, light pink glaze, Model No. 227, 1960 (ILLUS.) **38.00**

Wall pocket, flame shape w/sunburst at bottom rising to opening, white glaze, Model No. 691, 8½" h. **15.00**

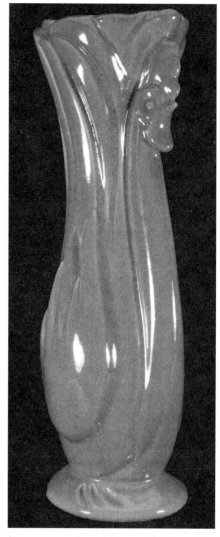

Model of Modernistic Rooster Vase

MAYER CHINA COMPANY

Joseph Mayer, an Englishman, came to New York in 1880 to begin a pottery importing company with his brother, Arthur. Less than a year later, he organized the Mayer Potteries Company, Ltd. with another brother named Ernest. Shortly thereafter, the business name would become Mayer China Company. At some point during this period, but for only a short time, the company was known as J. & E. Mayer.

In the late 1880s, Mayer was marketing white ironstone underglaze with a Lustre Band and Sprig (Tea Leaf). By the early 1900s, Mayer was producing semi-porcelain dinnerware, toilet sets and white granite. About 1915, Mayer discontinued dinnerware for home use and primarily concentrated on the manufacturing of hotel ware.

Shenango China Company of New Castle, Pennsylvania purchased Mayer China in 1964 but just four years later both companies were owned by Interpace. Then, in 1979, Shenango was bought by Anchor Hocking

Corporation and Mayer China added Walker China to their operation in 1980. In 1985, Syracuse China Company bought Mayer China.

Mayer CHINA CO.
© BEAVER FALLS PA

MAYER
CHINA
BEAVER FALLS, PA.
U.S.A.

Mayer China Marks

Bowl, 4½" h., made for the Northern Pacific Railway, exterior & interior borders of magenta & green leaves **$90.00**

Chamber pot w/lid, semi-vitreous, solid white high gloss, 11" d. **115.00**

Cup & saucer, Indian Tree design, pastel pinks on white ground, set **6.50**

Gravy boat, dainty yellow & pink rose buds on white ground, 7½" l., 4" h. **6.00**

Mug, child's, heavy restaurant ware, pink ground w/white elephant standing in a center ring at a circus, 3 ¾" h. **10.00**

Plate, 7¼" d., three sprays of pink & yellow flowers w/green leaves trailing from rim to the verge & partially into the center **8.00**

Plate, 7 ¾" d., children's motif, center shows child w/jack-in-the-box & rim has duck in fancy hat, musical top, bunny rabbit, clown, kitten & two dolls, Model No. 184 (ILLUS.) **30.00**

Children's Motif Plate

White Ground Plate with Scallops & Flowers

Plate, 7 ¾" d., made for the Northern Pacific Railway, exterior & interior borders of magenta & green leaves **210.00**

Plate, 10" d., white ground w/green rim design of small scallops & flowers & stems forming a chain, heavy restaurant ware, Model No. 459 (ILLUS. above) **8.00**

Platter, 11½" l., Western rodeo motif, white high gloss glaze w/dark brown & white branding irons on rim & bucking bronco rider in center **45.00**

Toothbrush holder, footed, round slightly bulbous body w/uneven rim, white, 5" h. **7.00**

References: "Chamber pots are collectible" by Grace C. Allison, *American Clay Exchange,* November 15, 1986

D. E. McNICOL POTTERY COMPANY

This company originally was the McNicol, Burton and Company but in 1892 it became D. E. McNicol Pottery Company operating out of East Liverpool, Ohio. They produced Rockingham-glazed wares, yellowware and white ironstone. Business was good and about 1920 they expanded into Clarksburg, West Virginia. They made a variety of products including dinner, hotel and toilet wares. Probably they are most well-known for their calendar and souvenir plates (heavily produced from 1916 through 1920) and decorated china for hospitals, hotels, railroads and restaurants.

The East Liverpool plant operated until about 1930 and the Clarksburg plant closed in 1954.

D.E. McNicoL POTTERY CO. EAST LIVERPOOL, OHIO

McNICOL, CHINA CLARKSBURG, W.VA.

D.E. McNicoL EAST LIVERPOOL, O.

McNicol China Marks

White Ironstone Restaurant Egg Cup

Bowl, 5½" d., white ironstone void of decoration except an initial "B" inside an oval on inside rim.......... **$5.00**

Egg cup, round foot w/curved sides & think rim, orange broad stripe, thin maroon & green stripes under rim, white ironstone restaurant ware, marked "McNicol China Clarksburg, W. VA., 1948," 3¼" h. (ILLUS. top, next col.) **10.00**

Pitcher & bowl, pitcher, 12" h., bowl, 17¼" d., white ironstone, pitcher w/one large orange flower encircled by oval shaped green chain, matching smaller flowers & chains in three areas on bowl, pr. **185.00**

Plate, child's 6½" d., w/alphabet around the edge, center decal shows, "Pussy Cat where have you been?" below a boy, girl & cat.. **25.00**

Plate, calendar, 7½" d., rim in green iridescent w/gold arrow points, inner circle has the 1916 calendar months & inside the circle is an Indian squaw, underneath the months is "Compliments of Louis Henne Co., New Braunfels, Texas" **15.00**

Plate, calendar, 8" d., gold edge w/1916 calendar months alternating w/bluebirds on rim, Dutch boy & girl in center w/"Luf is some nodings dot ickles two hearts mit de same somedings," below & "Compliments of Stebbins Store, Copeland, Kans." (ILLUS. top, next page) **23.00**

Plate, calendar, 8" d., "Victory" w/eagle below, 1920, each month around rim w/center having four flags & a globe intersected by the word "Peace," the date 28th June 1919 & 1914 on left w/1919 on right of flags, "The Great World War" underneath, marked on back "D.E. McNicol East Liverpool, O. 99" (ILLUS. bottom, next page) **28.00**

1916 Calendar Plate

1920 Calendar "Victory" Plate

Fruits and Chain Plate

Plate, 9" d., orange iridescent rim w/gold chains connecting a flower, center motif w/pear, strawberries, cherries & green leaves (ILLUS.)........................... **18.00**

Toothbrush holder, white ironstone w/tiny pink & yellow roses w/green leaves underneath rim & on slightly bulbous body inside a medallion, irregular rim, 5 ¾" h. ... **8.00**

Soap dish, round w/bluebirds in flight on inside bottom, white ironstone, 4½" d. **12.00**

References: "D.E. McNicol Pottery," by Susan N. Cox, *American Clay Exchange,* February 1981

METLOX POTTERIES

METLOX
MADE IN
U.S.A.

C Romanelli

MADE IN
Poppytrail
METLOX
CALIF.
U.S.A.

VERNONWARE
BY
METLOX
MADE IN CALIFORNIA

Miniatures
by METLOX
MANHATTAN BEACH
CALIFORNIA

Metlox Pottery Marks

While Metlox Potteries began operating in 1927, it was not until the late 1970s and early 1980s that collectors began to take particular interest in the products of this company.

T. C. and Willis Prouty, father and son respectively, began this company in Manhattan Beach, California and specialized in outdoor signs. In 1931 T. C. died and Willis began the production of dinnerware.

Over the years, Metlox has created an abundance of dinnerware including the line named California Pottery. Poppytrail, a table and kitchenwares line, was in production until about 1942; however, it was about six years before the Poppytrail line was produced that the company's trademark became known as "Poppytrail" also.

In 1947 when Metlox was purchased by Evan K. Shaw (American Pottery), dinnerware became the mainstay for the company.

Carl Romanelli joined Metlox as an artware designer and became well-known for his miniature animals and novelties. However, it is the Romanelli figurines, especially nudes and nudes with vases, that are eagerly sought by collectors.

While most of the Metlox dinnerware patterns have generally gone unnoticed by collectors who favored Fiesta, Bauer, LuRay *and other solid glazed colors, now more people are taking notice of the excellent dinnerware patterns they created.*

Poppets by Poppytrail are piquing the interest of collectors in today's market. They are stoneware flower-holders and planters created in doll-like fashion by Helen Slater. Metlox produced them during the 1960s and 1970s. The shelf-sitters and the individual Salvation Army band figures are among the most popular.

The Nostalgia Line suits many collectors who can parallel collect using Metlox's American Royal horses to complement other horse or animal collections. The Carriage collection, Santa & reindeer and old cars, are finding interest among those who collect vintage car memorabilia or Santa-related items.

In 1989, Metlox Potteries ceased operations.

Bowl, soup, 8" d., California Provincial patt., strutting rooster motif in maroon, leaf green & yellow w/a decorated green & brown border **$25.00**

Coffeepot, cov., Vernon Rose patt., pink roses w/green leaves on San Fernando shape, eight cup capacity **100.00**

Cookie jar, model of drummer boy head w/tall hat, red collar, white face, black brim on hat & chin strap, blue hat, red knob on top, 10 ¾" h. **475.00**

Cookie jar, model of an African-American Santa, standing **885.00**

Cookie jar, model of an owl, full-body, brown glaze, 9" h. **50.00**

Cookie jar, model of an owl, full-body, dark & pale blue, 10½" h. **75.00**

Cookie jar, model of a rag doll, boy in sitting position, 11" h. **215.00**

Cookie jar, model of a rag doll, girl in sitting position, 11" h. **225.00**

Cookie jar, model of a rose, pink & green, 7½" h. **375.00**

Cookie jar, model of a squirrel on pine cone, decorated, 11" h. **95.00**

Cookie jar, model of a whale w/small duck finial, blue glaze.... **425.00**

Creamer, California Provincial patt. **30.00**

Creamer, Fruit Basket patt., fruit & white flowers in brown basket, San Fernando shape w/scalloped edge & fluted verge **18.00**

Creamer, Pink Lady patt., small pink & purple posies w/green leaves, scalloped rims w/fluting, Vernon Ware, ca. 1965 .... **20.00**

Cup & saucer, California Ivy patt., set..................................... **15.00**

Cup & saucer, California Provincial patt., set **19.00**

Cup & saucer, Old Cathay patt., Oriental motif w/floral branch, blossoms & a bird h.p. w/rust, blue & green on a pale ivory background, set..........................**13.00**

Cup & saucer, Vernon Rose patt., pink roses w/green leaves on San Fernando shape, set **15.00**

"Barney" Poppets' Series Figure

Figure, Poppets' series, "Barney," bather boy lying on stomach, knees bent & balancing pot on soles of feet, Model No. 119, 8½" l. (ILLUS.) **60.00**

"Eliza" Poppets' Series Figure

"Casey" Poppets' Series Figure

Figure, Poppets' series, "Casey," policeman (sheriff), blue hat & jacket w/darker blue badge on hat & jacket, blue striped pants, brown hair & mustache, Model No. 019, 8" h. (ILLUS.).................................. **50.00**

Figure, Poppets' series, "Conchita," Mexican girl w/serape draped over her shoulders, open pot on her head & another pot beside her, open holes for her eyes, rough textured w/sand colored body, black hair, Model No. 309, 8 ¾" h. **65.00**

Figure, Poppets' series, "Effie," one of seven in Salvation Army band, standing w/her cymbals together, blue Salvation Army hat & coat, white skirt, yellow cymbals, Model No. 389, 7 ¾" h. **45.00**

Figure, Poppets' series, "Eliza," flower vendor, one large pot in front, one smaller at right foot & slightly behind, pots are brown & white, turquoise jacket & hat, white scarf around neck, Model No. 229, 5½" h. (ILLUS.)...................................... **60.00**

Figure, Poppets' series, "Huck," boy shelf-sitter fishing w/feet crossed, blue pants, brown shirt, yellow hat, Model No. 609, 6½" h. **50.00**

Figure, Poppets' series, "Jenny," shelf-sitter w/legs crossed at knees, yellow dress & bow in hair, Model No. 089, 8 ¾" h. **45.00**

Figure, Poppets' series, "Nellie," bird on her head, holding vase, holes for eyes & five holes around top of her hair, black hair & blouse w/black & turquoise circles on skirt, turquoise bird & vase, Model No. 169, 8¼" h. **55.00**

Figure, Poppets' series, "Nick," organ grinder w/monkey sitting atop grinder, man has yellow hat & kerchief around his neck, monkey has white vest & blue hat, Model No. 649 .... **50.00**

Figure of Flower Vendor and Wagon and Burro

"Sam" Poppet's Series Figure

Figures of Seated Man and Woman

Figure, Poppets' series, "Sam," attached pot on right, black shoes, turquoise jacket & blond hair, Model No. 269, 5 ¾" h. (ILLUS.) **40.00**

Figure of a man, flower vendor holding pot in left hand w/right arm raised, Nostalgia Line, 4½" h. (ILLUS. left above) **50.00**

Figure of a man, seated, (shelf-sitter), "Papa," Model No. 653 (ILLUS. next column, right)......... **55.00**

Figure of a Native American brave, standing w/arms folded across chest, Modern Masterpieces line, 9" h. **295.00**

Figure of a woman, seated, (shelf-sitter), "Mama," Model No. 652 (ILLUS. left).................. **55.00**

Figure of a woman, standing on a stylized ovoid base & holding an urn to the right side of her head & her left arm over her head touching the urn, left leg slightly bent at knee & in front of right leg, satin ivory glaze, "water bearer," "C. Romanelli" signed on base rim & "patent No. 125594" on bottom, Model No. 1816, 9¼" h........................ **225.00**

Flower frog to fit inside wagon, pale green, Nostalgia Line, 6" l., 3" h. (ILLUS. w/wagon & burro, previous page, top) **55.00**

Flower holder, figural, nude woman standing on oval base, right leg out in front & bent at knee, right hand under left breast, left arm bent w/hand at neck, head turned to left, vase w/three openings behind her, satin ivory glaze, "C. Romanelli" signed on base rim & also incised in script on bottom, "Poppytrail Made in California" incised on bottom, design patent No. 125593, Model No. 1806, 10" h. **260.00**

Flower holder, figural, woman standing on square base w/her arms behind her & wrapped around a cornucopia w/three openings, satin ivory woman w/satin pink cornucopia exterior & satin green & brown interior, "C. Romanelli" signed on base rim & "Metlox Made in U.S.A. Des Patent 122409" in stamped mark under the glaze, 8¼" h. **115.00**

Model of an angelfish on a base, olive green w/brown & rust glazes, marked "Romanelli" & "Metlox," Model No. 1814, 8½" h. **95.00**

Model of a burro, standing w/head down, white & grey body, yellow hat, Nostalgia Line, 7" l., 4½" h. (ILLUS. w/wagon previous page, top) **90.00**

Model of a circus horse, American Royal Collection series, white w/red trim, 6" l., 6" h. **125.00**

Model of a Clydesdale, American Royal Collection series, walking position, 9" l., 9" h. **200.00**

Model of a fish on a base, satin ivory glaze, paper label shows, 'Miniatures by Metlox Manhattan Beach, California,' 4¼" h. **75.00**

Model of a stork on a base, satin ivory glaze, stamp mark, "Metlox Made in U.S.A.," 6½" h. **65.00**

Model of a surrey w/metal fringe, pale green, Nostalgia Line, 10½" l., 9" h. **95.00**

Model of a wagon, dark brown w/pale green, white & pink glazes, Nostalgia Line, 10" l., 5½" w. (ILLUS. w/burro & flower vendor, previous page, top)...... **110.00**

Model of Seal Planter

Planter, model of a seal w/two front flippers hugging a round planter, pale blue satin matte, Model No. 456, 5¼" h. (ILLUS.)... **18.00**

Plate, 8½" d., Vernonware, Songs of Christmas limited edition series, White Christmas, 1978, eighth in the series, Della Robbia style carving of plate border of fruit, foliage & flowers, center has three carolers in front of a snow-covered home which is decorated for the holidays w/"Christmas 1978" on rim at bottom................. **30.00**

Plate, 10¼" d., California Ivy patt. **12.00**

Platter, 11" l., oval, California Provincial patt. **50.00**

Platter, 13" l., oval Mesa patt.,
Vernonware shape, Native
American designs & symbols,
rust, henna & brown colors......... **30.00**

Platter, 13½" l., oval, California
Provincial patt. **60.00**

Platter, 16" l., oval, Fruit Basket
patt., San Fernando
shape.. **50.00**

Salt & pepper shakers, handled,
Vernon Rose patt., San
Fernando shape, pr. **25.00**

Soup tureen, cover & ladle,
California Provincial patt: tureen
w/lid, beige basket design
w/open green handle on each
end, lid w/chicken sitting & in
maroon, green & yellow, 15" l.,
10" h.; ladle, basketweave, half
green, half yellow, 9" l.,
3 pcs.. **425.00**

Sugar, cov., California Ivy patt. **25.00**

Covered Gigi Pattern Sugar Bowl

Sugar, cov., Gigi patt., Country
French shape, footed w/grooves
in the shape, 4½" h.
(ILLUS.) **22.00**

Sugar, cov., Mesa patt.,
Vernonware shape **18.00**

Sugar, cov., Pink Lady patt.,
Vernon Ware shape, ca.
1965 .... **25.00**

Teapot, cov., Vernon Rose patt.
on San Fernando shape, six cup
capacity **100.00**

References: *Collector's Encyclopedia
of Metlox Potteries* by Carl Gibbs, Jr.,
Collector Books, 1995; "Metlox Poppytrail
Cookie Jars" by Susan N. Cox, *American
Clay Exchange,* September 30, 1987;
"California Provincial produced by Metlox
Potteries" by Delleen Enge, *The Glaze,*
September 1987; "Amusing Pottery Pieces"
by Letha Kopsas, *American Clay
Exchange,* June 30, 1984; Metlox Pottery
and Poppytrail Pottery correspondence and
catalogs

NICODEMUS FERRO-STONE CERAMICS

*Chester R. Nicodemus opened a pottery in
Columbus, Ohio around 1937. He worked his
way through Cleveland School of Art via a
paper route and graduated in 1925. He was
offered a job at the Ole King Cole Papier-
Mache factory for the first summer after
graduating and then he taught at the Dayton
Art Institute for about five years.*

*Mr. Nicodemus called his Ohio clay that
fired at high temperatures to an unusual
hardness "Ferro-Stone" which also served as
the name for his business. Ferro is the Latin
word for iron and Chester felt it enabled him
to fire stone hard. He was also able to
successfully produce glazes in ivory (a light
grey), pink, yellow, mottled green and
turquoise.*

*Animals, birds, vases, advertising
memorabilia, ashtrays and figurines were a
part of his product line.*

*As did John Frank of Frankoma Pottery
Company, Chester Nicodemus created
Christmas cards for his friends and
customers. He and his wife Florine started
this tradition in 1938. These mementos were
usually round, square or rectangular and had*

Chester's and Florine's names on them. They had a different greeting each year and the date.

Nicodemus designed the Distinguished Service Award given by the Columbus Art League in 1955; a twist of fate, he was also the recipient. Another achievement that Chester was proud of was the sculpture he created which is on permanent display at the Schumacher Gallery in the Capital University library. It is a figure of Christ.

In 1971, Chester Nicodemus semi-retired but by 1989 he went into full retirement at the age of 88. Mr. Nicodemus died in 1990.

Nicodemus used several marks and at least two labels. The marks are an "N" with a tiny letter to the upper left and a small numeral to the upper right. He also impressed his full last name on items. A paper label was used that was red and grey with the words "Nicodemus" and "Ferro-stone;" another label was silver with a purple line through the center and the word "Nicodemus" above it and "Ferro-stone" below it also in purple.

NICODEMUS

$^{c}N^{2}$

NICODEMUS

Nicodemus Marks

Ashtray, round w/four cigarette rests, advertising "Goucher College Founded 1885," impressed "Nicodemus" mark, 4½" d. (ILLUS. top, next column) **$23.00**

Bowl, 4½" d., round foot w/flared body, swirl lines inside, yellow, Model No. 554 .... **44.00**

Figure of angel praying, standing w/head down, no. 2 in a 9 piece nativity set, turquoise glaze, impressed "Nicodemus" mark, 7½" h. **90.00**

"Goucher College" Ashtray

Figure of angel w/harp, standing, no. 1 in a 9 piece nativity set, turquoise glaze, impressed "Nicodemus" mark, 7½" h. **95.00**

Figure of Joseph, no. 4 in a 9 piece nativity set, turquoise glaze, impressed "Nicodemus" mark, 7½" h. (ILLUS.) **115.00**

Figure of Joseph

Figure of Mary & Child, Mary seated w/head bowed, Child in Mary's lap, no. 3 in a 9 piece nativity set, turquoise glaze, impressed "Nicodemus" mark, 5½" h. **100.00**

Figures of three Wise Men, each kneeling, heads bowed, nos. 5, 6 & 7 of a 9 piece nativity set, turquoise glaze, impressed "Nicodemus" mark, 5½" h., set of 3 .... **140.00**

Model of a cat, curled up & sleeping, paper label, Model No. 650, 7" l. **145.00**

Model of a collie, standing on oblong base, impressed "Nicodemus" mark, 6" h. **165.00**

Model of a lamb, no. 8 in a 9 piece nativity set, turquoise glaze, 3" h. **25.00**

Model of a penguin, standing, head upward, black & white glaze, "Optimist," Model No. 91, 3" h. **95.00**

Model of Robin

Model of a robin, silver label & impressed "Nicodemus" mark, 3½" h. (ILLUS) **160.00**

Model of a robin, impressed "Nicodemus" mark, 5" h. **175.00**

Model of a rooster on round base, turquoise glaze, impressed mark "Nicodemus," 6" h. **135.00**

Model of a rooster on round base, crowing, tail up, ivory glaze w/red, Model No. 200, 22" h. **285.00**

Model of a squirrel, standing w/head bent, eating, tail up & against body, Model No. 139, 3" h. **90.00**

Model of a star, no. 9 in a 9 piece nativity set, turquoise glaze, unmarked, 2½" h. **20.00**

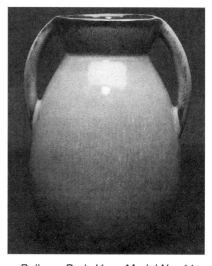

Bulbous Body Vase Model No. 44

Vase, 4" h., bulbous body w/handle on each side from center of body to rim, Model No. 44, red & grey label & impressed "Nicodemus" (ILLUS.) **100.00**

Vase, 4½" h., squatty, bulbous body tapering to a short stick neck, ivory glaze, Model No. 552, impressed "Nicodemus" mark...... **52.00**

Vase, 6" h., bottle-form, mottled green, Model No. 553 .... **75.00**

References: "A SaluteTo American Potters And Their Cats," by Marilyn Dipboye, *American Clay Exchange,* May 15, 1987; "Wallpockets-Popular Collectibles," by Grace C. Allison, *The Glaze,* November, 1986; A Letter from Wilbur Held, California, *American Clay Exchange,* April 15, 1985; "Chester R. Nicodemus Ferro-Stone Ceramics" by Betty Carson, *American Clay Exchange,* March 1983; "Artistic Suicide Scorned By Sculptor Nicodemus," by Ruth E. Dixon, *Ohio's Heritage,* March-April 1978; Correspondence between Chester R. Nicodemus and Susan N. Cox; Company catalogs

NORTH DAKOTA SCHOOL OF MINES

Also see: WPA

For additional information refer to: *American & European Art Pottery Price Guide*, edited by Kyle Husfloen, Antique Trader Books

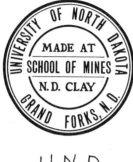

North Dakota Marks

The School of Mines was begun at the University of North Dakota in 1890. However, it hobbled along until 1898 when Earle Babcock became its director. Babcock used native North Dakota clay—a fact that remained throughout the university's production—but eastern companies actually produced the items from the clays sent to them by Earle Babcock. Sometimes North Dakota native artists would decorate the items returned to the School of Mines; sometimes they had already been decorated by the eastern firms. Mayer Pottery Company, Beaver Falls, Pennsylvania and Brockmann Pottery Company, Cincinnati, Ohio were two of the eastern companies that worked with Earle Babcock. At lease three known potteries from Zanesville, Ohio also worked with Babcock: Roseville Pottery Company, Ohio Pottery Company and the J. B. Owens Pottery Company. Earle Babcock worked diligently to prepare for the St. Louis Exposition in 1904 and, by any standards, it was considered a successful undertaking.

In 1910 things began to progress rapidly. Margaret Kelly Cable became the supervisor for the new ceramic department. Having studied with Frederick H. Rhead, it is easy to see his influence in some of Cable's Art Deco decorating style. She also studied under Charles F. Binns at Alfred University in Alfred, New York. Margaret Kelly Cable retired in 1949 but her almost forty years at the university had an effect on every person she encountered. In addition, her influence has produced some of the most beautiful sgrafitto-type ware known to exist. Margaret Cable died in October of 1960.

The most familiar mark used on this ware is the cobalt seal showing "University of North Dakota Grand Forks, N.D." in an outer circle and "Made at School of Mines N.D. Clay," dividing the inner circle. A slightly different seal is one that shows "The Cable Years" in place of "School of Mines."

Artists often signed their items or, at least, used their initials. Margaret Kelly Cable used "M. Cable," "Cable," "MKC," "MC," and two harder-to-find signatures, "Maggie" or "Maggie Mudd." Hildegard Fried used "Fried" or "HF." Flora Cable Huckfield, sister of Margaret Cable, used "Huckie," "Huck" or "Huck" in a circle, "FCH," "H," or "H" in a circle. Julia Edna Mattson simply used her last name or "JEM" or "JM." Freida L. Hammers used her last name or "FLH." Students who studied pottery making at the University marked their names or initials on pieces so collectors will find a variety of marking on various items.

Bowl, 2½" d., 1 ¾" h., high gloss blue-grey w/sgraffito-type flowers, marked w/cobalt seal & incised initials, "E.E." (ILLUS.) ... **$38.00**

Sgraffito-type Flowered Bowl

Figure of Bellhop

Figure of a bellhop w/tray in right hand, high gloss green, stamp marked "U.N.D. Grand Rapids, N.D." & incised "MC 19," 4½" h. (ILLUS.).................. **255.00**

Model of a lion, pressed, designed by Julia Edna Mattson, 1938, overall tan color, stamp "U.N.D. Grand Forks, N.D." & incised "49 JT," 3" l., 2" h. (ILLUS. below) **185.00**

Footed Off-White Pitcher

Pitcher, 7" h., footed, off-white glaze w/two blue bands separated by a green band near bottom of bulbous body & green & blue band at shoulder w/purple, blue & red flowers & light & dark leaves between the bands, green rim w/blue band inside rim & blue dots w/green scroll band between dots on handle, marked w/cobalt seal & incised "MC Cable 222;" several decorations were used on this item (ILLUS.) **345.00**

Model of Lion

Sugar Bowl

Sugar bowl, open, handleless, high gloss turquoise glaze interior, beige matte exterior w/wheat design in orange, rust & green, marked w/cobalt seal & incised "M Cable 242", 3" d., 2¾" h. (ILLUS. prev. page).......... **80.00**

Tray, irregular shape w/rounded corners, high gloss yellow, marked w/cobalt seal & "MJ" initials, 7½" l. **55.00**

Collecting Tips: North Dakota School of Mines items can cost over a thousand dollars for some of the larger, more intricately detailed pieces. However, those wanting to start a collection should not be hindered by price; many pieces can be found for less than a few hundred dollars. These items would not be considered inferior but rather they may be small, have a solid glaze or very little, if any, decoration. These characteristics do not detract from the pottery and serve as a basis for upgrading whenever possible.

References: "North Dakota School of Mines Pottery" by Scott H. Nelson and Kirk Carlson, *Journal of the American Art Pottery Association,* January-February 1986; "North Dakota School of Mines" pamphlet prepared by Margaret Kelly Cable, December 1926 and reprinted in the *American Clay Exchange,* November 1983; *University of North Dakota Pottery, The Cable Years* by Margaret Libby Barr, Donald Miller and Robert Barr, Knight Publishing Company, 1977

ONONDAGA POTTERY COMPANY

See: Syracuse China

PACIFIC CLAY PRODUCTS

Pacific Clay Products Company has been an enigma for so long that most writers prefer not to mention it or, at best, to skim the surface. However, in the last year or so, many new facts have come to light concerning this company. Much of the factual and informative material has come to me through Tillie Roman of South Dakota. Her persistence has paid off for collectors of Pacific Clay Products as well as Pacific Stoneware Company collectors. Not only is the information helpful to those collecting Pacific Clay items but those who own Pacific Stoneware cookie jars. Pacific Clay Products and Pacific Stoneware are not the same company.

Pacific Stoneware operated out of Portland, Oregon making stoneware crocks from one pint to twenty gallons, rabbit and chicken feeders, waterers, milk pans and bread bowls. They also made a complete line of flowerpots. In the 1950s, the company went out of business but in 1960, Bennett Welsh purchased it. With college students and artists, the People Lovers line became available. Six different cookie jars, three casseroles, planters, weed pots and wind bells were part of this line. Pacific produced a catalog and had national distribution. Displays were available at major gift markets such as Los Angeles, San Francisco, Seattle, Denver and so on. In 1973 Welsh sold his interest to his partner and the company continued for another ten years. Much of the People Lovers line can be found with a mark that has a copyright symbol, date and "Pacific Stoneware Inc., U.S.A. By Scarpino" (Ted Scarpino was the master mold maker for the People Lovers Cookie jars), a number (probably a stock number) and the word "Shagy." A sticker is attached to some of the items that shows, "People Lovers A handmade hand-decorated stoneware original, Pacific Stoneware, Inc. Est. 1883."

As to Pacific Clay Products, it was in the early 1920s that William Lacy merged several southern California potteries to form the Pacific Clay Products Company in Los Angeles. However, it was not until the early 1930s that Pacific began producing tableware and artware that has piqued the interest of today's collectors. Values for this company's products should increase greatly over the next few years. Their Hostessware line was large and came in solid glazes as well as decorated pieces. Colors were Apache Red, Pacific Blue, Lemon Yellow, Jade Green, Sierra White, Royal Blue and Delphinium

Blue. *Ceramic engineer, Frank McCann, and designer and head of the art department, Matthew Lattie, were largely responsible for Pacific's success. Pottery production ceased in 1942. The entries below refer to Pacific Clay Products only.*

PACIFIC
301
MADE IN USA

PACIFIC

Pacific Marks

Bowl, 12" l., oval, divided, Hostessware line **$28.00**

Candleholder, double, rectangular base w/rounded corners, curved pedestal the length of base arching upward at one end w/a round holder on top, then slanting down to the base w/a low round holder, jade green, 6" l., 4½" h. **33.00**

Candleholder, single lily rising in the center from a square base w/radical flaring leaf on each side of flower, white glaze, 5¼" h. **38.00**

Coaster, round, solid glaze, 4" d. **20.00**

Coaster, round, Dimity patt., blue & yellow, 4" d. **25.00**

Grease jar w/cover, round w/three rings near middle section of bottom, 5¼" h. **58.00**

Plate, 9" d., baby's, divided into three sections w/rabbits around rim **75.00**

Plate, 10¼" d., pie w/rim, deep blue, without clip-on handles **36.00**

Plate, 10½" d., divided, Hostessware line **50.00**

Plate, 11" d., grill, Hostessware line **35.00**

Platter, 15" d., round w/numerous rings, tab handles, yellow glaze **40.00**

Tray, oblong, Model No. 1063, pale blue interior, white exterior, 7½" l., 1½" h. **12.00**

Tumbler, bulbous bottom w/slightly inward curve at middle to form straight-sided top, 5" h. **17.00**

Tumbler, straight sides flaring slightly at rim, two rings near bottom, three rings near top, Hostessware line, 4⅛" h **15.00**

Vase, 3¼" h., 3" d., figural, model of a miniature cornucopia on a base w/six rings near middle of body & w/six rings at the narrow end, maroon glossy glaze, Model No. 3010, ca. 1930s **19.00**

Vase, 4¼" h., baluster shape w/elongated molded handles from center to under rim, maroon glaze............................. **20.00**

Vase, 5" h., bulbous body w/three horizontal rings near bottom & three horizontal rings at middle, jade green, Model No. 1500, raised circular mark, ca. late 1930s... **55.00**

Vase, 6½" h., graduated horizontal ribbing on front & back, Model No. 3108, pink high gloss (ILLUS. top, next page)..... **45.00**

Vase, 6½" h., oblong footed w/straight sides, three horizontal bands near foot w/flowers, leaves & stems in relief, ivory satin gloss or chartreuse gloss, Model No. 3052 .... **34.00**

Pacific Ribbed Vase

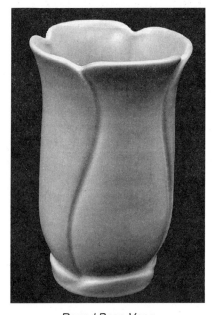

Round Base Vase

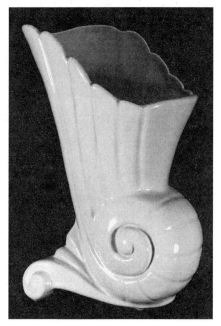

Cornucopia Vase

Vase, 8¼" h., model of upright cornucopia, scalloped rim, turquoise interior, white exterior (ILLUS.) **38.00**

Wall pocket, profile of George Washington, beading around his profile, two pistols on top of pocket, can also sit as a planter, Claire Lerner design, pink high gloss, Model No. 3060L, 5 ¾" h. (ILLUS. left, top next page) **14.00**

Wall pocket, profile of Martha Washington, beading around her profile, bow on top of pocket, can also sit as a planter, Claire Lerner design, pink high gloss, Model No. 3060R, 5 ¾" h. (ILLUS. right, top next page) **14.00**

Vase, 6½" h., oval foot, straight sides flaring gently to pleated & tiered rim, w/four vertical ribs, Model No. 3050, ca. 1938 .... **35.00**

Vase, 6 ¾" h., round base w/quatrefoil rim, matte green, Model No. 874 (ILLUS.).............. **45.00**

Vase, 7¼" h., 2 ¾" d., bottle-shaped w/molded handles on each side near middle, mint green, Model No. 886................. **28.00**

References: "The Secret to Pacific Pottery's Success," Susan on California Pottery column, by Susan N. Cox, *The Collector,* September 1994; Letter from Tillie Roman with copy of letter from Bennett Welsh, April 27, 1991; "Pacific Pottery," by Glenita Stearns, *The Depression Glass Daze,* November 1980; Company catalogs

Pacific Clay George and Martha Washington Wall Pockets

PENNSBURY POTTERY

In 1950 Pennsbury Pottery, named for the nearby home of William Penn, was founded by Henry Below and his wife, Lee in Morrisville, Pennsylvania. Henry had learned pottery making in Germany and was an expert in ceramic engineering and mold making. He designed some of the Pennsbury shapes and also managed the office. At one time, Mr. Below was associated with Stangl Pottery Company of Trenton, New Jersey. When Pennsbury Pottery opened, several workers at Stangl joined the Pennsbury operation. That may be one of the reasons that Pennsbury birds, the first items to be created, resembled the Stangl bird line.

Lee, also affiliated with Stangl Pottery at one time, was a talented artist who designed the well known Rooster pattern, almost all of the folk art designs and the Pennsylvania German blue and white dinnerware which was hand-painted. Workers and artists were trained at the pottery and many dedicated employees remained with the Belows during the seventeen years Pennsbury was in operation. Even though the pottery started with only a handful of employees, by the time the company closed nearly fifty people were working for Pennsbury Pottery.

Mr. Below died unexpectedly in 1959 and Mrs. Below died in 1968 after a long illness.

Pennsbury Pottery filed for bankruptcy in October, 1970. In April, 1971 the pottery was destroyed by fire.

Pennsbury is earthenware with a high temperature firing. Clays were used from Georgia and Tennessee and mixed with materials such as flint. Most of the designs are of the sgraffito type similar to Stangl's products. The most popular coloring, which is characteristic of Pennsbury, is the smear-type glaze of light brown after the sgraffito technique has been used.

The bird line is usually marked by hand with Pennsbury Pottery and most often the name of the bird. Dinnerware was made after the bird line became successful and was followed by art pieces, mugs, ashtrays and teapots. Commemorative merchandise for various organizations and companies was produced. Items, mostly trays, were made for the railroad companies to give as gifts to their passengers.

The first dinnerware line introduced was Black Rooster followed by Red Rooster. There was a line of cobalt blue decorations, named Blue Dowry, which has the same decorations as the brown Folkart pattern.

Collectors seem to appreciate any Pennsbury items but, probably due to its scarcity, the cobalt blue decorations on white do not sell as well as the regular brown glaze items. Popular among collectors are the items with cute saying and the Amish and Rooster patterns. Collectors consider real treasures such items as lamps, the large Christmas tree-shaped relish dishes, cookie jars with finial models of roosters and the bird line items.

Pennsbury
Pottery

Pennsbury

Pottery

morrisville, Pa.

Pennsbury Marks

Ashtray, Amish patt., 5" d. **$25.00**

Ashtray, dark grey w/mottling, dog's head in relief in center surrounded by dark green circle w/advertising "Fidelity Mutual Life Founded 1878," marked "Pennsbury Pottery" underglaze & "75th Anniversary 1878-1953," 5 ¾" w., 7" l. (ILLUS.) **55.00**

Ashtray with Dog's Head in Center

Hummingbird Candlestick

Ashtray, Such Schmootzers patt., boy & girl kissing, 5" d. **30.00**

Candleholder, Tulip patt., stylized tulips on round base, 5" d. **55.00**

Candlestick, hummingbird w/beak raised, wings back, on irregular oval base, white high gloss, Model No. 117, 5" h. (ILLUS.) **140.00**

Canister w/lid, Black Rooster patt. w/rooster finial on lid, "Flour" at top near rim, 9" h......................... **105.00**

Cookie jar w/lid, Harvest patt., 8" h. (ILLUS.)............................ **210.00**

Harvest Pattern Cookie Jar

Amish Head Stopper Cruets

Cookie jar w/lid, Red Barn patt.,
8" h. **205.00**

Creamer, Amish woman's head,
2" h. **20.00**

Cruets, oil & vinegar, Amish
head stoppers, 7" h., pr.
(ILLUS. top) **145.00**

Cruets, oil & vinegar, Black
Rooster patt. w/figural black
rooster stoppers, pr. 7" h. **195.00**

Cup & saucer, Hex patt., set **45.00**

Egg cup, Red Rooster patt.,
4" h. **50.00**

Lamp, pitcher shape, Hex patt.,
12" h. to the socket (ILLUS.) **285.00**

Model of a Barn Swallow,
marked "Pennsbury Pottery B.
Swallow #123, E.P." (Eleanor
Purcell)..................................... **200.00**

Model of a Blue Bird, marked
"Pennsbury Pottery #103 K.
Violet Kanivrael,"
4" h. **175.00**

Pitcher Shape Lamp

Rooster & Hen Models

Pennsbury Duck Model

Boy and Girl Pattern Pie Plate

Model of a duck, standing on round green base, marked "Pennsbury Pottery" on unglazed bottom, 6½" h. (ILLUS.) **185.00**

Models of a rooster & hen, White Leghorn, rooster Model No. P202, hen Model No. P201, may be found with Model Nos. 127 & 128 respectively, 10½" h., pr. (ILLUS. top) **710.00**

Mug, Delft Toleware patt., white exterior w/blue fruit & leaves, dark blue interior, 4½" h. **45.00**

Pie plate, 9" d., Boy & Girl patt., wording "Whispered words beneath the bower, holding hands at some late hour, usually lead as you well know to raising young ones, crops and dough," (ILLUS.) **100.00**

Pitcher with Eagle on Obverse

Harvest Pattern Plate

Round Wall Plaque

Pitcher, 5¼" h., eagle on obverse w/shield on reverse (ILLUS.) **65.00**

Plate, 8" d., Harvest patt., (ILLUS.) **70.00**

Plate, 10" d., Red Rooster patt..... **37.00**

Relish tray, model of a Christmas tree, five sections, Red Rooster patt., 14½" h. **135.00**

Salt & pepper shakers, pitcher-shaped w/brown tops & Amish man & woman patt., 2½" h., pr.... **41.00**

Tile, Black Rooster patt., 6" sq. **40.00**

Wall plaque, round w/saying, "What giffs What ouches you?" Amish boy sitting w/Amish woman bending over him, marked "Pennsbury Pottery, Morrisville, PA. NFBPWC Philadelphia, PA. 1960," 4¼" d. (ILLUS. next column).................. **35.00**

Wall plaque, locomotive in relief, "Baltimore & Ohio R.R. 1837" above locomotive, "Lafayette" below locomotive, 7½" l.............. **85.00**

Wall pocket, square w/house & "God Bless Our Mortgaged Home" dark green border, 6½" d. **38.00**

Wall pocket, square w/cowboy riding gingham horse, 6½" **40.00**

Wall pocket, square w/Distlefink deep rose border, 6½" d............. **35.00**

Wall pocket, square, Tulip patt., deep rose border, 6½" d............. **35.00**

References: *Pennsbury Pottery* by Lucile Henzke, Schiffer Publishing Ltd., 1990; *Pennsbury Pottery Book I Video* by B. A. Wellman & Shirley Graff; "Investing in and decorating with Pennsbury Pottery" by Susan N. Cox, *American Clay Exchange,* July 15, 1987; "Pennsbury Pottery" by Esther Myers, *American Clay Exchange*

January 30, 1986; "Pennsbury Pottery Pictorial" by Susan N. Cox, *American Clay Exchange* June 15, 1985; "Pennsbury Pottery Birds" by Esther Myers, *American Clay Exchange* February 28, 1985; "Pennsbury Pottery Update," *American Clay Exchange* August 30, 1984; Correspondence and telephone conversations with Lucile Henzke; Company catalogs and invoices dating circa 1959 through 1965; Antiques Research Development Pennsbury Report, Susan N. Cox owner, El Cajon, California

Peters & Reed

see Zane Pottery under "Additional Companies to Consider"

HOWARD PIERCE CERAMICS

HOWARD
PIERCE

Pierce

Hp

Howard Pierce
Claremont, Calif

Pierce Marks

Howard Pierce began his studio in 1941 in Claremont, California. Before that, he had worked for William Manker also of Claremont. Occasionally collectors can see the similarity in Manker and Pierce items, especially the two color, high gloss bowls and small vases. This business relationship lasted about three years. By 1950, Mr. Pierce had national representation for all his products.

From the beginning, wildlife and animals were the major output of Pierce's artware. In the early years, Pierce produced some polyurethane pieces, mostly birds or roadrunners on bases, but an allergic reaction forced him to stop using it. He also created a small amount of merchandise in a Wedgwood-type Jasper ware body in matte pale pink and light green. A few years later, in the same Jasper ware body in white, Pierce designed porcelain bisque animals and plants that were placed in or near the open areas of high-glazed vases. These bisque items are well done and delicate. When Mt. St. Helens volcano erupted, Pierce obtained a small quantity of the ash and developed a sandy, rough-textured glaze. Not to be confused with this, there was also a 'lava' glaze unrelated to the Mt. St. Helens treatment. Mr. Pierce described 'lava' as "...bubbling up from the bottom."

He created a few pieces in gold leaf; however, there was a gold treatment of the 1950s which, for lack of a better name, I have called "Sears gold." Sears, Roebuck & Company ordered a large quantity of assorted Pierce products from his distributor with the request that they be done in an overall gold finish. I remember a telephone conversation in late 1993 between Howard and myself about this gold treatment. He was certain none of those pieces had the "Howard Pierce" mark but I told him I was holding a large gold duck that carried his mark. He said that either a few had gotten out with the mark or it was not the gold done for Sears. Rather, he felt that the duck could be a gold leaf he had personally done. Unable to resolve the mystery, we agreed that I would bring the duck on my next visit to his home and we could solve it then. Howard did tell me that he was not satisfied with the Sears gold product as much of the undercoat red treatment showed through. He died just a few months later and we were never able to finish our discussion in person. Several companies, including Freeman-McFarlin, used a gold leaf finish. Collectors can easily know if they have a Pierce creation by studying his product line. To my knowledge he never created an item especially for Sears but, rather, took the merchandise from his regular pieces.

In the late 1970s, Mr. Pierce began incising a number in the clay of experimentally glazed products. From this numbering system he was able to successfully recreate various glazes in blues, deep greens, pinks, purples, yellows and blacks which are highly collectible. Howard particularly liked the greys, browns and whites for his pieces and felt any experimental colors should be classified as "seconds." Collectors have shown a preference for these unusual glazes.

A set of three individual angels were probably one of the shortest runs of the Pierce porcelain lines. The angels' wings were often damaged in the kiln and because of the intricacy of the work, they were time-consuming and, therefore, more costly than he wanted them to be. (Howard always felt his products should be inexpensive so everyone who desired could have a piece of his work.) Only the three angels with black faces have proven to be more scarce than the three angels with white faces.

In November 1992, due to health problems, Howard and Ellen Pierce destroyed all the molds they had created over the years. But Howard was an artist and wanted to work a few hours a week, so in 1993, he purchased a small kiln and began on a very limited basis creating smaller versions of his larger past porcelain items. These pieces are simply stamped "Pierce." Howard Pierce passed away in February, 1994.

Bowl, 4¼" d., 2½" h., gradually flaring sides to a scalloped rim, burgundy exterior, chartreuse interior, incised mark, "Howard Pierce P-1, Calif." (ILLUS. below, top left) **$25.00**

Bowl, 5" d., 1 ¾" h., oval base flaring to a straight rim, light pink exterior, mint green interior, incised mark, "Howard Pierce P-6, Calif." (ILLUS. below, bottom right) **20.00**

Bowl, 9" d., 2½" h., round base w/flared, deep sides, dark brown exterior, brown & white "lava" treatment interior, signed in script "Pierce" **70.00**

Figure of an Eskimo man, standing, crude face features, arms indistinct against body, brown face & feet over white body, Model No. 206P, ca. 1953, 7" h. **85.00**

Figure of a girl, kneeling w/bowl in left hand, right arm extended, palm raised & open, "Sears gold," no mark, 7" h. **15.00**

Figure of a girl w/non-descript face & goose (one piece), girl standing w/right hand on goose, pot in left hand, rough textured grey glaze, 6" h. **95.00**

Howard Pierce Bowls and Vases

Three Angel Figurines

Figure group of a black boy &
girl holding hands, white glossy
glaze, ca. 1985, 4½" h. **50.00**

Figure group of Madonna &
Child busts on square base,
modernistic bust of Mother &
Child, white, rough texture,
5" h. **55.00**

Figurines, three angels, one
standing w/hymn book, one
kneeling in prayer, w/bare soles
of feet showing behind her, one
sitting w/hands on chin, white
glaze; standing angel, 6¼" h.,
kneeling angel, 4½" h., sitting
angel, 3 ¾" h., set
(ILLUS.) **135.00**

Magnet, model of a dolphin, grey
or brown, 3¼" l., 1½" h. **27.00**

Magnet, turtle, blue experimental
glaze, 2¼" l., 1½" h. **30.00**

Model of a bird on a branch,
standing, polyurethane, 4 ¾" l.,
3½" h. **80.00**

Model of a circus horse, head
down, tail straight, leaping
position w/middle of body
attached to small, round center
base, white w/grey accents,
7½" l., 6½" h. (ILLUS.)............. **100.00**

Model of Circus Horse

Model of a duck, head turned
slightly, "Sears gold" stamp
marked "Howard Pierce,"
7 ¾" h. **48.00**

Model of an eagle, standing on
small, rectangular base w/head
turned to side, black w/white
neck & head, 1950s, 3¼" l.,
7½" h. (ILLUS. next page)......... **110.00**

Model of an egret, standing, feet
& legs obscured by leaf base,
neck long & curved,
9½" h. **75.00**

Model of an elephant, seated,
trunk raised, "Mt. St. Helens"
ash treatment, 4 ¾" h. **28.00**

Model of Racoon

Model of Eagle

Model of an ermine, seated
upright w/tail curled upward
behind & against body, brown
eyes, ears, nose & tip of tail
w/white body, ca. early 1950s,
9" h. **145.00**

Model of a fawn, sitting, head &
ears up, legs folded under body,
dark brown eyes, experimental
tan glaze, ca. 1985, 5½" h. **36.00**

Model of a frog, sitting, green
high gloss w/black mottling,
stamp marked "Howard Pierce
Porcelains," 5¼" l., 4¾" h. **55.00**

Model of a giraffe, head turned
to side, modernistic design, legs
slightly apart, no base, 12½" h. .. **46.00**

Model of a goose, seated
w/head stretched upward,
mouth open, "Sears gold,"
no mark, 3¾" h. **7.00**

Model of a leopard, pacing
position, h.p. spots, tawny body,
dark brown spots, limited
production, 11½" l., 2¾" h. **510.00**

Model of a panther, pacing
position, black glaze, 11½" l.,
2¾" h. **95.00**

Model of a pelican, beak
attached to body, 1980s, 7" h. **75.00**

Model of a pelican, beak away
from body, 1950s, 8" h. **125.00**

Model of a polar bear, walking
position, 7¼" l. **55.00**

Model of a raccoon, seated,
head turned slightly, full face,
brown glaze w/four stripes
around tail, 9" l., 3½" h.
(ILLUS.) **70.00**

Model of a roadrunner, standing
on wire legs, tail pointed
upward, head held high,
polyurethane, 8" h. **165.00**

Model of a seal, seated, head
up, black glaze, 5½" l., 5" h. **55.00**

Model of a tiger, pacing position,
cream body, brown h.p. stripes,
limited production, 11½" l.,
2¾" h. **515.00**

Wall Pocket of Running Deer

Models of a fish, purple w/black stripes, 5" l., 4¼" h.; 3½" l., 3¼" h., pr. **75.00**

Pencil holder, nude women in relief around outside, one year limited production, 1980, 3½" d., 4¼" h. **25.00**

Sign, advertising, shows "Copper Mountain Campus" w/initials "CMC" in black cut-out & on top of sign, 4½" l., 3½" h................... **47.00**

Sign, dealer advertising, smooth surface, triangular shape, "Pierce" at top in 1½" block letters, "Porcelain" underneath Pierce in ½" letters, 6" l., 2½" h.. **135.00**

Sign, dealer advertising, rough surface resembling tree bark, "Howard Pierce" in script on upper line, "Porcelain" in block letters on second line, grey or brown glaze, 6" l., 2½" h........... **100.00**

Vase, 3½" h., 3½" l., slightly flaring sides to a straight oval rim, burgundy exterior, chartreuse interior, incised mark "Howard Pierce P-5 Claremont, Calif." (ILLUS. top right, page 169) **45.00**

Vase, 3 ¾" h., 2½" l., square w/straight sides, light green exterior, yellow interior, incised mark, "Howard Pierce P-4, Claremont, Calif." (ILLUS. bottom left, page 169) **38.00**

Oblong Vase

Vase, 5" h., 6½" l., oblong w/circle in center w/bisque girl w/basket, dog & small platform, chartreuse w/black flecks, incised mark "Howard Pierce 201P Claremont, Calif." (ILLUS.)........ **125.00**

Vase, 7½" h., rectangular black base w/straight-sided glossy vase on one end, white porcelain bisque fawn & tree on other end w/three tree branches attached to vase, underside of recessed base divided in half w/one side incised in script underglaze "Howard Pierce" & the other side incised "302P Claremont, Calif." **125.00**

Wall plaque, model of two raccoons on tree branch w/leaves, one raccoon above the other raccoon, "Pierce" on front bottom right, cement, 10½" w., 16" h. **375.00**

Wall pocket, oblong, dusty pink
bisque rim & bottom, dark pink
center w/five white bisque
running deer molded in relief,
7¾" l., 3½" h. (ILLUS. top,
previous page)......................... **155.00**

Whistle, bird shape w/hole at tail,
brown w/white glaze, 3½" h........ **20.00**

References: "An Obituary For The
Artist Who Kept The Little Guy In Mind" by
Susan N. Cox, *Collector* newspaper col-
umn Susan on California Pottery, April
1994; Numerous interviews with Howard
and Ellen Pierce and Bob and Susan
Cox; Catalog sheets, fliers from distribu-
tors, photos from the Pierces to Susan
Cox; Howard Pierce Horses by Susan N.
Cox, American Clay Exchange, June 15,
1985; "Howard Pierce Porcelains" by
Susan N. Cox, *The Antique Trader
Weekly,* August 3, 1983

RED WING POTTERY

Red Wing Pottery Marks

The Red Wing Stoneware Company was
organized in 1868 in Red Wing, Minnesota.
Many other potteries operated in the area and
when some of them merged with the Red
Wing Stoneware Company in 1894, the
joining of these companies comprised the Red
Wing Union Stoneware Company. When
interest began to fade for stoneware items,
Red Wing introduced an art pottery line and
the name was once again changed. It became
Red Wing Potteries, Inc. in 1930. In 1947
stoneware was no longer made but
dinnerware in a variety of patterns, vases,
planters, ashtrays and cookie jars were made
until August 24, 1967 when all production
ceased.

In the early 1930s, George Rumrill of the
Rum Rill Pottery Company in Little Rock,
Arkansas approached Red Wing about
making Rum Rill Pottery. An agreement was
formalized and most of the pieces produced
were named "RumRill by Red Wing."
However, this association lasted only about
eight years.

Belle Kogan created some whimsical,
"stretched" figurines for Red Wing.
Sometimes the only mark is a "B" followed by
a four digit number. These were created in
various glazes, including a white glaze.
Many of them are hand-decorated and others
can be found in all-bisque or in all-high gloss
colors. It is possible to find a combination of
high gloss and bisque.

Saffron ware, introduced in the late 1930s
and Red Wing's solution to yellowware that
was being produced by many other
companies, is popular among collectors today.
To produce a variety of items in Saffron, Red
Wing used many of the molds they used on
their Gray Line kitchenware which has a
sponge band decoration.

Belle Kogan also designed the Fondoso
shape that is popular with collectors today. It
is part of Red Wing's Gypsy Trail Hostess
Ware. Pieces were produced in red, yellow,
dark blue, light blue, off-white, green, and
pink. Bowls were also made in russet.
Hollowware in the early Fondoso was glazed
one color; later items were white glazed on
the inside.

Bob White, a hand-painted pattern, was
introduced in 1956 with production
continuing until the company closed in 1967.

While *Tweed Tex* is a pattern name that is void of any design, it also refers to a rough surface basketweave texture that Red Wing used to add certain pattern designs. The decorated *Tweed Tex* appeals to many collectors today.

Roundup, introduced in 1958, is a popular patern today with its cowboys and chuck wagons motif.

The *Concord* shape, which was introduced in 1947 and had modified squares with rounded corners on flatware, can boast the largest number of patterns created by Red Wing. There were flower patterns with such names as *Lexington Rose*, *Zinnia*, *Iris*, *Magnolia*, *Chrysanthemum*, and *Morning Glory*.

Of all the dinnerware patterns produced by Red Wing, the *Provincial Oomph* bowls, all *Labriego* pieces, and the tumblers and trivets in *Bob White* are the hardest to find.

Batter Set

Batter set, tray, syrup pitcher w/lid & batter pitcher w/lid: tray 12" l., 7¼" w., marked "Red Wing Potteries Inc. Design Pat. Pending" & a copyright symbol; pitcher w/lid 5 ¾" h., incised underglaze "Red Wing" & copyright symbol, pitcher w/lid 9" h., marked "Red Wing Potteries Inc.," & copyright symbol, pale green high gloss, designed by Belle Kogan, Fondoso shape, 5 pieces (ILLUS.) **$175.00**

Bean pot w/cover, handled, high gloss dark brown w/aqua cover, Village Green patt., marked underglaze "Red Wing U.S.A." 6¼" d., 5½" h. **45.00**

Beater jar, Saffron ware, fluted panel in center w/rust sponge band under rim, 5½" d., 5½" h. **125.00**

Bowl, 6½" d., Bob White patt. **10.00**

Bowl, mixing, 7" d., Fondoso shape, pastel blue glaze............. **30.00**

Bowl, salad, 12" d., Bob White patt. **40.00**

Bowl with Lug Handle

Bowl, 12¼" l., w/lug handle, white rough texture overall (Tweed Tex), Country Garden patt. w/assorted colored flowers & leaves, marked "Red Wing Handpainted USA 243," & wings, reddish brown clay (ILLUS.) **7.00**

Candlestick, pink w/mottled brown, marked "Red Wing USA M1471," 3¼" d., 4 ¾" h. (ILLUS. next page) **12.00**

Casserole w/cover, Bob White patt., incised "Red Wing U.S.A." 12½" l. from handle to handle, 6½" h. **30.00**

Tampico Pattern Sugar & Creamer

Candlestick M1471

Casserole w/cover, Saffron ware w/overall blue & brown sponged design, recessed button knob on lid, 3 pint, 7¼" d.................. **225.00**

Cookie jar, Apple, 8½" h. **70.00**

Cookie jar, Chef, yellow glaze w/brown hair, eye, mustache, & shoes, marked w/wings, "Red Wing Pottery hand painted patent, D-130-228, D-130, 329, D130-330" (ILLUS. next column)...................................... **65.00**

Cookie jar, Dutch Girl, yellow & brown glaze............................ **90.00**

Cookie jar, Dutch Girl, tan & brown glaze **125.00**

Cookie jar, Grapes....................... **60.00**

Chef Cookie Jar

Cookie jar, Saffron ware, plain yellow glaze resembling the saffron spice **135.00**

Creamer & cov. sugar Bob White patt., pr. **29.00**

Creamer & open sugar, Tampico patt., colorful melons & leaves, marked "Red Wing U.S.A." creamer 4¼" h., sugar 3½" h., pr. (ILLUS. top).............. **17.00**

Creamer & cov. sugar, Lexington Rose patt. on Concord shape, discontinued ca. 1950s, pr. **15.00**

Planter with Raised Leaf Design

Figurine, 9½" h., Oriental Goddess, Model No. B1308, grey high glaze **100.00**

Figurine, 10¼" h., Dancing Girl w/tambourine, standing w/left arm bent above her head, right arm across waist w/hand holding tambourine, Model No. B1416, grey high glaze **120.00**

Figurine, 10½" h., Model No. B1414, "stretched" cowgirl on round base, head up, arms bent w/hands at waist **150.00**

Figurine, 11" h., Model No. B1415, "stretched" cowboy on round base, one hand on thigh, other hand at waist **150.00**

Pitcher, 12" h., Random Harvest patt., front w/orange, lime, brown & coral leaves & flowers, reverse, brown, aqua & beige leaves & flowers w/a brown flecked overall glaze, incised "Red Wing USA" (ILLUS.) **38.00**

Planter, octagonal shape, high gloss aqua outside, high gloss yellow inside, marked underglaze, "Red Wing U.S.A. 1347," 9½" l. **25.00**

Planter, quatrefoil rim, high gloss grey outside, high gloss maroon inside, marked "Red Wing USA 1206," 12" l. **39.00**

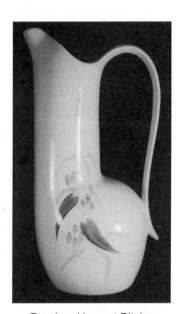

Random Harvest Pitcher

Planter, white high gloss outside, aqua glaze inside, raised leaf design near bottom, marked "Red Wing U.S.A. B1402," 7½" l., 3½" h. (ILLUS.) **28.00**

Plate, 6½" d., Lexington Rose patt. on Concord shape **5.00**

Plate, 9½" d., Fondoso patt., pastel blue **12.00**

Plate, 10½" d., Roundup patt. **22.00**

Platter, oval, 12", Fondoso patt., pastel green................................. **23.00**

Tampico Pattern Platter

Platter with Cover

Platter, 15" l., Tampico patt.
(ILLUS. top) **16.00**

Platter w/cover, 15" l., 8" h.,
Provincial "Oomph" patt., platter
dark brown underside, aqua
inside & rim, cover dark brown
outside, aqua inside, marked
"Red Wing USA," (ILLUS.
center) **120.00**

Salt & pepper shakers, Fondoso
shape, pink glaze, pr. **15.00**

Teapot, 7½" h., Bob White patt.
(ILLUS.) **65.00**

Bob White Pattern Teapot

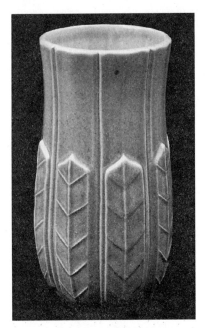

Arrow In-Relief Design Vase

Angular Red Wing Vase

Vase, 4½" h., "V" shaped raised design & rim, aqua glaze, incised on unglazed bottom, "899 Red Wing" **16.00**

Vase, 8" h., arrow in-relief design from bottom to center, mustard colored flecked glaze outside w/grey glaze inside, incised "Red Wing U.S.A. M1519" (ILLUS. top, left column)............. **45.00**

Vase, 8½" h., beige w/brown wash, marked "Red Wing 1181 U.S.A." **48.00**

Vase, 9¼" h., sharp angular sides, high gloss yellow outside & grey inside (ILLUS., bottom, left column)................................. **23.00**

No. 3 Water Cooler

Water cooler, No. 3, white stoneware w/blue decoration, iron handles, "wing" in rust, Red Wing mark in blue on front of cooler, spigot missing, 10½" d., 12" h. (ILLUS.)......................... **425.00**

References: "Red Wing Portrait Figurines," by Lucile Hentzke, *American Clay Exchange,* October 1987; "Falconer Hopeful of Reviving Red Wing's Creations," by Gini Gramm, *American Clay Exchange,* September 30, 1987; "Red Wing Soars," by Marcie Leitzke, *American Clay Exchange,* May 15, 1986; "Saffron Ware: Red Wing's Answer To Yellowware," by Jo Anne Hagen,

American Clay Exchange, December 1983; "Red Wing Fever," by Marcie Leitzke, American Clay Exchange, February 1982; Red Wing-Past, Present and Future, by David A. Newkirk, American Clay Exchange, December 1981; Red Wing Potters & Their Wares by Gary and Bonnie Tefft, privately printed 1981; Red Wing Dinnerware by Stanley J. Bougie and David A. Newkirk, privately printed, 1980; "Red Wing Dinnerware" by David A. Newkirk, The Antique Trader Weekly, March 12, 1980; A Guide to Red Wing Markings by David A. Newkirk, privately printed 1979; "Some Advertising Items Made in Red Wing," by Jo Irwin, The Antique Trader Weekly, November 23, 1977

Collectors' Club: Red Wing Collectors' Society, Inc., P. O. Box 124, Neosho, WI 53059 includes monthly newsletter

Museums: Goodhue County Historical Society Museum, Red Wing, MN; Kenosha Public Museum, Kenosha, WI

ROSELANE POTTERY

$Roselane$

PASADENA, CALIF

$Rose fane$
©
U.S.A.

Roselane Pottery Marks

William "Doc" Fields and Geogia, his wife, began Roselane Pottery in 1938 as a home-based operation. In 1940 the Fields moved the operation to Pasadena, California. The Roselane enterprise was moved again in 1968 to Baldwin Park, California where it remained for six years. When William died in 1973, Georgia sold Roselane to Prather Engineering Corporation and it was moved to Long Beach, California. In 1977 the business closed completely. Several marks were used as well as paper labels. However, even if a piece is unmarked, experience and a trained eye will alert you to Roselane's products.

The items produced by Roselane were varied and included several different treatments and glazes. The pottery successfully manufactured such items as ashtrays, bowls, candlesticks, covered boxes, figurines, sculptured animals on wood bases, vases and wall pockets. They had lines such as Aqua Marine, Chinese Modern and the Sparkler series.

The Sparkler series, introduced in the 1950s, was a popular product for the company. Today, even though imported reproductions were made, collectors appreciate the airbrushed decorated semi-porcelain children and animals. Originally the Sparklers had rhinestone eyes but the later ones came with plastic eyes.

Chinese-Modern is not as popular as some of Roselane's other products. Certain pieces, particularly the vases, are plentiful on the secondary market. Probably this is due to Roselane having produced so many of them.

Aqua Marine, a buffet serving line with pieces such as large, deep bowls and trays, was created in a sgraffito technique. These items with motifs such as fish or snowflakes are much in demand today. They were created from the mid-1940s until the early 1950s.

The childrens' line has not been recognized yet for its collectible value so prices remain on the low side. That will change as collectors grow to appreciate the uniqueness and availability of the items. Right now there seems to be an ample supply of them; however, collectors will find their favorites within this group and prices will reflect that preference.

About the time Doc Fields was discontinuing his childrens' line, he was creating ceramic animals on walnut bases. Having a stylistic concept, this series was not well-received by the public and was discontinued shortly after introduction. The discontinuance of those items has created a demand for them in today's market.

The deer groups that were produced by Roselane would rival any company's similar items. The lightweight deer have become masterpieces for some and their fragility only enhances their beauty. Also, many of the deer are not single items but, rather, two or three small deer on one base with the base often times having raised flowers. The high gloss glazes are most often pale blue, ivory, brown or pale green.

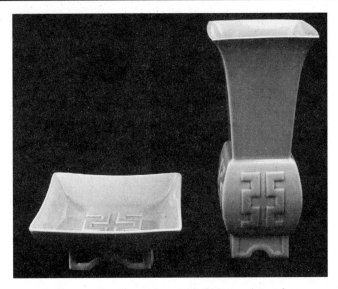

Square Bowl and Vase with Chinese Artwork

Bowl, 6¼" square, pedestal base w/Chinese openwork, grey outside, lime green inside, Model No. 200 (ILLUS. top left) **$29.00**

Bowl, 9" d., 2" h., high-glaze grey underneath, pink inside w/sgraffito-type grey "snowflakes" design, scroll mark, Model No. A-9 (ILLUS.) **55.00**

Bowl, 13" l., 2½" h., rectangular shape w/vertical ribs on center base, maroon high gloss glaze bowl w/maroon base, Model No. 213, in-mold mark **29.00**

Bowl, 15" d., 8" w., shallow, rectangle w/butterfly, bird, tulip & marigold in each corner in-relief underglaze & "Chinese Modern" footed base, deep purple inside w/light purple on decorations, scroll mark, Model No. 52 .... **65.00**

Candleholder, double "Chinese Modern" openwork base w/two lily-shaped holders, one slightly higher than the other, deep purple, 6½" l., 5¼" h. **35.00**

"Snowflakes" Design Bowl

Candleholder, square center base w/vertical ribs, grey w/maroon candleholder section, marked "Roselane" in-mold, Model No. C1, also w/sticker, 2½" h., pr. **45.00**

Figure of a boy in diving position on square base, beige & brown satin matte, "Lo Diver" incised on base edge, "Roselane U.S.A." w/copyright symbol incised on bottom, 4½" h. (ILLUS. next page) **22.00**

*Figures of
Man and
Woman
Balinese
Dancers on
Bases*

Figure of Boy in Diving Position

Figure of a girl, kneeling, arms folded over chest w/hands together in prayer, head slightly raised, eyes closed, reverse of girl shows ponytail & bottoms of feet & toes, satin matte beige & brown, incised "Roselane U.S.A." w/copyright symbol, 4½" h. **23.00**

Figure of a newsboy, standing, left hand in pocket, newspaper tucked under right arm, knee patch on left trouser, beige & brown, incised on back bottom of left pant leg, "Roselane" & incised on right pant leg bottom "USA" w/copyright symbol, 5" h. **28.00**

Figure of a nurse, holding & feeding baby, beige & brown satin matte, marked w/copyright symbol & U.S.A. 4½" h. **24.00**

Figures of a man & woman Balinese dancers on bases, high gloss grey; man signed "A.A. Tagaris" on top of base near right foot, Model No. 401, 12½" h.; woman, Model No.a 402, 11" h.; each w/in-mold Roselane mark, pr. (ILLUS. top) **155.00**

Figure of a boy, seated & holding open cookie jar w/cookies in it & left hand holding one cookie near mouth, legs folded under body w/right foot showing, satin matte beige & brown, incised "Roselane U.S.A." w/copyright symbol, 3½" h. **24.00**

Model of Cat

Model of Deer Group

Model of a bear, seated, head facing forward & tilted slightly, ears up, arms & hands in front of body but not touching, rough textured, light to dark brown, Model No. 2635, 5½" h. **29.00**

Model of a bulldog, seated, glossy beige, brown, light blue, w/pink plastic eyes, "Sparkler" series, 2½" h.............................. **24.00**

Model of a cat, modernistic, w/head turned back & slightly down over body, mottled tan high gloss w/green eyes, marked w/copyright symbol & "U.S.A." on unglazed bottom, 7½" h. (ILLUS. above) **28.00**

Model of a cockatiel on round base, head down almost to bottom of base, tail feathers up, face features non-descript, brown & beige high gloss, marked "Roselane Pasadena, Calif." 9 ¾" h. **25.00**

Model of a deer group, two deer on oval base w/flowers, one deer slightly taller than the other, chocolate brown high glaze, Model No. 210, 5¼" h. (ILLUS.) **32.00**

Model of a deer on oval base, stylized design, standing w/back legs together & bent, front legs together & straight, head turned, ears straight, weighs 2 ounces, glossy green glaze, 5" h. **30.00**

Model of a dog, sitting, yellow glass eyes, marked w/copyright symbol & "U.S.A.," "Sparkler" series, 3" h. **16.00**

Model of a goose on stump, back view, wings spread, neck & head up & over right wing, yellow w/brown accents, incised "Roselane 126," 3½" wing span, 5" h. **19.00**

Model of a goose, seated w/head & neck over back w/bill touching back, light & dark grey satin-matte, incised "USA" w/copyright symbol, 2¼" l., 3½" h. **18.00**

Model of an owl, blue glass eyes, feet well-defined, "Sparkler" series, beige & brown matte, 3¼" h. (ILLUS. next page) **22.00**

Model of "Sparkler" Owl

Model of an owl, modernistic
design w/large head & tapering
body, plastic eyes, semi-
porcelain, teal w/black highlights,
"Sparkler" series, marked
"Roselane U.S.A." on unglazed
bottom, 7" h. **38.00**

Model of a giraffe, seated, two
front legs folded under, back
legs not visible, tail up & over
back, long neck twisted w/head
turned to look behind, glossy
cream glaze w/dark brown
spots, Model No. 264, ca. 1960,
4 ¾" l., 9" h. **35.00**

Model of a horse standing on
oval base, stylized, light grey
w/brown, ca. 1949-53,
8½" h. **34.00**

Model of a raccoon, seated,
head turned, tail up, semi-
porcelain brown & black,
"Sparkler" series, 4¼" h. **24.00**

Sign, dealer advertising, scroll
design, glossy light grey,
12½" l., 3" h. **175.00**

Vase, 6½" h., "Chinese Modern"
openwork on small square base
rising to straight sides w/tiny
flare at rim, glossy grey outside,
maroon inside **18.00**

Vase, 10" h., "Chinese Modern"
square foot w/bulbous lower
body w/raised design & rising to
gently flaring sides w/straight
rim, grey outside, lime green
inside (ILLUS. right w/bowl,
page 180) **32.00**

ROSEMEADE POTTERY
*See Wahpeton Pottery Company
See WPA*

ROSEVILLE POTTERY COMPANY

Founded in 1890 as the Roseville Pottery Company in Roseville, Ohio, this business quickly became a success and today the products that were made then are considered one of the most sought after in the ceramics collecting field. The items, having survived many decades, are examples of the workmanship that went into Roseville's various lines. George Frank Young, hired in 1891 at age 27, served as secretary and general manager until he was able to buy all the company stock, making him its sole owner. The operation was moved to Zanesville, Ohio in 1898. In the 1930s the name was changed to Roseville Pottery, Inc. If there is any confusion among new collectors it is the difficulty in deciding which patterns or which items they prefer to collect. Numerous collectors buy the many flower patterns produced over the years while the futuristic shapes of the Futura pattern have been the chosen design for other collectors. The Juvenile line is popular today among young married adults starting their families and grandparents wanting to give something of lasting value to their grandchildren. In the early 1980s, Roseville's popularity seemed to decline; however, those who knew that collecting interests seem to run in seven or eight year cycles, encouraged people to hold on to what they had and to keep buying. Those who followed that advice are now reaping the benefits of high-ticket prices which show no signs of a slow down in the near future.

Items listed here are by patterns or lines.

APPLE BLOSSOM (1948)

Pink, blue or green backgrounds with pink and white apple blossom buds in relief and brown tree branch handles, green leaves accent embossed designs.

Basket w/circular handle, green
ground, No. 309-8", 8" h. **$185.00**

**Basket w/asymmetrical
overhead** handle, pink ground,
No. 310-10", 10" h. **195.00**

Bowl, 4" d., pink ground,
No. 300-4" **90.00**

Bowl, 6½" l., 2½" h., flat handles,
No. 326-6................................. **105.00**

Creamer & open sugar bowl,
pink ground, Nos. 371-C &
371-S, pr.................................**130.00**

Ewer, ovoid, green ground,
No. 316-8", 8" h. **125.00**

Jardiniere, two-handled, pink
ground, No. 342-6", 6" h. **130.00**

Teapot, cov., overhead handle,
pink ground, No. 371-P **235.00**

Vase, bud, 7" h., base handles,
flaring rim, No. 379-7"................. **95.00**

Vase, 9½" h., 5" d., asymmetrical
handles, cylindrical w/disc base,
blue ground, No. 387-9" **165.00**

ARTWOOD (ca. 1950)

High gloss mottled grey with wine, green with brown, or yellow with brown, predominantly vases and planters with cut outs of sculptured flowers and tree branches.

Planter, footed, shaped rim,
flower within cut-out, grey
w/wine high gloss, No. 1056-
10", 10½" w., 6½" h. **55.00**

BANEDA (1933)

Mottled raspberry pink high gloss or a green matte background with a deep blue wide panel embossed pattern resembling pumpkin vines with white or yellow flowers, green leaves and small orange fruit.

Two-Handled Baneda Jardiniere

Bowl, 10" l., 3½" h., two-handled,
raspberry pink ground **280.00**

Jardiniere w/two handles from
mid-bulbous body to under rim,
raspberry pink ground, 9½" h.
(ILLUS.) **550.00**

Urn, small rim handles, bulbous,
raspberry pink ground, 5" h. **325.00**

Urn, small rim handles, green
ground, 7" h. **395.00**

Tapering Baneda Vase

Vase, 4½" h., tiny rim handles,
sharply canted sides, raspberry
pink ground, No. 603-4"
(ILLUS.) **250.00**

Vase, 5" h., two handles, footed
ovoid body w/green ground **250.00**

BITTERSWEET (1940)

Faintly textured grounds of grey blending to rose, rose and green, yellow with terra cotta, or a solid green on a green with russet berries, green leaves and brown handled branches complete the design.

Basket w/high overhead inverted "V" shaped handle, green ground, No. 807, 8½" h. **140.00**

Basket, low overhead handle, shaped rim, green ground, No. 810-10", 10" h. **225.00**

Cornucopia-vase, grey & rose ground, No. 857-4", 4½" h. **75.00**

BLACKBERRY (1933)

Embossed band of clustered deep colored blackberries with ivory leaves faintly touched in green and terra cotta on a thick true-to-life textured background of green mottling.

Bowl, 8" d., tiny rim handles **300.00**

Candleholders, two handles at midsection, domed flaring base, straight candle nozzle w/wide rim, 4½" h., pr. **435.00**

Vase, 4" h., bulbous body w/slightly flaring rim, two small handles **250.00**

Vase, 4" h., bulbous body tapering to a short neck, two slightly angled handles **375.00**

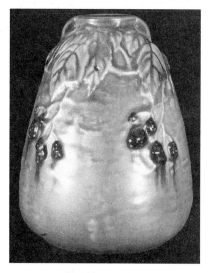

Blackberry Vase

Vase, 5" h., jug-type, swelled cylindrical body tapering to two tiny handles (ILLUS.) **300.00**

Vase, 5" h., two-handled squatty bulbous body tapering to a straight, wide neck **300.00**

Wall pocket, 8½" h. **900.00**

BLEEDING HEART (1938)

Shaded blue, green or pink grounds with pink blossoms and green leaves.

Basket w/circular handle, blue ground, No. 360-10", 10" h. **325.00**

Ewer, pink ground, No. 963-6", 6" h. **155.00**

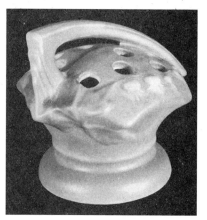

Bleeding Heart Flower Frog

Flower frog, pink ground w/green leaves, angled overhead handle, No. 40 (ILLUS.) **125.00**

Jardiniere, small pointed shoulder handles, blue ground, No. 651-3", 3" h. **95.00**

Vase, 4" h., two-handled, pink ground, No. 138-4" **65.00**

Vase, 8" h., two pointed handles rising from base to midsection, blue ground, No. 969-8" **150.00**

Wall pocket, angular pointed overhead handle rising from midsection, pink ground, No. 1287-8", 8½" h. **325.00**

BURMESE (1950s)

A line of wall pockets, book ends, candleholders and console bowls in white, green or black, usually associated with Oriental faces.

Wall pocket, bust of woman,
white, 7½" h. **200.00**

BUSHBERRY (1948)

Embossed green leaves with a touch of ivory and orange berry clusters over a bark-textured ground of blue, green or terra cotta with branch-type handles.

Basket w/asymmetrical overhead
handle, green ground, No. 371-
10", 10" h. **200.00**

Book ends, angled back
w/branch handle over leaf &
berry cluster, green ground, No.
9, 5¼" h, pr. (ILLUS.)................ **355.00**

Bowl, 10" d., russet ground,
No. 414-10" **120.00**

Cornucopia-vase, upright on
round base, one handle, blue
ground, No. 153-6", 6" h. **100.00**

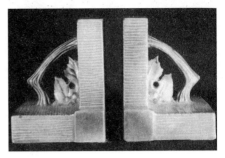

Bushberry Book Ends

Ewer, russet ground, No. 1-6",
6" h. ILLUS. left) **125.00**

Ewer, blue ground, No. 2-10",
10" h. (ILLUS. right).................. **275.00**

Ewer, russet ground, No. 3-15",
15" h. (ILLUS. center).............. **325.00**

Vase, 6" h., angular side handles,
low foot, globular w/wide neck,
blue ground, No. 156-6" **120.00**

Vase, 14½" h., asymmetrical side
handles, blue ground, No.
39-14" **350.00**

Wall pocket, high-low handles,
blue ground, No. 1291-8",
8" h. **275.00**

A Group of Bushberry Ewers

CAPRI (late line)

Red semi-matte, yellow or light green matte finishes in leaves, petals, shells or tulip designs.

Ashtray, shell-shaped, multiple cigarette rests on rim, light green ground, No. 598-9", 9" w. .. **35.00**

Bowl, 7" d., light green ground **35.00**

CARNELIAN I (1910-1915)

Satin matte in two color or light and dark shades of the same color with the dark glaze always dripping over the lighter one with ornate and elaborately treated handles.

Console bowl, two handles rising from above foot to under rim, light & dark blue, 14" l............... **135.00**

Vase, 8" h., base handles, fan-shaped, light & dark green ... **125.00**

Vase, 10" h., squatty bulbous base w/tall slender gently flaring neck, long angled handles at lower sides, light & dark blue.... **135.00**

Wall pocket, ornate side handles, fan-shaped rim, five rings at center, light & dark green, 8" h. **150.00**

CARNELIAN II (1915)

Mottled or intermingled colors of rose, blue, lilac and green layered thickly in various combinations.

Ewer, pink & purple, 12½" h. **175.00**

Vase, 6½" h., fan-shaped, blue & pink................................. **75.00**

Wall pocket, green w/shades of lilac, straight side handles, 8" h. **150.00**

CHERRY BLOSSOM (1933)

White blossom sprigs with yellow centers and brown or terra cotta twigs with blue ground and pink lattice or yellow ground

with brown lattice resembling a fence which dominates the lower two thirds of each piece.

Basket, hanging-type, blue & pink ground, 8" **600.00**

Candleholders, side handles near midsection, yellow w/brown ground, 4" h., pr....................... **275.00**

Vase, 5" h., two-handled, slightly ovoid, pink & blue ground **225.00**

Vase, 7" h., slightly ovoid body, no handles, yellow w/brown ground **350.00**

Cylindrical Footed Vase

Vase, 7" h., footed cylindrical body w/two handles near rim, blue ground (ILLUS.) **275.00**

Vase, 10" h., two-handled, ovoid w/short wide neck, terra cotta ground **430.00**

CLEMANA (1934)

Velvet-like matte glaze in blue, mint green or yellow with small white flowers with pink or yellow centers and pale, muted green leaves surrounded by a lattice-type design. Pieces normally have small angled handles with tiny open circles.

Candleholders, green ground,
No. 1104-4½", 4½" h., pr. **295.00**

Vase, 6½" h., cylindrical
w/handles rising from
midsection, blue ground,
No. 749-6" **210.00**

CLEMATIS (1944)

*Satin-matte vertical-textured backgrounds
of green, tan or blue with stylized heart-
shaped leaves and large blossoms with yellow
centers - green and ivory blossoms on brown,
pink blossoms on green or white blossoms on
blue.*

Clematis Hanging-Type Basket

Basket, hanging-type, brown
ground, No. 470-5", 5" h.
ILLUS.) **175.00**

Bowl, 4" d., bulbous body
w/closed side handles **55.00**

Cookie jar, cov., blue ground,
No. 3-8", 8" h. **325.00**

Cookie jar, cov., brown ground,
No. 3-8", 8" h. **275.00**

Cornucopia-vase, green ground,
No. 190-6", 6" h. **70.00**

Ewer, brown ground, No. 18-15",
15" h. **300.00**

Flowerpot w/saucer, green
ground, No. 668-5", 5½" h. **105.00**

Flower frog, brown ground,
No. 50, 4½" h............................. **60.00**

Vase, double bud, 5" h., two
cylinders joined by a single
clematis blossom, blue ground,
No. 194-5" **85.00**

Vase, 7" h., brown ground, two
angular handles, No. 188 .... **75.00**

Wall pocket, angular side
handles, green ground,
No. 1295-8", 8½" h. **200.00**

COLUMBINE (1940s)

*Matte backgrounds complement the
different colored embossed blossoms - yellow
blossoms on blue, pink blossoms on pink
shaded to green and blue blossoms on tan
shaded to green with mostly pointed handles
and irregular shaped rims.*

Basket, hanging-type, pink
ground, 8½" h. **225.00**

Candlesticks, flat disc base
w/handles rising to nozzle,
green & pink ground, No. 1146-
4½", 5" h., pr............................. **105.00**

Cornucopia-vase, pink ground,
No. 149-6", 5½" h. **90.00**

Ewer, sharply angled handle,
blue ground, No. 18-7", 7" h. **150.00**

Jardiniere, squatty body w/tiny
handles, tan ground, No. 655-3",
3" h. **75.00**

CORNELIAN (early 1900s)

*Simple shapes with relief-molded designs
and overall sponged decoration.*

Mug, shaving, yellow
spongeware, 4" h........................ **95.00**

COSMOS (1940)

*A band of embossed flowers over matte
glazes that have horizontal ridges against a
lightly textured background above the band
and a heavily textured ground below the
band. Grounds of green or light brown have a
blue band with white and orchid blossoms
while the blue ground has an ivory band with
yellow and orchid flowers.*

Basket, hanging-type, handles
rising from midsection to rim,
blue ground, No. 361-5", 7" h. **305.00**

Candleholders, loop handles rising from disc base to midsection of nozzle, low, blue ground, No. 1136, 2" h., pr. **90.00**

Vase, 4" h., two-handled, globular base & wide neck, blue ground, No. 944-4" **70.00**

Vase, 5" h., loop handles rising from footed base, chalice-form, green ground, No. 945-5" **95.00**

CREMONA (1927)

Embossed flowers of many varieties on textured or mottled backgrounds of light green with pale blue or pink with ivory— very few examples have handles.

Console bowl, square w/rounded corners, light green w/blue ground **80.00**

Flower frog, round form w/dome top, light green w/blue ground **25.00**

Vase, 10½" h., jug-type, two angular handles, pink w/ivory ground **130.00**

DAHLROSE (1924-1928)

A band of white daisies with green leaves over a mottled tan and green ground or a predominately green ground.

Dahlrose Vase

Basket, hanging-type, 7½" **225.00**

Bowl, 10", oval, two-handled...... **225.00**

Jardiniere, squatty bulbous form w/tiny rim handles, tan ground, 6" h. **200.00**

Vase, 8" h., round footed cone-shaped body w/two tiny handles, tan ground (ILLUS. lower left)..................... **210.00**

DAWN (1937)

Incised flowers with slender petals void of leaves—green ground with blue-violet tinted blossoms, pink or yellow ground with blue-green blossoms, all with yellow centers. Simple handle projections are without openings and round objects sit atop square bases.

Centerpiece, square pedestalled base w/bulbous body & wide mouth, projecting flat handles near rim hold a round candleholder on each tab, No. 319-6", 6" h. **315.00**

Ewer, square pedestalled base w/four spires at bottom of cone-shaped body, No. 834, 16" h. **430.00**

Flower frog, cylindrical, pink ground, No. 31-3 x 4", 3" d., 4" h. **100.00**

Vase, 8" h.,, angled squatty base tapering to a tall cylindrical neck w/small tab handles, raised on a square foot, No. 829-8" **160.00**

DONATELLO (1915)

Vertical fluting in ivory and green with a wide brown band of embossed playful and pensive cherubs and trees.

Basket, high pointed overhead handle, globular body, 15" h. **350.00**

Basket, hanging-type, No. 327, 8" h. **165.00**

Chamberstick, deep saucer base w/ring handle, No.

1011 .... **145.00**

Flower frog, No. 14-2½", 2½" h. ... **30.00**

Pitcher, 6½" h. **255.00**

Wall pocket, 10" h..................... **170.00**

Wall pocket, 11½" h.................. **195.00**

EARLY EMBOSSED PITCHERS (before 1916)

High gloss glaze with various embossed scenes on this utility line of pitchers which received heavy duty use when introduced. The daily handling caused most pitchers to have some damage which collectors tolerate. However, big chips, poorly defined motifs, open hairlines or broken spouts or handles are not generally acceptable to collectors.

"The Cow" Pitcher

Pitcher, 6" h., "The Bridge" **155.00**

Pitcher, 6½" h., "The Cow," green base, rim w/heavily embossed branches & handle, brown tree trunk & brown cow over white ground, one cow positioned on each side of handle, one tree trunk positioned on each side of spout, rare, note the two other cow pitchers below (ILLUS.)..... **375.00**

7½" size, same as above but not as rare **325.00**

"The Cow" with Painted Limbs Pitcher

"Landscape" Pitcher

Pitcher, 7¼" h., "The Boy," standing & playing flute on one side, boy w/stein in right hand & right leg up on other side.......... **370.00**

Pitcher, 7½" h., "The Cow" w/head up facing front w/the tree to the side of cow; other side has cow grazing, head down & tree behind cow, tree limbs & branches are painted, not heavily embossed (ILLUS.).................................... **325.00**

Pitcher, 7½" h., "Landscape," cottage surrounded by trees (ILLUS.).................................... **145.00**

"Tulip" Pitcher

Pitcher, 7½" h., "Tulip" w/caramel
colored base, handle & rim, blue
flowers w/green leaves
(ILLUS.) **155.00**

Pitcher, 8" h., "The Mill"
windmill.................................... **350.00**

"Poppy" Pitcher

Pitcher, 9" h., "Poppy," white
ground w/rust-colored flowers or
caramel & beige ground w/tan
flowers, ornate handle
(ILLUS.) **195.00**

Pitcher, 9½" h., "Goldenrod,"
green rim & base w/green
extending slightly up to bottom
of handle, brown flowers &
butterflies over white ground ... **150.00**

"Wild Rose" Pitcher

Pitcher, 9 ¾" h., "Wild Rose,"
pale blue base, rim & handle or
caramel color base, rim &
handle w/brown flowers & green
leaves; gold tracing may be
found on some of the caramel
colored pitchers (ILLUS.).......... **145.00**

FALLINE (1933)

*Blended backgrounds of tan gradually
shading to green and blue, or tan to darker
brown with evenly curved panels separated
by half-opened vertical peapod decorations
and semi-scallops and with ear-like handles
on most pieces.*

Falline Loop Handle Vase

Candlestick, 4" h. **150.00**

Vase, 6" h., half-opened seed pods vertically encircling the body, deep purple fading to green to terra cotta at rim, two wide loop handles (ILLUS. bottom, previous page)............. **290.00**

Vase, 9" h., footed ringed bulbous body tapering slightly to a wide-mouthed rim, two large ear-like handles, brown ground............. **375.00**

FERELLA (1931)

Cut-outs alternating with impressed shell designs at top and base in a mottled brown or a deep rose glaze with turquoise mottling.

Candlestick, goblet-form w/candle nozzle rising from center, brown ground, No. 1078-4", 4½" h......................... **245.00**

Ferella Vase

Vase, 6" h., footed body w/gently flaring sides w/wide neck, two-handled, rose ground (ILLUS.) .. **325.00**

Wall pocket, brown ground, No. 1266-6½"., 6½" h. **875.00**

FOXGLOVE (1940s)

Matte glaze background of pink, blue or green with spires of embossed pink and white foxgloves.

Basket w/overhead handle, blue ground, No. 375-12", 12" h. **325.00**

Basket, hanging-type, blue or green ground, No. 466-5", 6½" h., each **250.00**

Book ends, pink ground, No. 10, pr................................. **265.00**

Candleholder, blue ground, No. 1149, 2½" h......................... **85.00**

Candleholder, pink ground, No. 1150-4½", 4½" h. **175.00**

Console bowl, No. 425, 14" l. **240.00**

Ewer, swelled body on short pedestal base, pink ground, No. 4-6½", 6½" h. **125.00**

Ewer, green ground, No. 5-10", 10" h. **225.00**

Flower frog, cornucopia-form, No. 46, 4" h.............................. **100.00**

Tray, easel-shaped w/irregular openings on each end, blue ground **145.00**

Vase, double bud, 4½" h., gate-form, No. 160-4½" **140.00**

Wall pocket, two-handled, pink ground, No. 1292-8", 8" h. **370.00**

FREESIA (1945)

Satin matte finish background of wavy impressed lines of green, blue or terra cotta with embossed blossoms and blade-like leaves; understated handles.

Basket w/low overhead handle, flaring sides, terra cotta ground, No. 390-7", 7" h. **125.00**

Basket, hanging-type, terra cotta ground, No. 471-5", 5" **225.00**

Book ends, blue ground, No. 15, pr. **235.00**

Candleholders, tiny pointed handles, domed base, blue ground, No. 1160-2", 2" h., pr..... **65.00**

Candlesticks, disc base, cylindrical w/low handles, terra cotta ground, No. 1161-4½", 4½" h. (ILLUS. top, next page) ... **135.00**

*Freesia Low Handled
Candlesticks*

Cookie jar, cov., blue ground,
No. 4-8", 10½" h. **425.00**

Cornucopia-vase, blue ground,
No. 198-8", 8" h. **65.00**

Creamer, green ground,
No. 6-C **80.00**

Ewer, green ground, No. 20-10",
10" h. **185.00**

Jardiniere, bulbous body w/tiny
rim handles, green ground,
No. 669-4", 4" h. **75.00**

Sugar, green ground, No. 6-S **80.00**

Teapot, cov., terra cotta ground,
No. 6-T **175.00**

Vase, 6" h., two angled handles,
green ground, No. 117-6"
(ILLUS.) **135.00**

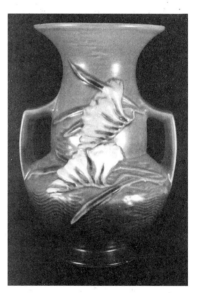

Freesia Globular Base Vase

Vase, 8" h., globular base &
flaring rim, handles at
midsection, terra cotta ground,
No. 122-8" (ILLUS.) **150.00**

Wall pocket, angular handles,
terra cotta ground, No. 1296-8",
8½" h. **165.00**

FUCHSIA (1939)

*Satin matte glaze grounds with blue
shading to yellow, green shading to terra
cotta, or terra cotta shading to gold; embossed
blooms of blue, green or tan and serrated
leaves.*

Freesia Angled-Handled Vase

Cornucopia-vase, blue ground,
No. 129-6", 6" h. **115.00**

Flower frog, blue ground,
No. 37 .... **150.00**

Jardiniere, footed bulbous body
w/two handles, green and terra
cotta ground, No., 645-3", 3" h. ... **95.00**

Vase, 8" h., footed bulbous base
w/tapering cylindrical neck, loop
handles, blue ground,
No. 898-8" **255.00**

Wall pocket, fan-shaped w/two
handles, blue ground,
No. 1282-8", 8½" h. **425.00**

GARDENIA (late 1940s)

White blossoms with green leaves on smooth backgrounds of green, grey or tan with incised vertical lines at top and bottom.

Basket, hanging-type, grey
ground, 6" h. **175.00**

Basket, overhead handle, green
ground, No. 610-12", 12" h. **270.00**

Book ends, grey ground,
No. 659, 5" h., pr. **180.00**

Cornucopia-vase, tan ground,
No. 621-6", 6" h. **70.00**

Tray, lobed-form, tan ground,
No. 631-14", 15" l. **175.00**

IRIS (1938)

Satin matte backgrounds with combinations of light and dark blue, rose and green, or tan shading to green or brown with white or yellow blossoms and green leaves; layered handles have canted corners.

Basket w/pointed overhead
handle, compressed ball form,
rose & green ground, No. 354-8",
8" h. **330.00**

Ewer, bulbous body, cut-out rim,
rose & green ground,
No. 926-10", 10" h. **300.00**

IXIA (1930s)

Bell-shaped flowers with yellow centers and slender leaves; lavender blossoms on green or yellow ground or white blossoms on pink ground, closed wing-shaped handles are prevalent.

Basket, hanging-type, pink
ground, 7" d. **225.00**

Flower frog, yellow ground,
No. 34 .... **110.00**

JONQUIL (1931)

Textured background of terra cotta mottled in ivory and blended green with green leaves that rise from the base and white blossoms that bloom at the top of items.

Basket, footed base w/cylindrical
body rising to short flaring neck
w/overhead handle, 10" h. **275.00**

Bowl, 10½" d., shallow,
w/attached flower frog,
No. 98-10" **200.00**

Vase, 3⅛" h., squatty body
w/canted sides, two handles
rising from base to rim **100.00**

Wall pocket, open handles rising
from pointed base & extending
above flaring rim to form a
pointed top, 8½" h. **475.00**

JUVENILE
(introduced circa 1916)

Painted transfer-printed creamware decorated with motifs to catch the attention of children. They include chicks, sad-eyed puppies (dogs), Santa Claus, sitting rabbits (ears up), standing rabbits (ears back and wearing a jacket), pigs (standing and wearing clothes), floppy ducks (with red hat and red boots), ducks (without hats or boots), sunbonnet girls, fancy cats and bears. The names listed above are those given by collectors. Unusual items such as side-pour pitchers, divided plates, two-handled mugs,

Bowl with Three Evenly Spaced Chicks

and especially egg cups command higher prices than the more common pieces. There are several band colors with green being the most common.

Bowl, 5 ¾" d., 2" h., plain cream glaze inside, wide green band separated by two narrow black bands w/three chicks evenly spaced around outside, marked "RV 14" (ILLUS.).........................**130.00**

Bowl, 5 ¾" d., 2¼" h. w/slightly flaring sides & rim, three brown rabbits w/ears back standing around inner sides, rust jackets, green rim, marked "Rv" (ILLUS.) **155.00**

Bowl, 5 ¾" d., 2¼" h. w/slightly flaring sides & rim, three sunbonnet girls around inner sides, yellow bonnets, pale blue dresses, orange rim, marked "Rv" (ILLUS.) **140.00**

Egg cup, goblet shape, No. 1, 2½" h. **275.00**

Sunbonnet Girls Bowl

Rabbit Egg Cup

Egg cup, sitting rabbits, black piping surrounds wide green band at rim w/black piping near base, No. 2, 3" h. (ILLUS.) **235.00**

Feeding dish w/rolled edge, sitting rabbits, four brown rabbits, ears up, sitting on wide green band in bottom of dish, orange rim separated by two narrow bands, black narrow band on outer rim, unmarked, 6½" d., 1¼" h. (ILLUS. next page) **135.00**

Rabbits with Jackets Bowl

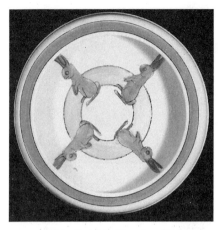

Sitting Rabbits Feeding Dish

Standing Rabbits Feeding Dish

Feeding dish w/rolled edge, standing rabbits, three brown rabbits w/rust jackets, green rim & green circle in bottom connecting the rabbits, thin black line circling middle of outside, marked "Rv," 7" d., 1¼" h. (ILLUS.) **145.00**

Feeding dish w/rolled edge, chicks, three chicks inside bottom standing on wide green band, two black thin lines separated by a wide green band on outside edge, marked "Rv," 7¼" d., 1¼" h. **135.00**

Feeding dish w/rolled edge, pigs wearing clothes, 8" d. **260.00**

Yellow Chick Mug

Feeding dish w/rolled edge, Santa Claus walking w/toy sack over his back, 8½" d. **375.00**

Mug, fancy cats, 3" h. **150.00**

Mug, plain creamware glaze inside, narrow black band near base & rim & separating wide green band w/a yellow chick on each side of handle, marked "Rv 7," 3" h. (ILLUS.) **100.00**

Pitcher, 3" h., Santa Claus **165.00**

Pitcher, 3" h., side pour, chicks **160.00**

Pitcher, 3" h., sunbonnet girls **95.00**

Pitcher, 3¼" h., bulbous body w/angular handle rising slightly above rim, chicks **150.00**

Pitcher, 3½" h., seated dog, sad-eyed brown puppy sitting on each side of spout w/black narrow band at base & rim & extending in a "V" shape under spout, wide grey band separated by black narrow bands near puppy's neck, marked "Rv" (ILLUS. next page) **90.00**

Pitcher, 3½" h., ducks, yellow duck w/red shoes & hat on each side of spout w/black narrow band at base & rim & extending in a "V" shape under spout, wide blue band separated by black narrow bands near duck's back, marked "Rv" (ILLUS. next page) **200.00**

Seated Dog Pitcher

Duck Pitcher

Standing Rabbit Pitcher

Pitcher, 3½" h., standing rabbit, brown rabbit w/rust colored jacket on each side of spout, black narrow band at base & rim & extending in a "V" shape under spout, wide green band separated by black narrow bands near rabbit's tail, marked "Rv" (ILLUS.) **85.00**

Pitcher, milk, 3 ¾" h., bulbous body, chicks, green bands........ **185.00**

Pitcher, 4" h., bears, green bands....................................... **140.00**

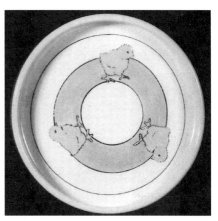

Chicks Plate

Plate, 8¼" d., chicks, thin black lines separating wide green band on verge, four yellow chicks, unmarked (ILLUS.) **125.00**

LA ROSE (1924)

Satin matte gently textured ivory background against embossed swags of green vines and small red roses; rim borders gently beaded.

Basket, hanging-type, No. 338-6", 6" h. **175.00**

Vase, double bud, 4½" h., gate-form **100.00**

Wall pocket, fan-shaped, No. 1234, 7½" h........................ **150.00**

Wall pocket, long teardrop-form, No. 1235, 12" h......................... **275.00**

Magnolia Console Bowl

MAGNOLIA (1943)

Faintly textured & gently mottled backgrounds of green, blue or tan and with embossed white blossoms, rose flower centers and black stems.

Ashtray, two-handled, low bowl form, blue ground, No. 28, 7" d.. **135.00**

Book ends, green ground, No. 13, pr.................................. **200.00**

Console bowl, stepped ends w/blossoms rising slightly above rim, tan ground, No. 452-14" l. (ILLUS.) **195.00**

Cookie jar, cov., shoulder handles, blue ground, No. 2-8", overall 10" h............................. **430.00**

Cornucopia-vase, blue or tan ground, No. 184-6", 6" h., each .. **95.00**

Ewer, squatty body rising to a long, tapering neck, tan ground, No. 15-15", 15" h. **350.00**

Model of a conch shell, tan ground, No. 453-6", 6½" w. **125.00**

Pitcher, cider, 7" h., footed bulbous body w/large handle blue ground, No. 132-7" **325.00**

Vase, double bud, 4½" h., gate-form, green ground, No. 186-4".. **110.00**

Wall pocket, overhead handle w/pointed ends, tan ground, No. 1294-8½", 8½" h. **250.00**

MING TREE (1947)

Eastern influences of high-gloss glazes and softly textured backgrounds of vertical ridges in mint green with pink or white puffed blossoms, blue with white blossoms or white with green blossoms; gnarled branches form handles.

Ming Tree Vase

Ashtray, shaped square w/indented rest at each corner, No. 599, 6" d............................. **110.00**

Basket, hanging-type, green ground, No. 505-8", 6" h. **210.00**

Basket, blue ground, No. 509-
   12", 13" h. **195.00**

Book ends, white ground, No.
   559, 5½" h., pr. **150.00**

Candleholders, squat melon-
   ribbed body w/angular branch
   handles at shoulder, blue
   ground, No. 551, 2¼" h., pr. **85.00**

Ewer, wide short base w/slender
   bottle-form body and branch
   handle, blue ground,
   No. 516-10", 10" h. **115.00**

Model of a conch shell, white
   ground, No. 563, 8½" w. **165.00**

Vase, 8" h., asymmetrical branch
   handles, on undulating
   cylindrical body, blue ground,
   No. 582-8" (ILLUS. previous
   page) **125.00**

MISCELLANEOUS

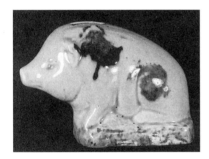

Pig Bank

Bank, model of a pig, large,
   recumbent, high gloss,
   spongeware-type base, beige
   body w/black & brown
   splotches, 5½" l., 4" h.
   (ILLUS.) **295.00**

Candlestick, shield-form, child in
   night gown carrying a candle &
   the words "Good Night," on
   inner light reflector shield, heart-
   shaped leaves on front rim &
   trailing down each side of
   handle, black piping, unmarked,
   7" h. (ILLUS. top, next col.) **425.00**

"Good Night" Candlestick

Dutch Line Creamware Mug

Mug, Dutch line creamware, boy
   on one side, girl on reverse,
   9½" h. (ILLUS.) **100.00**

Mug, Holland line creamware,
   boy on one side, girl on reverse,
   4" h. (ILLUS. next page) **65.00**

Umbrella stand, blended high
   gloss, No. 727, 9½" d.,
   19½" h. **550.00**

Holland Line Creamware Mug

MODERNE (1930s)

Matte-glazed backgrounds of ivory with pink, turquoise with gold, or brown with green adds authenticity to the already realistic Art Deco styling of vertical lines, swirls and circles.

Bowl-vase, low foot, compressed ball-form, ivory w/pink, No. 299-6", 6½" h............................ **155.00**

Flower frog, bell-shaped w/holes on mid-rim & three graduated circles at top w/two vertical waterfall-like lines from top to base, ivory w/pink, No. 26-7", 7" h. **105.00**

Moderne Bud Vase

Moderne Cylindrical Vase

Vase, triple bud, 7" h., turquoise w/gold, No. 792-7" (ILLUS.) **295.00**

Vase, 8" h., swelled cylindrical form w/tiny handles at rim, ivory w/pink ground, No. 797-8" (ILLUS.) **135.00**

Vase, 19" h., footed squatty base rising to a bottle form, two wing-shaped handles at base, brown w/green, No. 800-10"............... **185.00**

MONTACELLO (1931)

A Native American appearance dominates this pattern with black and white trumpet flowers bound together with a ribbon-like band; backgrounds are a tan or light green mottled in blue and fading to ivory with the shapes sturdy and strong. The line has been reproduced for several years. Originally the reproductions carried a paper label.

Basket w/pointed overhead handle, tall collared neck, blue ground, No. 332-6", 6½" h. **275.00**

Basket w/overhead handle, flared neck, No. 333, 6½" h. **250.00**

Vase, 7" h., two-handled, slightly ovoid, wide mouth, terra cotta ground, No. 561-7" **325.00**

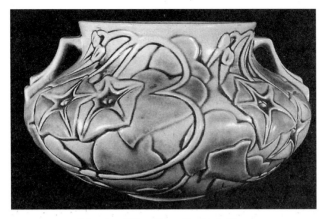

Morning Glory Squatty Body Vase

MORNING GLORY (1935)

Stylized pastel open-faced blossoms and green vines against a green or white ground with brown on the white to distinguish and separate the design.

Basket w/high pointed overhead handle, globular body, white ground, 10½" h. **415.00**

Candlesticks, flaring base, small angular handles at midsection, green ground, 5" h., pr. **425.00**

Vase, 4" h., squatty body, small shoulder handles, white ground, (ILLUS. top) **275.00**

Vase, 7" h., pillow-shaped, base handles, white ground **290.00**

Wall pocket, double, green ground, 8½" h. **900.00**

PEONY (early 1940s)

Blossoms with green leaves in relief on a textured, slightly shaded, background of gold with brown, rose with blue or green.

Basket, hanging-type, rose ground, No. 467-5", 5" h. **170.00**

Book ends, gold ground, No. 11, 5½" h., pr. **235.00**

Creamer, gold ground, No. 3-C, 3" h. **68.00**

Ewer, bulbous base w/short neck and spout, green ground, No. 7-6", 6" h. **86.00**

Ewer, squatty body w/long bottle neck w/cut-outs and long spout, rose ground, No. 8-10", 10" h. ... **210.00**

Peony Flower Frog

Flower frog, fan-shaped w/angular base handles, rose ground, No. 47-4", 4" h. (ILLUS.) **95.00**

Mug, bulbous body w/angled handle, gold ground, No. 2-3½", 3½" h. **115.00**

Sugar bowl, open, gold ground, No. 3-S **75.00**

Teapot, cov., gold ground, No. 3-T **200.00**

Wall pocket, two-handled, gold
ground, No. 1293-8", 8" h. **180.00**

PINE CONE (1931)

*Embossed bronw pine cones and green
pine needles on grounds of blue, brown or
green; twisted handles incorporate themselves
into the design of many pieces.*

Ashtray, pendant-shaped w/one
cigarette rest at smallest point
w/pine needles on the outer rim
of two sides, green ground,
No. 499, 4½" l. **135.00**

Basket, low overhead branch
handle, flat disc base, flared rim,
blue ground, No. 338-10",
10" h. **400.00**

Basket, hanging-type, brown
ground, No. 352-5", 5" h. **350.00**

Candlesticks, disc base w/one
candle nozzle, brown ground,
No. 1099C-4½", 4½" h., pr. **195.00**

Cornucopia-vase, blue ground,
No. 126-6", 6" h. **120.00**

Mug, green ground, No. 960-4",
4" h. **225.00**

Plate, 7½" d., blue ground **550.00**

Tumbler

Tumbler, brown ground,
No. 414, 5" h. (ILLUS.) **215.00**

Umbrella stand, blue ground,
No. 777-20", 20" h. **2,550.00**

Vase, 6" h., brown ground,
No. 748-6" **150.00**

Vase, 9" h., blue ground,
No. 705-9" **350.00**

Triple Wall Pocket

Wall bracket, blue ground,
No. 1-5 x 8" **495.00**

Wall pocket, double, blue
ground, No. 1273-8", 8½" h. **375.00**

Wall pocket, triple, blue ground,
No. 466-8½", 8½" w. (ILLUS.
above) **415.00**

POPPY (1930)

*Shaded backgrounds of blue, green or pink
with embossed blooms, buds and foliage.*

Basket, wide trumpet-form w/high
& wide arched handle, pink
ground, No. 347-10",
10" h. **350.00**

Ewer, pink ground, No. 880-18",
18" h. **500.00**

Ewer, ornate cut-out lip, green
ground, No. 876-10",
10" h. **225.00**

Wall pocket, triple, tapering
center section flanked by small
tapering cylinders, blue ground,
No. 1281-8", 8½" h. **350.00**

PRIMROSE (1932)

*Embossed single blossom clusters on long
stems and leaves with grounds in blue, pink
or tan.*

Cornucopia-vase, tan ground,
No. 125-6", 6" h. **85.00**

Vase, 12" h., blue ground, No.
771-12" **395.00**

Vase, 12" h., pink ground, No.
771-12" **415.00**

RAYMOR (1952)

Modernistic shapes designed by Ben Seibel in colors of black, ivory, tan, grey, dark green and medium green.

Bowl, salad, 11½" d., grey,
No. 161 .... **40.00**

Coffee server, swinging-type
w/base, dark green,
No. 176 .... **385.00**

Cup & saucer, dark green,
Nos. 150 & 151, set **30.00**

Plate, salad, ivory, No. 153 .... **28.00**

Plate, dinner, black, No. 152 .... **30.00**

Plate, bread & butter, grey,
No. 154 .... **20.00**

ROZANE ROYAL (1904)

Paperweight, artist-signed G.
Gerwick on rim edge, applied
Rozane Royal seal, 4" l., 2½"
w., ½" h. (ILLUS. right) **385.00**

Paperweight, artist-signed V.
Adams, applied Rozane Royal
seal, 4" l., 2½" w., ½" h.
(ILLUS. left) **385.00**

Vase, 5" h., holly w/leaves
decoration, artist-signed,
applied Rozane Royal seal
(ILLUS. right) **420.00**

Vase, 5" h., flowers, buds &
leaves, artist-signed, applied
Rozane Royal seal (ILLUS.
left) **420.00**

Rozane Royal Vases

SILHOUETTE (1952)

Combed pattern backgrounds in recessed shaped panels decorated with female nudes or floral designs. Grounds are rose, tan, turquoise blue or white with turquoise.

Ashtray, square w/indentations
at corners, turquoise blue,
ground, No. 799 .... **75.00**

Basket, hanging-type, female
nudes, white ground **275.00**

Basket flaring cylinder w/pointed
overhead handle, florals, tan
ground, No. 708-6",
6" h. **150.00**

Rozane Royal Artist-Signed Paperweights

Cornucopia-vase, florals, white, ground, No. 721-8", 8" h. **80.00**

Ewer, bulging base, florals, white, ground, No. 716-6", 6" h. **55.00**

Ewer, sharply canted sides, florals, tan, ground, No. 717-10", 10" h. **160.00**

Vase, 7" h., fan-shaped, female nudes, tan, ground, No. 783-7".. **275.00**

Vase, 10" h., small open handles between square base & waisted cylindrical body, shaped rim, female nudes, turquoise, ground, No. 787-10" **290.00**

Wall pocket, bullet-shaped w/angular pierced handles, florals, rose, ground, No. 766-8", 8" h. **170.00**

Wall pocket, bullet-shaped w/angular pierced handles, female nudes, rose, No. 766-8", 8" h. **230.00**

SNOWBERRY (1946)

Green leaves, brown branches and white berries embossed over spider-web designs in backgrounds of blue, green or rose.

Ashtray, round, shaded blue ground, No. 1AT **95.00**

Basket w/asymmetrical overhead handle, shaded rose ground, No. 1BK-8", 8" h. **200.00**

Candlesticks, angular side handles, shaded green ground, No. 1CS2-4½", 4½" h., pr. **140.00**

Vase, bud, 7" h., single base handle, asymmetrical rim, shaded blue ground, No. 1BV-7" **70.00**

Wall pocket, angular handles rising from base, shaded blue ground, No. 1WP-8", 8" w., 5½" h.. **160.00**

Wall pocket, angular handles rising from base, shaded green ground, No. 1WP-8", 8" w., 5½" h. **170.00**

Wall pocket, angular handles rising from base, shaded rose ground, No. 1WP-8", 8" w., 5½" h. **150.00**

SUNFLOWER (1930)

A repeating band of yellow flowers in low relief circling the top of each piece on a shaded mottled background of royal blue to light green at the base and ivory and terra cotta at the top form the motif for this line. Green leaves further enhance the striking appearance of this pattern.

Candlesticks, handles from midsection to under rim, 4" h., pr. **165.00**

Sunflower Globular Urn

Urn, globular w/small rim handles, 4" h. (ILLUS.) **435.00**

Vase, 9" h., 7" d., two-handled, bulbous **875.00**

Wall pocket, curved openwork double handle, 7½" h............... **700.00**

THORN APPLE (1930s)

Trumpet-like white blooms with green leaves appear on one side with leaves and thorny pods on the reverse against shaded backgrounds of blue, brown or pink.

Basket, hanging-type, shaded blue ground, No. 355-6", 7" d. ... **400.00**

Basket w/pointed overhead handle, conical w/low foot, shaded pink ground, No. 342-10", 10" h. **265.00**

Candlesticks, leaf base w/thorny burr short chandle socket, blue ground, No. 1117, 2½" h., pr. **95.00**

Vase, 4" h., squatty body w/short narrow neck, angular pierced handles rising from midsection, shaded brown ground, No. 808-4" **140.00**

Vase, triple bud, 6" h., shaded brown ground, No. 1120-6" **155.00**

Wall pocket, shaded brown ground w/pattern above bowl, 8½" h. **525.00**

Wall pocket, triple, shaded blue ground, No. 1280-8", 8" h. **475.00**

VELMOSS (1935)

Embossed clusters of leaves over three wavy horizontal lines with an occasional white berry or two over satin matte grounds of green, raspberry red or turquoise. The sparsely trimmed decoration is usually found at the top but, occasionally, can be found rising from the base.

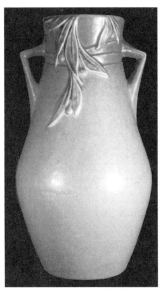

Velmoss Vase

Candlesticks, disc base w/one candle nozzle, mottled turquoise ground, No. 1100-4½", 4½" h., pr. **125.00**

Cornucopia-vase, disc base, mottled raspberry red ground, No. 115-7", 7" h. **98.00**

Vase, double bud, 8" h., mottled green ground, No. 116-8" **145.00**

Vase, 12½" h., mottled raspberry red ground, No. 721-12" (ILLUS. previous column) **235.00**

Wall pocket, high-low pockets conjoined by leaves at bottom & at top for hanging, mottled green ground, 8½" h. **495.00**

VENETIAN (early 1900s)

See: Blue & White Stoneware

WATER LILY (1940s)

High-relief embossed open white flowers on lily pads against a horizontal ridged ground of blue, brown or green.

Basket w/pointed overhead handle, cylindrical w/flaring rim, shaded blue ground, No. 380-8", 8" h. **175.00**

Basket, hanging-type, gold shading to brown ground, No. 468-5", 9" h. **225.00**

Candleholders, flat base, angular handles rising from base to midsection of nozzle, shaded blue ground, No. 1155-4½", 5" h., pr. **175.00**

Cookie jar, cov., angular handles, gold shading to brown ground, No. 1-8", 8" h. **375.00**

Cornucopia-vase, shaded blue ground, No. 178-8", 8" h. **95.00**

Ewer, compressed globular base, tall neck w/long spout and angled handle, gold shading to brown ground, No. 11-10", 10" h. (ILLUS. next page) **180.00**

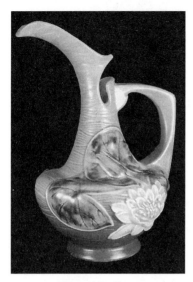

Water Lily Ewer

Model of Conch Shell

Jardiniere, two-handled, pink
shading to green ground,
No. 663-3", 3" h. **80.00**

Model of a conch shell, gold
shading to brown ground,
No. 445-6", 6" h. (ILLUS.)......... **175.00**

WHITE ROSE (1940)

*Flower sprays and green leaves against a
textured background of blue, brown shading
to green or pink shading to green.*

Candleholders, double, pink
shading to green ground,
No. 1143, 4" h., pr. **175.00**

Ewer, semi-ovoid w/high pointed
handle at shoulder, blended
blue ground, No. 990-10",
10" h. **175.00**

Ewer, globular base w/long neck
& sweeping lip, brown shading
to green ground, No. 993-15",
15" h. **370.00**

Flower frog, basket-shaped
w/overhead handle, blended
blue ground, No. 41 .... **95.00**

Vase, double bud, 4½" h., two
cylinders joined by an arched
bridge, blended blue ground,
No. 148 .... **145.00**

WINCRAFT (1948)

*Embossed in floral or animal designs
(animals being harder to find) using shapes
from other lines such as Cremona, Pine Cone,
Primrose and others. High gloss glazes in
bright shades of apricot, blue, grey, tan,
turquoise or yellow.*

Book ends, green ground,
No. 259, 6½" h., pr. **175.00**

Bowl, 10" l., canoe-form w/high
shaped ends, glossy mottled
yellow w/grasses in relief
around base, No. 231-10" **110.00**

Wincraft Cornucopia-Vase

Cornucopia-vase, low
rectangular base, relief florals
against a yellow ground, No.
221-8", 9" l., 5" h. (ILLUS.) **90.00**

Ewer, branch handle, blue,
ground, No. 217-6", 6" h. **60.00**

Wall pocket, globular, green ivy
vine in relief on glossy tan
ground, No. 267-5", 5" h. **135.00**

ZEPHYR LILY (1946)

*A swirled-textured background of blue,
green or tan satin matte against embossed
lilies of yellow, rose or white.*

Ashtray, round w/leaves forming
cigarette rests, blue ground,
No. 27 .... **95.00**

Cookie jar, cov., blue ground,
No. 5-8", 10" h. **425.00**

Tray, stylized pear-shaped
w/stem handle, green ground,
14½" l. **175.00**

Vase, bud, 7½" h., handles rising
from conical base, terra cotta
ground, No. 201-7" **80.00**

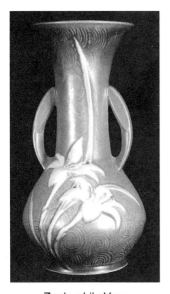

Zephyr Lily Vase

Vase, 10" h., handles rising from
shoulder of bulbous base to
middle of wide neck w/flaring
mouth, terra cotta ground,
No. 137-10" (ILLUS.) **170.00**

Wall pocket, two handles at
base, blue ground, No. 1297-8",
8" h. **195.00**

References: "The Waxing and Waning
of Wall Pockets" by Mae L. Strom,
American Clay Exchange, May 30, 1987;
"Roseville's Cherubic Donatello" by Gini
Gramm, *American Clay Exchange,* July
1986; "The Dutch of Roseville" by Susan N.
Cox, *American Clay Exchange,* April 30,
1986; "Versatile Potter-Frederick Hurten
Rhead" by Grace C. Allison, *American Clay
Exchange,* January 15, 1986; "Embossed
Pitchers" by Randie Page, *American Clay
Exchange,* July 1985; "Roseville Repro's"
by John Pitts, *American Clay Exchange,*
March 1984; "Roseville Memories" by
Susan Hannibal, *American Clay Exchange,*
February 1984; "Ring Around the
Rose(y)ville" by Susan N. Cox, *Spinning
Wheel,* July/August 1983; "Roseville's
Bushberry" by Jim Duke, *American Clay
Exchange,* April 1983; "Uncommon
Roseville Pottery" by Ed Gisel, Jr.,
American Clay Exchange, September
1981; *The Collector's Encyclopedia of
Roseville Potery—First Series* by Sharon &
Bob Huxford, Collector Books, 1976; *The
Collector's Encyclopedia of Roseville
Potery—Second Series* by Sharon & Bob
Huxford, Collector Books, 1980; *Roseville
Pottery for Love or Money* by Virginia
Hillway Huxton, Gymbre Hill Publishing
Co., 1977.

Collectors' Club: Contact Jack and
Nancy Bomm, Roseville's of the Past, P.O.
Box 656, Clarcona, Florida 32710-0656,
$19.95 includes membership and bi-month-
ly newsletter. Club has American Art
Pottery show once a year in January.

SANTA BARBARA
CERAMIC DESIGN

*This company is comprised of artists and
potters who work together to create an
unusual line of porcellaneous stoneware. Ray
Markow founded the studio in 1976 and the
techniques used by the studio were developed
by him during the 1973-1976 period
following his graduation from the University
of California at Santa Barbara where he
majored in ceramics. The artists at Santa
Barbara Ceramic Design (SBCD) made
numerous discoveries that enhanced the look
of the work. Each SBCD item was*

handpainted with original designs created by the artists. The designs were rigorously evaluated before becoming a part of the shop repertoire. According to SBCD, their work was closely aligned with the work of turn of the century art potteries, such as Rookwood. From its beginning in 1976 until circa 1986 when they turned out work reminiscent of the Arts and Crafts period, the artists and their initials as signed are shown. Don Tate made all the pots on a potter's wheel for the artists to design. If his initials appear on a vase, they are usually incised. Almost without exception, items will be marked "SBCD," in a stylized script, the date created and the artist's initials. Special request items were also done during the first ten years. Collectors can tell the difference in a "special request" piece by the elaborate detailing in various places which carry through the main theme. Generally, the additional places would be on the rim or neck of a vase; wide rim of a plate; foot up to the body of a lamp base; and the rims of candlesticks. SBCD is still producing items. However, collectors tend to amass vases, candlesticks, lamps with original shades designed by Sara Soltau, and so on from their early years 1976-1986. The artists initials (as they would appear on items) are listed below with the names of the artists.

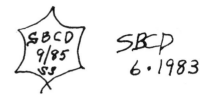

Santa Barbara Marks

Candlesticks, white ground w/pale pink rim & edge, black band above & below pink rose buds w/green leaves, marked "AA" (Allison Atwill) & SBCD 6.1983," 7¼" h., pr. (ILLUS.) **$175.00**

Lamp base, round foot w/bulbous body, white ground w/pink lilies, blue miniature lilies & green leaves, signed "SS" (Shannon Sargent) 6½" h. **125.00**

Lamp base, Model No. 5130, rust & yellow nasturtiums w/green leaves over beige ground, 12" h. (ILLUS. right next page) ... **165.00**

w/original shade **185.00**

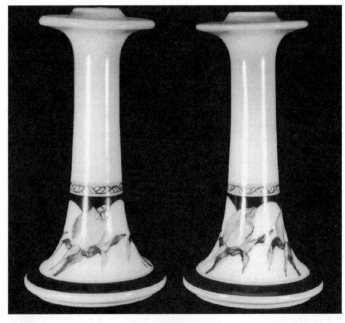

Candlesticks Marked "AA"

*Vase and Lamp
Base Model No.
5130*

Vase with Two Penguins

Plate, 9" d., white edge w/white Calla Lily buds & muted green leaves over a pale grey rim, center w/three large Calla Lilies & two large muted green leaves over a black background **22.00**

Tile, white water lily w/yellow center, blue & green leaves w/green frog leaping, small moon overhead, "SBCD" on front lower left & initials "SS" on front lower right, 4 x 5" **40.00**

Vase, 5" h., spice glazed background w/autumn & golden peach nasturtiums (ILLUS. left above) **80.00**

Vase, 7" h., golden beige background w/an orange wild rose & green leaves, signed "LEC 1980 SBCD" **110.00**

Vase, 7½" h., muted blue
background w/two penguins & a
baby penguin on front vase body
& mountains, water & iceberg on
reverse, elaborate motif of
swimming fish & penguins in a
wide band near rim indicates
"special request" marked "SBCD
9/83 SS PNV33" & incised "DT"
(Don Tate) (ILLUS. previous
page) **275.00**

References: Meetings between
Raymond Markow and Susan N. Cox;
Correspondence between SBCD artists,
B.J. Duke and Susan N. Cox; Santa
"Barbara Ceramic Design-Traditions of the
Past" by Susan N. Cox, *Journal of the
American Art Pottery Association,* July-
August 1985

Artists and their signatures who have worked at
Santa Barbara Ceramic Design.

Ray Markow	Ray		
Barbara Rose	B. Rose		
Darcy Neal	A̶J̶		
Laurie Cosca	ℒℰC		
Kat Corcoran	KAT		
Kathleen Crea	KC		
Shannon Sargent	SS		
Jim Hardman	J. H.		
Suzanne Tormey	S. T.		
Laurie Linn Ball	L.L.B.	Earlier L.L.	h. L.
Dorie Knight Hutchinson	D̶H̶	Earlier B̶	
Elena Dhyansky	ED		
Margaret Gilson	M̶G̶		
Mary Favero	M̶E̶F		
Susan Dray	"Zetta"		
Michelle Foster	MF	MF	
Gary Ba-Han	GBH	G	
Allison Atwill	A̶A̶		
Bill Pasini	WP	WP	
Itoko Takeuchi	9t		
Anne Collinson Fitch	A̶C̶	Earlier A CF	
Don Tate	d̶T̶.		

SCHOOP (HEDI) ART CREATIONS

Hedi Schoop

HEDI SCHOOP
HOLLYWOOD, CALIF.

Hedi Schoop Marks

Hedi Schoop began producing ceramics in 1940 in Hollywood, California. Practically all figurines, from that date until a fire in 1958 resulted in the closing of the pottery, were designed and modeled by Hedi Schoop even though almost fifty decorators worked at her studio. A variety of items were made including animals, ashtrays, bowls, boxes with lids, candlesticks, figurines, lamps, planters, and wall plaques. Hedi Schoop products range from those with crude characteristics to those with intricate details to others with delicate, fragile traits.

The first time I met Hedi Schoop I was in awe of the graciousness of the woman. During our conversation, Hedi told me she would autograph one of my pieces if I wished. I picked my favorite figurine but when she tried to sign the glazed bottom, of course, the ink would not penetrate the glossy surface. Finally, she opened her purse, pulled out an eyebrow pencil and carefully penned her name. Collectors have used adjectives such as feminine, gracious, elegant and sophisticated to identify Schoop's work. Perhaps her figurines are mirrors of the woman who created them.

There were a variety of marks ranging from the stamped or incised Schoop signature to the hard-to-find Hedi Schoop sticker. The words "Hollywood, Cal." or "California" can also be found in conjunction with the Hedi Schoop name.

Schoop was imitated by many artists; some were people who had worked for her, then left to pursue their own businesses. Kim Ward and Yona were two whose works are becoming collectible in their own right. Ynez is another, but collectors have not begun yet to collect those marked items in any great number. Novices wanting to collect only

Schoop pieces should buy the marked items since almost all of her pieces were identified or, at least, obtain verification from a reputable source that you have the genuine product.

Bowl, 10½" l., 6" h., figural, duck sitting w/body forming bowl, dark brown w/gold trim **$45.00**

Bowl, 10 ¾" d., 3" h., low, round sides w/fluted edges, woman sitting in middle w/one flower in her hands, dress sleeves have hand-painted flowers, hair w/rough texture **85.00**

Bust of a Child

Bust of a child, angel-like w/wings & w/finger at mouth indicating "quiet", eyes closed, pink, white, blue glazes, 8" h. (ILLUS.) **45.00**

Casserole w/lid, individual, canoe-shaped, brown high gloss w/leaves & fruit decoration on lid, white glaze inside, Model No. 510, marked "Hedi Schoop California," 9½" l., 3½" h. (ILLUS. next page) **32.00**

Figure of a ballet dancer, pink w/platinum trim, platinum ring on each arm, one leg extended, other slightly bent, 10" h. (ILLUS. next page) **160.00**

Casserole with Lid

Figure of Ballet Dancer

Figure of Clown with Barbell

Figure of a clown standing, one leg crossed over other leg, one hand to head, other hand to mouth, bucket & mop at his side, 10½" h............................... **95.00**

Figure of a clown w/legs apart, one hand over head holding barbell, other hand on waist, turquoise & pink w/platinum trim, 13" h. (ILLUS.).................. **150.00**

Figure of a Dutch boy on round white base, hands in pockets, body tilted slightly back, blue shoes, yellow pants & shirt, blue buttons, scarf & hat, 10" h. **65.00**

Figure of a girl standing, bell-shaped skirt w/scalloped edges, sunflower-shaped face & yellow hair, green blouse, yellow skirt, Model No. 703, 9" h. **40.00**

Figure of a girl standing, holding bowl over her head, one leg raised slightly, the other leg on base, white glossy overall glaze w/blue & green striped skirt, blue scarf around head & tied at neck, blue shoes, 13" h.. **85.00**

Figure of Girl Standing

Woman with Mirror

Figure of a girl standing
w/yellow bird in left hand, bisque
basket in right hand, black hat &
dress w/black bodice & vertical
bisque stripes alternating
w/black, yellow & white high
gloss stripes, bisque basket,
stamp mark "Hedi Schoop,
Hollywood, Cal.," 9½" h.
(ILLUS.) **75.00**

Figure of a woman on a base
w/an oval upright glass mirror
behind her, reflecting her back,
all black except white hair,
blouse, purse & trim on hat &
dress, w/mirror in good condition,
4 ¾" l., 8" h. (ILLUS.).................. **160.00**

Figure group, cowboy & lady,
dancing, bisque faces & hands,
he has hat & kerchief, she is
holding up her long ruffled dress
w/right hand & has bow in hair
at back, green, black & yellow
glazes, 11" h. **185.00**

Figure group, girl & tree on a
base, girl w/head up looking at
top of tree w/her arms raised,
rough texture, mint green
w/white glaze, brown leaves on
girl's skirt, 7½" l., 11½" h. **115.00**

Masks TV Lamp

Flowerpot, miniature w/one hole
on each side to attach a cord,
cloth, or string to form a handle,
an accompaniment for the
figurines w/hands positioned to
carry a pot in one or two hands,
glazes complement the
figurines, unmarked, 2¼" h. **22.00**

Lamp, figural, TV-type, Comedy &
Tragedy masks on a base w/full
comedy, part tragedy conjoined,
dark green w/gold trim, ca. 1954,
10 ¾" l., 12" h. (ILLUS.) **325.00**

Model of a cat, sitting, two bells
in-relief on collar, bow on collar
forms two small pots at back of
head, rough textured white
w/dark brown pots & yellow
bells, 4½" l., 7½" h. **55.00**

Tray, divided w/irregular leaf-
shaped raised edges, w/fairy on
her knees, arms outstretched
beside her, head tilted, beige &
gold tray, beige w/pink tinge
angel, gold wings, rose on left
wrist, belt of roses around her
waist w/rose-glazed bowl & rose
hair, bottom of tray also in a
rose high gloss, 11½" l., 6" h.
including angel **89.00**

References: "Hedi Schoop Art
Creations," by Susan N. Cox, *Collector*
newspaper column, September 1995;
Antiques Research Development report,
January 1988; Correspondence and inter-
view with the artist; Company photographs
and catalog sheets; Column by B. A.
Wellman, *The Depression Glass Daze,*
February 1987; *American Clay Exchange*
Calendar for 1988, printed December,
1987; "Hedi Schoop Dancer" by Susan N.
Cox, *American Clay Exchange,* August 15,
1986; "Collectors Recent Finds," *American
Clay Exchange,* July 1986

SHAWNEE POTTERY

See: Antique Trader Books
*Pottery & Porcelain - Ceramics
Price Guide*

STERLING CHINA COMPANY

Sterling China Company got its start in
1878 in Wellsville, Ohio when John
Patterson and two sons, Jefferson and John,
began producing artware and Rockingham—
glazed ware. Four more sons would join John
and the company name was changed to
Patterson Brothers Pottery. However, the
plant closed in 1914. Three years later, C. C.
Pomeroy, William Wells and a group of
businessmen took over the Patterson pottery
and renamed it Sterling China Company.

Primarily, Sterling China created hotel
ware, making once-fired mugs, cups and
bowls. By 1940, they had a complete line of
hotel china. Since it was successful, they
concentrated their efforts on hotels,
steamships, airlines, restaurants and
railroads. Pink and blue Willow ware, since it
was popular at the time, was made for many
hotels.

In the early 1950s, Sterling took over
Caribe China Corporation. Also, about that
time, Russel Wright designed a restaurant-
hotel line for Sterling. It was available only a
short time and was produced in green, grey,
brown, white and yellow. Today it is not easy
to find. Many times the items were not
marked but those who have studied Russel
Wright's designs and techniques would have
no difficulty in identifying the Sterling china
he created.

In 1955 Sterling purchased the assets of
Scammell China and again, in 1960, they
acquired yet another company, the Wellsville
China Company.

Sterling China Marks

Biscuit jar w/lid, cobalt blue &
gold decoration on lid & jar, six-
sided panels w/squared
handles, marked w/crown &
"Sterling China," 5½" h.
(ILLUS. next page) **$145.00**

Bowl, 6¼" d., white w/a gold leaf
border & a diesel streamliner
going through a green circle **35.00**

Bisquit Jar with Lid

Blue Rim Bowl

Gravy Boat with Crown

Bowl, 7" d., white w/wide navy blue rim & narrow navy blue inner rim bands, one blue anchor (ILLUS. middle) **8.00**

Cup & saucer, Russel Wright design, comma-shaped finger hold, yellow **35.00**

Cup & saucer, white w/a gold leaf border & a diesel streamliner going through a green circle **50.00**

Cup, white w/yellow shading from middle of cup to rim, restaurant ware, marked "Sterling Vitrified China, East Liverpool, Ohio U.S.A.," Model No. M-3 .... **6.00**

Gravy boat, footed, white w/three maroon bands w/center band wider than top or bottom bands, gold crown divides the bands, Model No. Q4, marked "Sterling China Wellsville, OH. U.S.A.," 8" l. (ILLUS.bottom previous column) **12.00**

Mug, Irish coffee, footed, 7" h. **8.00**

Plate, 9½" d., grill w/three sections, Willow patt., blue **12.00**

Plate, 10½" d., white w/a gold leaf border & a diesel streamliner w/wings going through a green circle **60.00**

Plate, 11" d., Willow patt., pink design **15.00**

Salt & pepper shakers, white w/miniature pink flowers & green leaves on base & around rim, 5¼" h., pr. **19.00**

Sugar, cov. railroad china, white w/a gold leaf border & diesel streamliner w/wings going through a green circle in center **80.00**

Tray, 7¼" l., octagon shape, railroad china, ivory w/two blue-green bands & yellow thin band on border **30.00**

SYRACUSE CHINA COMPANY

SYRACUSE
China
U.S.A.

SYRACUSE CHINA
ECONO—RIM
T-1
TRADE MARK
PATENTED

Syracuse China Marks

Syracuse China's history goes back to 1841 when W. H. Farrar decided to make Rockingham-glazed animals, butter crocks, bowls and jugs. In 1855 and for over fifteen years it was known as Empire Pottery. In 1871, a group of businessmen bought Empire and changed the name to Onondaga Pottery Company. Again, in 1966, the name was officially changed to Syracuse China Company, although the "Sycracuse China" mark had been used on one line of hinca since 1879.

When legalized gambling hit Atlantic City, New Jersey, many of the hotels along the boardwalk were torn down which has enabled collectors to reap the benefits of purchasing china that became available. About 1929 Syracuse designer Douglas Bourne created a new china pattern for Haddon Hall. The pattern was a group of flowers around a mottled brown border with an inner motif of fruit joined by a black and brown stripe. The pattern was named "Rutland" and copyrighted by Syracuse in May 1929. Haddon Hall was not pleased with it so they contacted their supplier, John Wanamaker, asking him to find another supplier. Wanamaker chose Emil Schnepf, head designer at Scammell China. Minor changes were made to the design (stars were added to the brown border) and Scammell's design was patented May 1933. The Syracuse China owners were upset so the president of Syracuse visited Wanamaker. The result was that John Wanamaker was no longer a supplier of Syracuse China. Look for the Rutland pattern. It can be found by collectors eager to hang onto a piece of our heritage.

When R. Guy Cowan closed Cowan Pottery in 1932, he became art director, designing for the Syracuse China Company. It was also at this time that Viktor Schreckengost designed several restaurant and hotel ware patterns for this company.

In 1970, Syracuse discontinued their home china line and within a year they became one of the largest manufacturers of airline, commercial, hotel and restaurant wares. This has been a boon to collectors of advertising memorabilia, especially Western motif designs, and particularly railroad china and restaurant ware.

In 1959, Syracuse acquired Vandesca-Syracuse Ltd., of Jolliette, Quebec, Canada, another large manufacturer of hotel china. In 1984, Syracuse purchased the Mayer China Company.

Bowl, 3¾" d., ivory ground w/alternating brown cows & brown fence sections, marked "Syralite," part of an assortment of items for "Rod's Steak House, Williams, Arizona," Wallace China also used this decal for the same company (ILLUS. left) **$35.00**

"Rod's Steak House" Bowl and Plate

Bowl with Flowers & Bird

Bowl, 4½" d., colorful rim
w/alternating rust flowers &
yellow & tan foliage, orange,
blue & yellow flowers w/green
leaves around verge & center of
bowl w/yellow bird (ILLUS.) **10.00**

Bowl, 4 ¾" d., white w/cobalt &
light blue sailboats around
verge, Adobe Ware (ILLUS.) **9.00**

Bowl, 8" d., Country Garden
patt., large embossed
hollyhocks & foliage in rose,
yellow, purple & green over an
ivory body, ca. 1944 .... **21.00**

Butter pat, white w/floral sprays
of violets & daisies, made for
Chicago Burlington & Quincy
Railroad, w/backstamp,
3½" d. **115.00**

Same without backstamp **40.00**

Cup & saucer, demitasse,
Arcadia patt., set **25.00**

Cup & saucer, Baroque pattern
scroll motif inside rim of cup &
around well edge of saucer,
normally grey design but made
in other colors, plain swirl
Berkeley shape, set.................... **14.00**

Cup & saucer, open rose
w/leaves inside cup & in center
of saucer, single rose buds on
rim of saucer in two places & on
outside of cup, gold trim, set **15.00**

Creamer & cov. sugar bowl,
Econo-Rim line, vertical panels,
ivory glaze w/mustard, rust &
tan horizontal lines across two
panels, creamer 5¼" l., 3½" h.
(ILLUS.) **12.00**

Egg cup, footed, tan glaze
w/flowerpots at top edge,
Econo-Rim line, may have
Great Northern backstamp,
2½" h. **175.00**

Mug, child's, blue pinstripe border
w/animals dressed colorfully,
made for Great Northern
Railway, 3" h............................. **515.00**

Mug, white w/brown cattle
brands, 3½" h.) **15.00**

Plate, 5" d., Coralbel patt., center
motif w/light & dark green
leaves & purple & pink tulips
w/grey stems, purple rim & three
rings of grey, purple & green on
verge **13.00**

Econo-Rim Covered Sugar Bowl & Creamer

Plate, 5 ¾" d., white ground w/friar w/halo above his head, fishing pole over his left shoulder, basket w/large fish in it, brown clothes & shoes, green fish **14.00**

Plate, 6¼" d., ivory ground w/alternating brown cows & fence sections, cow in center w/"Rod's Steak House, Williams, Arizona" above cow & "Gateway To The Grand Canyon" below cow, Wallace China also used this decal for the same china (ILLUS. right, page 216) **140.00**

Broadmoo Golf Club Plate

Plate, 6¼" d., scalloped edge, pale pink rim & edge w/white separated by a maroon circle, advertising "The Broadmoo Golf Club" w/a golfer holding gold club behind him in swinging position, marked "Syracuse China U.S.A.," 3" d. (ILLUS.) **10.00**

Plate, 7" d. advertising "Skychef", pale grey fading to white background, sall baker man in tin glaze **10.00**

Plate, 8" d., Arcadia patt., a gold line on the rim & one on the verge w/a chain of tiny pink roses w/pale green foliage & touches of blue between the two gold lines, Winchester shape **18.00**

Child's Plate with Alphabet

Plate, 8½" d., child's w/alphabet around rim, leaping white lamb w/black accents & pink ribbon around neck w/bell attached, blades of dark green grass under lamb, pale green shading to light blue, marked "Syracuse China U.S.A." (ILLUS.) **42.00**

Plate, 9" d., Dogwood patt. w/white & pink petals & foliage from rim to plain center, ca. 1950 .... **9.00**

Plate, 9½" d., Baroque patt., grey scroll motif between rim & verge, plain swirl Berkeley shape **8.00**

Plate, 10" d., Governor Clinton patt., gold rim w/silver ring slightly inside rim & gold ring on verge, gold & silver singular center geometric Empire Period motif, ca. 1946 .... **17.00**

Plate, 10" d., Shellridge shape, w/overall white, orange blossoms in center of flatware w/pie crust edge, ca. 1940 .... **17.00**

Plate, 10" d., Portland patt. w/sprays of old fashioned flowers in powder blue, rose, lavender, yellow & pale green w/a gold edge & wide rim fluted at six evenly spaced intervals, introduced in 1949 .... **10.00**

Nature Study Poppies Plate

Plate, 10½" d., white border
w/black rim & white center
w/gold ring, green foliage,
white, blue & pink poppies,
"Nature Study Poppies" marked
& "Old Ivory O.P. Co." &
"Syracuse China" in scroll mark
(ILLUS.) **22.00**

Lady Louise Pattern Plate

Plate, 11½" d., Lady Louise patt.
in sterling silver rim, marked
"Made in America, O.P. Co.,
Old Ivory" (ILLUS.) **35.00**

Platter, 16½" l., Coralbel patt.,
platinum rim w/green, platinum
& green rings above verge,
tulips & leaves in center **30.00**

Tray, celery, Dogwood patt.,
10" l. **23.00**

References: "Onodaga Pottery—
Syracuse China" by Don Brewer, *American
Clay Exchange,* February 28, 1985;
Mementos of an Elegant Era...Atlantic
City's Hotel China and Silver" by Larry R.
Paul, *Spinning Wheel,* March-April 1983;
"Nothing Was Finer Than Dining Car
China" by Stanley L. Baker, *The Antique
Trader Weekly,* February 21, 1979

TAYLOR, SMITH & TAYLOR

*This company began in 1899 when C. A.
Smith and Colonel John Taylor used the
Taylor, Smith & Lee Pottery facilities. In
1903 a reorganization occurred and John
Taylor's interests in the company were
purchased by W. L. Smith and his son, W. L.
Smith, Jr. The Smith family owned the
business until 1973 when Anchor Hocking
Corporation purchased it.*

*Taylor, Smith & Taylor (T. S. & T.) could
be considered a giant in their production of
dinnerware. At one time they employed over
500 people. Earthenware and fine china
bodies were used but the china body was
discontinued in the early 1970s.*

*Vistosa, made from 1938 until the early
1940s, was produced to thwart the
competition that Homer Laughlin's Fiesta
was creating. Vistosa came in cobalt blue,
pale green, mango red and a deep yellow. The
pieces had pie crust edges.*

*Lu-Ray is probably the most important
line T. S. & T. created. It was in production
from about 1938 until 1955. Soft, pastel
glazes were Chatham Gray, Persian Cream,
Sharon Pink, Surf Green and Windsor Blue.
The hardest-to-find pastel is the Chatham
Gray. Lu-Ray was made on two different
shapes: Laurel or Empire.*

*Taverne was produced by several
companies and T. S. & T. was no exception.
Their Taverne line, which company brochures
sometimes referred to as Silhouette, was used
on their Laurel shape and became available
circa 1933 and lasted about fifteen years.*

*Wheat was a popular pattern with
homemakers and can be found on the Empire*

or *Laurel* shape. Red Wheat was available first, probably about 1938 and Green Wheat about 1940. Whether with three red or green wide leaves, the additional motif and colors were a combination of grey and black "weeping" sprays with all the pieces trimmed in platinum.

The company closed in 1981 citing recession problems as the cause.

Taylor, Smith & Taylor Marks

Ashtray, Reveille patt., yellow speckled ground w/orange rim, orange, green, tan & rust rooster w/tail feathers apart, flowers & leaves of same colors, 4½" d. **$20.00**

Bowl, 6" d., Vistosa patt., cobalt blue **4.00**

Bowl, 9" d., Lu-Ray, Sharon Pink **18.00**

Bowl, 9" d., Taverne patt. **15.00**

Bowl, 9" l., oval, Taverne patt. **19.00**

Butter dish, cov., round, Taverne patt. **160.00**

Creamer, Lu-Ray, Empire shape, Persian Cream (ILLUS. right) **7.00**

Creamer, Lu-Ray, Laurel shape, Persian Cream (ILLUS. left) **8.00**

Mug, white exterior, pale blue interior, marked "Taylor Mug, Genuine, Made in USA," 3½" h. ... **4.00**

Pickle dish, Taverne patt., 9½" l. .. **16.00**

Plate, 5" d., Magnolia patt., Conversation shape **2.00**

Plate, 5" d., Petit Point Bouquet patt. **5.00**

Plate, 6" d., Lu-Ray, Surf Green..... **4.00**

Plate, 6" d., Taverne patt................ **5.00**

Plate, 6" d., Vistosa patt., pale green... **4.50**

Conversation Shape Plate

Plate, 6¼" d., Conversation shape, dark green wide rim band, white center w/white & pink flowers w/green leaves, designed by Walter Dorwin Teague, 1950s (ILLUS.) **3.00**

Plate, 7" d., Taverne patt............... **6.00**

Lu-Ray Creamers

Petit Point Bouquet Pattern Plate

Reveille Pattern Plate

Plate, 9" d., Lu-Ray, Sharon Pink .. **8.00**

Plate, 9½" d., Magnolia patt.,
Conversation shape **4.00**

Plate, 10" d., Petit Point Bouquet
patt. (ILLUS.) **6.00**

Plate, 10" d., Reveille patt.,
yellow speckled ground
w/orange rim, orange, green,
tan & rust rooster w/flowers &
leaves of same colors
(ILLUS.) **8.00**

Plate, 14" d., Lu-Ray, Surf Green .. **28.00**

Plate, 14" d., Vistosa patt., deep
yellow **19.00**

Salt & pepper shakers, Lu-Ray,
Sharon Pink, Empire shape,
4" h., pr. (ILLUS.)........................ **15.00**

Salt & pepper shakers, Taverne
patt., 5" h., pr. **70.00**

Salt & pepper shakers, Green
Wheat patt., Empire shape,
4" h., pr. **13.00**

References: "Lovely Lu-Ray Pastels"
by B. A. Wellman, *American Clay
Exchange,* October 30, 1986; "China sou-
venirs - East Liverpool, Ohio" by Grace C.
Allison, *American Clay Exchange,* June 30,
1986; "Table Top Fashions of Bygone
Days" by Norma Rehl, *National Journal,*
June 1981

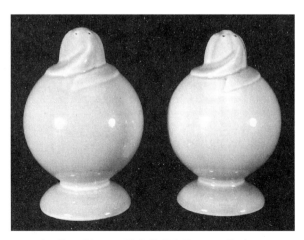

Lu-Ray Sharon Pink Salt & Pepper Shakers

TECHNICAL PORCELAIN AND CHINAWARE COMPANY

The most familiar mark this company used was "Tepco" and many collectors are beginning to notice the variety of restaurant ware they created. Operating from El Cerrito, California from 1922 until the mid-1970s, Tepco had not piqued the interest of collectors until the Western motif craze became so popular. Notice the mark that shows "Blue Ridge China" which is similar to the Blue Ridge Pottery collected today. There was no connection between the two companies. However, items produced by Tepco bearing that backstamp are on a white ground as opposed to their more popular beige ground and their Blue Ridge marked items are not as heavy as the items marked in a different manner.

Technical Porcelain Marks

Western Traveler Bowl

Bowl, 6" d., Western Traveler patt., beige w/brown Western branding irons & boots (ILLUS.) **$29.00**

Butter pat, beige w/orange ovals w/interlocking chains around rim, 2½" d. **4.00**

Brown Pine Cone Cup & Saucer

Cup & saucer, brown pine cones w/green pine needles, set (ILLUS.) **15.00**

Gravy boat, off-white w/pink & yellow flowers & green leaves in center of one side, 6½" l. **11.00**

Mug, branding irons, cowboy hats & longhorn, brown over beige, 2¾" h. **20.00**

Western Theme Mug

Mug, Western theme w/stagecoach, horses, riders on horseback & a small inset with horse & rider, lasso trim on handle, 3½" h. (ILLUS.) **35.00**

Plate, 6¼" d., white ground w/branding irons, boots, cowboy hat, longhorn & yoke around rim w/saddle on rail in center & rider on bucking bronco in background, Blue Ridge China mark (ILLUS. next page) **17.00**

TWIN WINTON

Western Theme Plate

Maroon Design Plate

Plate, 7¾" d., maroon design on
rim and verge w/white ground
(ILLUS.) **9.00**

Plate, 9¾" d., beige w/green
scroll design on rim **10.00**

TEPCO
*See: Technical Porcelain and
Chinaware Company*

BW^s BURKE
        WINTON

WINTON Twin Winton
        Pasadena

Twin Winton Marks

Twin brothers, Don and Ross Winton began a partnership with Helen Burke in 1936 in Pasadena, California. She decorated and sold many of the products in a display room at the pottery. Don created small, slip-cast figurines and Ross took care of the everyday operations that the steadily growing business entailed. By 1946 a third brother, Bruce, came aboard. However, around 1952, the twins sold their interests in the business to Bruce.

In the late 1950s Twin Winton was located in San Juan Capistrano, California. Ownership changed again in the mid-1970s when William F. Bowermaster and Fred Bowermaster purchased the company.

The Hillbilly line began in the late 1940s. It consisted of mountain folk figures on various items with many of the pieces having figural Hillbilly handles. Pieces include lamps, pitchers, shakers and ice buckets as well as planters in the form of outhouses. While the Hillbilly series is popular today, it is the Open Range series that has captured the interest of many collectors. Open Range features a Western motif which includes bucking broncos, figural cowboy handles, steers, branding irons and so on.

Bruce had moved the company to El Monte, California and by the mid-1950s, Twin Winton was producing cookie jars in brown-stained bisque highlighted with colored glazes. Numerous items such as wallpockets, spoon rests, napkin holders and icebuckets can be found with this treatment.

Most of these were designed by then freelancer, Don Winton.

In the mid-1970s, the Collectors' Series began. It included eighteen different cookie jars and all of them carried the Collectors' Series mark.

Items marked "Twinton" and usually with a stock number and the year 1972 are figurines of children on a base usually doing something such as playing football, shoveling sand, and so forth. These items also were designed by Don and Ross had them created in the Orient and imported to the United States. They were not profitable and the line was in existence only a short time.

Early pieces are usually marked on unglazed bottoms "Burke Winton" or "BW" and also an impressed "Burke Winton" can be found. After 1952 most items were incised "Twin Winton Calif. USA," although variations existed.

Big Boy Cookie Jar

Cookie jar, Big Boy, light brown w/oval glazed blue eyes, hard-to-find, 10 ⅜" h. (ILLUS.) **$325.00**

Cookie jar, Cookie Counter w/poodle lid **95.00**

Cookie jar, Cookie Shack, Model No. 97 .... **135.00**

Cookie jar, Elephant Sailor, medium brown w/white sailor hat & pink & blue accents, 11½" h. **70.00**

Cookie jar, Elf Bakery, light wood finish w/yellow & white accents, Model No. 50, 12¼" h. **125.00**

Cookie jar, Gun Fighter Rabbit, wood finish **135.00**

Cookie jar, Mother Goose, 1962 .... **125.00**

Cookie jar, Noah's Ark, wood finish w/glazed accents, 11" h. **95.00**

Cookie jar, Persian Kitten, wood finish, kitten's right front leg raised, Model No. 44 .... **60.00**

Cookie jar, Ye Old Cookie Bucket, bronw w/painted flowers **38.00**

Figure of Boy Sitting

Figure of a boy sitting on round base hugging a bear, boy has blond hair, blue eyes & wears blue pajamas, brown bear w/blue bow at neck, "Twin Winton" incised on base rim, Model No. T-11, 2 ¾" d., 3 ¾" h.(ILLUS.) **50.00**

Figure of African-American girl standing on round base w/sack in right hand behind her back, head tilted slightly, right stocking down & around ankles, sucker in left hand, "Twinton" incised on base rim, Model No. T-9, 5½" h. **64.00**

Figure of African-American football player w/number 15 jersey, football under right arm, left arm outstretched w/palm bent to ward off opponent, "Twinton" incised on base rim, Model No. T-10, 5½" h. **65.00**

Figure of girl sitting on round base playing w/red pail filled w/sand & red shovel in right hand, legs in front of her w/pail between them, blond pigtails, "Twinton" incised on base rim, Model No. T-12, 4" h. **55.00**

Model of Baby Chick

Model of a Bear Cub

Figure of Mythological Pan

Figure of mythological Pan w/musical pipes sitting on brown & beige high gloss stump, bisque body w/grey bisque instrument & goats hoofs, marked in relief on glazed bottom, "Twin Winton Pasadena Cal." 11¼" h. (ILLUS.) **375.00**

Model of a baby chick w/oversized brown shoes, blue tail & coat, blue & green bonnet tied at neck, Model No. 41, 3¼" l., 3" h. (ILLUS.).................... **67.00**

Model of a bear cub standing on four legs w/head turned, dark brown high gloss w/beige head, paws & tail, Model No. 38, 2½" l., 2" h. **36.00**

Model of a bear cub walking, right front paw out in front of body, left arm resting on body, brown & beige high gloss w/black accents, 1½" l., 2 ¾" h. (ILLUS. second above).............. **30.00**

Model of a doe lying down w/head up & long ears out from sides of face, dark brown body w/ecru face & avocado & dark brown accents, Model No. 129, 5" l., 4¼" h. (ILLUS. next page).. **75.00**

Model of a Doe

Model of a raccoon, sitting w/paws in front of him, beige, tan & black glazes, Model No. 113, 2¼" l., 2½" h. (ILLUS.)........ **37.00**

Model of a squirrel walking, dark brown body w/beige, blue & rust accents, flower & leaves between his eyes, Model No. 12, 3" l., 3" h. (ILLUS.)............... **42.00**

Model of a Squirrel

Model of a Raccoon

Model of a squirrel w/paws out from sides of body, dark green, beige & brown high gloss, 2¼" h. **35.00**

"Authentic Twinton Figurines" Advertising Sign

Model of a squirrel w/paws out from sides of body, rust & beige glazes w/avocado & black accents, tail behind & up above head, 2½" h. **52.00**

Sign, advertising, fence-type w/girl standing on right side w/her right arm near top where bird is sitting & boy standing on left side w/left arm toward top of fence feeding squirrel, flowers near base, "Authentic Twinton Figurines," on front of sign, 12½" l. (ILLUS. bottom, previous page) **450.00**

Collecting tips: The older small animals are still within the price range of almost any collector. These animals are well-made, have charming appeal and will surely rise in value. Look for the ones with the "BW" or "Winton" mark. The "Twinton" childrens' series may well be the Hummels of tomorrow and should be worth consideration.

References: Conversations with Don Winton; company catalogs and brochures

VALLEY VISTA POTTERY
See: Maddux of California

WAHPETON POTTERY COMPANY
(ROSEMEADE)

Also see: WPA

$\mathcal{R}osemeade$

NORTH DAKOTA
$\mathcal{R}osemeade$

Wahpeton Marks

Laura A. Taylor attended school at the State Teachers College in Valley City, North Dakota, studying pottery-making under Glen Lukens, a ceramic artist and college instructor. In 1931 she studied special arts and ceramics at the University of North Dakota and was fortunate to have Margaret Cable as her teacher. Margaret Cable was a talented artist, concerned teacher and, most importantly, instrumental in spearheading the ceramics division at UND.

Laura Taylor worked for the Dickota Pottery Company in Dickinson, North Dakota for a short time. She also exhibited some pottery at a Ceramic Exposition in Syracuse, New York in 1934. By 1936, Laura Taylor's career was gaining momentum. She was appointed State Supervisor of the Federal Clay Project at Mandan, North Dakota

under the Works Progress Administration (WPA). In 1939, the WPA suggested and encouraged Laura to use her talents at the potter's wheel during the New York World's Fair.

In 1940, Laura Taylor and Robert J. Hughes, whom Laura had met a the New York World's Fair, opened the Wahpeton Pottery, naming it after the North Dakota county and town of Wahpeton where it was located. The more common name quickly became **Rosemeade.** Hughes and Taylor married three years later.

The pottery did a thriving business and it became necessary to hire a ceramic engineer. Howard S. Lewis from Iowa State College in Ames, Iowa was chosen as a partner and served as Wahpeton's engineer formulating all the glazes for the pottery. Mr. Lewis had worked at Niloak Pottery Company and would shortly create the swirl clay for Wahpeton that had been so successful for Niloak. Laura Taylor designed the items and perfected the glazes. Her animal and bird figures were popular from Wahpeton's inception and remain so today among collectors.

Wahpeton Pottery, even though a small scale operation, endured until Laura's death in 1959. The company continued until 1961 and stock was sold from the salesroom until 1964. Mr. Hughes died in 1970.

Items can be found with or without the Prairie Rose (North Dakota's state flower) sticker and a majority of items have a stamped mark.

Ashtray, two cigarette rests on rim, bucking bronco w/rider in relief, yellow high gloss, 4¼" d. ...**$45.00**

Ashtray, North Dakota state shape.. **40.00**

Ashtray w/fox attached, oval shape w/three cigarette rests, forest green ashtray, brown fox w/white tip of tail & white inside ears, 6" l., 3¼" h **155.00**

Basket, pale turquoise matte w/shades of pink, sticker on handle, 5" d., 4¼" h. **19.00**

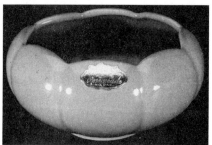

Chartreuse Bowl

Bowl, 4" d., 2 ¾" h., chartreuse high gloss, stamp marked "Rosemeade" & sticker (ILLUS.,) **45.00**

Bowl, 4" d., 2½" h., free-form w/flared sides rising to a quatrefoil rim, high gloss lavender, stamp-marked "Rosemeade" **36.00**

Creamer, figural corn cob............. **34.00**

Model of a bear, red glaze......... **200.00**

Model of a pheasant, 11" h. 14" l. **235.00**

Planter, deer standing in front of bud vase, matte beige, pale green & blue, 7¼" h................... **30.00**

Salt & pepper shakers, figural corn cob, pr. **35.00**

Salt & pepper shakers, model of a Mallard duck, pr....................... **41.00**

Salt & pepper shakers, model of a pelican, pr............................... **76.00**

Salt & pepper shakers, model of a tulip, pr.................................... **25.00**

Sugar bowl, open, handleless, pale matte blue, stamp-marked "Rosemeade North Dakota," & sticker, 2¼" h. (ILLUS.) **24.00**

Handleless Sugar Bowl

Tulip-shaped Vase

Vase, 2 ¾" h., tulip shape w/six holes for hanging, blue high gloss, stamp-marked "Rosemeade" (ILLUS.) **42.00**

References: *Beautiful Rosemeade Pottery* by Shirley L. Sampson and Irene J. Harms, privately printed, 1986; "Rosemeade Pottery Part One" by Susan N. Cox, *American Clay Exchange,* July 1982; "Rosemeade" by Susan N. Cox, *American Clay Exchange,* September 1982

Museum: Richland County Historical Museum, Wahpeton, North Dakota

WATT POTTERY

See: Antique Trader Books *Pottery & Porcelain - Ceramics Price Guide*

WEIL WARE

The California Figurine Company came into existence when Max Weil opened the business near the end of the 1930s. In 1945 Weil purchased the California Art Pottery and the name became Max Weil of California. It has been noted that Mr. Weil bought discontinued Catalina Pottery greenware vases and planters from Gladding, McBean around 1942. Weil then decorated and glazed them at his plant.

About 1946 Max Weil entered the dinnerware field. It was at this time that Malay Bambu (the spelling "Bamboo" is incorrect) was introduced. By 1950 Weil Ware was considered one of the six largest dinnerware manufacturers in California.

Dinnerware came in square or round configurations. The most common pattern seems to be Malay Bambu. However, there are many others such as "Brentwood," "Birchwood," "Malay Blossom," "Malay Mango," and "Malay Rose." On the Malay patterns generally, only the "Blossom," "Rose," or "Mango," will be included in the mark. The decorations are handpainted under a high gloss and the backgrounds usually are pale green, grey or yellow. In a 1946 advertisement, Malay Bambu came in coral Bambu (yellow stalks, green leaves and a coral band), Aqua Bambu (black stalks, white leaves on an aqua background) and Dawn Bambu (yellow stalks and green leaves with a dawn grey band).

Vases, candleholders, bowls and planters were produced in two-tone glazes while the Modern Chinese Ming Tree pattern was created in bowls, planters, lidded containers and ginger jars with a decorated ming tree pattern which was done in a coralene treatment.

Max Weil's company started out as the California Figurine Company and he certainly created his share of them. Children, women, men, planter girls and boys, wall pockets, women carrying pots, standing near vases and pushing carts can all be found in a wide assortment of glazes. After the company became Max Weil of California, dinnerware was the key word in almost all factory brochures and catalogs with bowls, vases and figurines printed in smaller type.

Max Weil died in 1954. Under the direction of Frederick Grant, the corporation lasted until 1960 when it was dissolved.

Weil Ware Marks

Creamer & cov. sugar bowl,
Rose patt. w/pale green background, brown & white flowers w/green leaves, brown on outer rim of handle, creamer 3" h., pr. (ILLUS.) **$14.00**

Cup & saucer, Rose patt., brown flower w/green leaves over a pale yellow ground, square saucer 5 ¾" l., cup 2½" h., set **6.50**

Rose Pattern Creamer & Sugar Bowl

Figure of Girl Standing

Rose Pattern Plate

Teapot with Bamboo and Leaves

Figure of a girl standing &
holding a large pot on each
side, long pale green dress
w/pink flowers & green leaves,
pink scarf around her head &
tied at neck, black hair, white
ringed pots, incised "4024 ELA
Z5" & burro mark (ILLUS.) **35.00**

Figure of girl standing w/left
arm resting on large vase that
extends from bottom of her
dress to her waist, pink & white
dress w/pink & blue flowers,
blue ribbon tied at waist, bonnet
on her head, brown hair, Model
No. 4023, 10 ¾" h....................... **28.00**

Jelly jar w/lid, Rose patt., brown
& beige flowers w/green leaves
& brown stems over pale green
body, lid has opening for spoon,
4" h. **7.00**

Plate, 9 ¾" sq. Rose patt.
w/brown & tan flowers, green
leaves & brown stems (ILLUS.
top, next column) **8.00**

Teapot, cov, 7¼" h., grey
background w/yellow bamboo &
green leaves (ILLUS.) **24.00**

Vase, 4¼" h., Rose patt. w/one
light & dark brown flower, green
leaves & brown stems over
white background, burro mark
w/"Des. Pat Appl. For" also on
bae **11.00**

Vase, 6" h., upright cornucopia on
shell-type base, Model No. 719,
light green high gloss exterior
w/white glaze interior **12.00**

Vase, 6½" h., Ming Tree patt.,
pink to white shading high gloss
ground w/brown & green
coralene-type tree (ILLUS.
next page) **23.00**

Vase, 8" h., footed base w/four
indentations in body & rising to
a quatrefoil rim, pale green
w/brown tree & pink coralene-
type blossoms **25.00**

Ming Tree Vase

Wall pocket, Ming Tree patt.,
flared sides w/squared one inch
rim, Model No. 937, 4¼" h.......... **15.00**

References: "Weil Ware Wets
Collectors' Tastes," California Pottery col-
umn, by Susan N. Cox, *Collector,*
November, 1995; American Pottery, Glass
and China column by Susan N. Cox, *The
Antique Trader Weekly,* November 20,
1985; "Weil Ware" by Helen Brink,
American Clay Exchange, October 30,
1984; "Weil of California" by Maxine
Nelson, *The Daze,* November 1980; Weil
Ware company catalogs

Weller Pottery
*See "American & European Art
Pottery Price Guide" (Antique
Trader Books, 1995)*

WPA/FAP POTTERY

(Works Progress Administration/
Federal Arts Project)

W P A
CERAMICS   W P A
N. DAK.

WPA Ceramics Marks

Technically speaking, what has become
known as WPA Pottery was in reality the
Works Progress Administration/Federal Arts
Project program begun by President Franklin
D. Roosevelt and his associates. While not
limited to artists—the WPA also helped to
build bridges, housing and other important
necessities—collectors generally think of the
program as being used for the betterment of
the arts.

Feeling that the talents of artists were a
valuable resource for our country and its
future, Roosevelt wanted to financially assist
them. So, in circa 1934-1935 the WPA/FAP
was begun. It gave jobs to many artists in
diversified fields with pay averaging

approximately $100.00 per month. In 1939,
Congress intervened and from then until the
projects ceased, twenty-five percent of its
financial backing had to come from sources
other than the government. Even though the
programs were tapering off by 1942, some
have been recorded as lasting through 1945
since funding had already been earmarked
and allocated for them.

Many colleges, universities and museums
across the United States were involved with
the WPA pottery projects. It seems that
practically every state had some form of WPA
assistance program for artists. Talented and
distinguished teachers', historians' and
artists' names have been associated with the
WPA. Some of these people had their own
businesses such as Laura Taylor of Wahpeton
Pottery and others, such as Charles Grantier,
were designers for companies working under
the auspices of the WPA.

Most WPA pieces are well-marked;
sometimes one item will be marked two or
three times with the same words. However,
some pottery will show only the WPA
initials. Naturally, items well marked will
bring a higher value than those with only a
WPA mark.

CALIFORNIA WPA

Artists in California were some of the fortunate people whose programs lasted through 1945. The regional center for the Northern California WPA was located in San Francisco and in 1937 was under the guidance of John Magnani who supervised various projects of ceramics, painting, sculpture, woodworking and weaving. Mr. Magnani was born in New York, attended high school in San Francisco and studied at the University of California. One artist, Beniamino Bufano, worked for the San Francisco project and did mostly Eastern sculpture work. However, he has been credited with making many small animals that were produced by the Walrich Pottery of Berkeley, California. In the pottery programs, ashtrays, decorative objects and vases were created for use by various governmental offices. Most of this work was hand-thrown. Molds were made and produced by casting. Clays and glazes were developed and fired in gas kilns which had been constructed by the artists. Many of the states, including California and Ohio, allowed the artists to function in all phases of work.

Albert H. King, another supervisor of the California WPA, was in charge of the Mosaic project at Long Beach. He also volunteered as a writer who worked on the project's publication Mosaics and Allied Techniques. This was an undated mimeographed publication which was written circa 1940.

NORTH DAKOTA WPA

As Director of the Department of Ceramic Engineering at the University of North Dakota, Laura Taylor additionally accepted the State Supervisor's appointment for the WPA project in 1936. She held this position until 1939.

As did Edris Eckhardt, Taylor also used nursery rhymes for her creations. These included Humpty Dumpty, Old King Cole, Mother Hubbard, Peter, Peter Pumpkin Eater and the Fiddlers Three.

After finishing her time with the WPA, Laura Taylor opened Wahpeton Pottery.

Charles Grantier was born in North Dakota and graduated from the University of North Dakota in 1932. He taught school for a short time but in 1935 accepted a position with the Dickinson Clay Products Company. Dickinson was just beginning to branch out into the field of art pottery using local clays. Grantier was hired as a designer for their Dickota Pottery.

In 1939 Grantier went to work for the WPA. Because of the vacancy left by Laura Taylor in 1939 when she went to New York for the WPA, Charles Grantier became the State Supervisor for this project. He remained in that position until 1942 when the project ended.

While the WPA headquarters was in Mandan, North Dakota, it had been necessary for the firing of the pottery to be done either at the university or at Fort Yates. When Grantier became State Supervisor he acquired a kiln and from then on all firing was done in Mandan.

Numerous items with varying designs were made at Mandan for the WPA. Besides the statues and other work created by Laura Taylor, Charles Grantier produced Mary Had A Little Lamb, Little Boy Blue, Three Little Pigs, Red Riding Hood and others. All of these items were distributed by the government to nursery schools in the state. This may account for today's scarcity of these pieces. If a school offered a hot lunch program, they received WPA pottery in the form of milk pitchers, fruit and custard cups, cereal bowls and miscellaneous functional pieces.

Under Charles Grantier's direction other items such as lamps, vases, paperweights, candleholders and so on were created.

OHIO WPA

Edris Eckhardt is probably one of the most talented, yet least known artists to work with the WPA. She was a 1932 graduate of the Cleveland School of Art and the leader of a workshop sponsored by the Cleveland WPA. This workshop encompassed three institutions —the Cleveland Museum of Art, Cowan Pottery and the Cleveland School of Art— where Eckhardt was in charge of all the ceramics produced at those places.

Between 1933-1939 Edris struggled to gain recognition for her students. She wanted their work to serve as a legitimate fine art form. However, the WPA was basically a *work relief project for a multitude of artists and craftsmen. Eckhardt was faced with the blending of such diversified talents of students, painters, sculptors and commercial artists to satisfy the federal authorities and yet maintain a product suitable for the public.*

Ingenuity and Lewis Carroll (as well as a few other writers) played a large role in solving Eckhardt's problem. She made molds for the Alice in Wonderland characters in sizes from five to seven inches. Also, characters such as the Three Little Pigs, Mary Had A Little Lamb, Humpty Dumpty, Mother Hubbard, Baa Baa Black Sheep and others were created. Each artist was allowed the freedom to express their creativity so probably no two, of the more than 125 designs, were alike.

Edris Eckhardt was probably more fortunate than most other leaders of the various WPA projects. In 1939, when Congress decreed that twenty-five percent of funding had to come from outside sources, Ernest Bonn, the Director of the Cleveland Metropolitan Housing Authority, stepped in with financial backing to help Edris and her group. It was during this period that the name was changed to the WPA Ohio Art Program and they began making playground equipment figures for a government housing development. Tiles were also created which have been credited to Henry Keto and Emily Schrivens.

Bowl, 7½" d., ruffled edge, dark green glaze, marked in a circle "Ceramics Project Works Progress Administration" **$345.00**

Figure of "Big Bad Wolf" standing on base & leaning against tree trunk w/right leg crossed over left leg & right arm behind back, high gloss ivory glaze, marked "WPA Ceramics N. Dak.," 7" h. **955.00**

Figure of Humpty Dumpty sitting on a wall, beige high gloss, stamp mark in cobalt on bottom, "WPA Ceramics N. Dak." & initials "MC" (Margaret Cable) on back of Humpty's head, 4¼" l., 5¼" h. (ILLUS.).... **675.00**

Figure of Humpty Dumpty

Figure group, boy standing w/left hand on hip, lamb standing at boy's right side & ewe behind boy, "Baa Baa Black Sheep" in ink on base rim, marked "Federal Art Project Cleveland, Ohio, Edris Eckhardt," 21" l., 6½" h... **1,025.00**

Figure group, man w/boy carried on his back, small girl standing w/arms around man's waist w/a white dog in jumping position, marked "Christmas Carol, 40 WPA" & "Edris Eckhardt," 9¼" h. **1,100.00**

Jug, 8" h., bulbous body w/short bottle neck, handle from mid-body to shoulder, ivory glaze, produced at Mandan, North Dakota under the direction of Charles Grantier...................... **215.00**

Plate, 8½" d., North Dakota Capitol Building motif in mustard glaze, rust plate, ca. 1940-1942, produced at Mandan, North Dakota under the direction of Charles Grantier **150.00**

Swelled Cylindrical Vase

Vase, 4½" h., 3½" d., swelled cylindrical form w/short flaring neck, pale green high gloss exterior, matte ivory interior, stamp mark in cobalt "WPA Ceramics N. Dak." & pressed "WPA Ceramics N. Dak." & incised initials "PH" & incised "N.D." (ILLUS.) **375.00**

Vase, 6" h., 3 ¾" d., swelled cylindrical form w/short flaring neck, dark green w/black overtones exterior, ivory matte interior, stamp mark "WPA Ceramics N. DAK." w/initials "HD" incised, weighs over two pounds **415.00**

Vase, 7 ¾" h., cylindrical body w/rounded shoulder & base w/short neck & closed rim, Native American dark grey design over a white ground, Mandan, North Dakota **525.00**

References: *The Diversions of Keramos: American Clay Sculpture, 1925-1950,* Everson Museum of Art, Syracuse, New York, 1983; "WPA Pottery, Part One" by Susan N. Cox, *American Clay Exchange,* July 1982; WPA Pottery, Part Two by Susan N. Cox, American Clay Exchange, September 1982; "A Collector Finds Special Pieces" by Betty Carson, *American Clay Exchange,* November 1982; WPA Pottery by Betty Carson, *American*

Clay Exchange, December 1981; *The Potter's Art in California: 1885-1955* by Hazel V. Bray, The Oakland Museum Art Department 1980; Papers, correspondence and photographs between Mrs. Charles Grantier and Susan N. Cox

ADDITIONAL COMPANIES TO CONSIDER

The pottery companies included in this section are worth your consideration. They are here because of two noticeable trends: Many collectors have decided they want to start a collection of the pieces from one or more of the companies or because there has been little buying and selling activity even though books have been written about the firms. As examples, DeLee Art is causing a great deal of interest but little is known about the company and just recently a book specializing on Vallona Starr products has become available so interest should grow within the next few months. Neither Peters & Reed (Zanesware) nor LePere Pottery have had books devoted exclusively to them but there are many collectors who quietly go about buying items produced by both companies. Their products were made by talented artists who played a huge part in the history of the industry. Still, there are not many collectors for either group.

There are many companies worthy of your consideration that are not included in this price guide. That is due to lack of space, time or that the items have not had enough activity to study fair pricing.

CALIFORNIA ORIGINALS

This company, originally located in Manhattan Beach, California and named Heirlooms of Tomorrow in 1944, was known more for their cookie jars than other items. The owners, William Bailey, who had started the company, and Harold Roman of Roman Ceramics in Kentucky and maker of Cumberland Ware, must have had a particular fascination for frogs; they produced many frog cookie jars in assorted sizes, glazes and positions. It could be that California Originals' major buyers, such as J. C. Penney, Montgomery Ward, S & H Green Stamps, Sears and Top Value Stamps, requested frogs. California Originals was on a par with Metlox Potteries in producing a variety of cookie jars. Figurines and animal statues were also created by this company. Under the Heirlooms of Tomorrow business name, Victorian clothing and clothing with losts of lace and gold work can be found on figurines. Many items are unmarked but those that are have a three or four digit number and, most often, "USA." After Roman Ceramics bought the business in 1979, it lasted only until 1982.

USA
CALIFORIG
CALIF ORIGINALS

California Originals Marks

Cookie jar, cov., Dog, "458," 11½" h. (ILLUS.) **$55.00**

Dog Cookie Jar

CEMAR CLAY PRODUCTS COMPANY

This company originated in Los Angeles, California about 1944 and was in business until circa 1958. During those few years they produced a variety of items. The company made dinnerware, some cookie jars and condiment sets, advertising memorabilia, animals, Art Deco figurines and planters. If a product is marked it generally is incised underglaze and will show "Cemar" and a number which probably indicates a company stock number.

cemar

Cemar Clay Products Mark

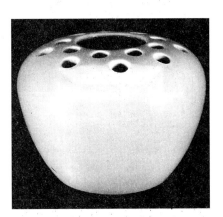

Cemar Flower Arranger

Flower arranger w/eighteen holes, pale blue high gloss, marked "Cemar 404," 5" d., 3¾" h. (ILLUS.) **$9.00**

Model of a bird, white satin glaze, marked "Cemar 541," 8" h. (ILLUS. next page) **26.00**

Planter w/three individual pots on a decorated base, light grey exterior, pink high gloss interior, Made in several colors including majolica marked "Cemar H," 6½" l., 3½" h. **20.00**

Bird Model

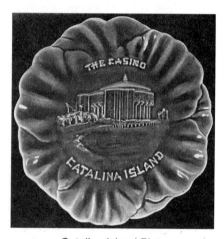

Catalina Island Plate

Plate, 7" d., bright rose high gloss, advertising the Catalina Island (California) Casino w/the Casino pictured w/"The Casino" above the building & "Catalina Island" below, marked "Cemar 629." (ILLUS.) **45.00**

CLAYCRAFT POTTERIES

Claycraft operated in Los Angeles, California from about 1921 until the late 1930s. They made stoneware, decorative art tiles, garden pottery and so on. Collectors are more interested in Claycraft's tiles than their other products. Care should be used not to confuse this company with the Clay Craft Studios of Winchester, Massachusetts.

Claycraft Mark

Tile with Flower Motif

Tile with Relief Scene

Tile w/flower motif in blue, brown, green and white, marked "Claycraft," 2 x 4" (ILLUS.) **$50.00**

Tile w/in-relief scene of seagull in flight over ocean waves, cliffs in background. 4" sq. (ILLUS.) ... **95.00**

References: Claycraft Potteries of California by Douglas Scott, American Clay Exchange October 1983; Claycraft Potteries Tile Catalog from the company, circa 1925

Continental Kilns Covered Sugar Bowl & Creamer

CONTINENTAL KILNS

Continental Kilns operated in Chester, West Virginia from 1944 until 1957. The company made dinnerware in a variety of patterns and their peices are well-marked with the Continental Kilns name, the pattern name and "USA." The company was formed by Vincent Broomhall who had been the art director for E.M. Knowles Company and three other investors who helped front most of the capital. Pieces are generally semi-porcelain but it ws Broomhall's desire to create a Belleek-type ware. This ware was to be named "Vencent" but I have not seen this type of product marked with the company's name.

Creamer & cov. sugar bowl,
h.p. floral decoration, floral bud finial, marked "Continental Kilns" w/ teapot backstamp logo, pr. (ILLUS.) **$17.00**

References: Continental Kilns, Inc. 1944-1957 by Doris and Burdell Hall, American Clay Exchange, December 1983

DELEE ART

Of all the California potteries specializing in figurines that have been enigmas, DeLee Art has to be in the top ten. There are several known facts and lots of assumptions concerning this studio-type company. Facts are that it operated in several California locations: two different Los Angeles addresses and a Hollywood address. The company was owned by Delores and Lee Mitchell. Their

products included many figurines, some with planters attached; miniature animals; and a skunk line. The figurines are favorites among collectors. This partiality is probably because most of the items are marked, leaving no doubt as to their maker, and they are inexpensive when compared to some other more well-known California companies' figurines. The skunk line does not share the same enthusiasm for collectors, however. This is due in part to their plentiful supply except perhaps for the boy skunk with blue hat and the matching girl skunk with her large, wide brim blue hat. Being harder to find, these two skunks are sought by collectors.

$d e \, bec \, Art$
© 1938

delee Art

Delee Art Marks

Figures of a boy & a girl lying on their backs w/legs crossed, marked w/a black & silver paper label, "DeLee Art, California, Hand decorated," 2½" l., pr. (ILLUS. top, next page) **$85.00**

Model of a bunny w/ears up, partial label reading "Bunny Hug" and marked "DeLee," 6" h. (ILLUS. next page, center) **27.00**

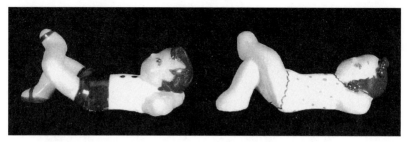

Boy and Girl Figures

Model of Bunny

Girl Planter

Planter, figure of girl leaning over the planter, label. Unusual in that most planter people are holding a tiny pot. 5" h., 4¼" l. (ILLUS. front) **55.00**

Planter, figure of girl standing, overall white high gloss w/brown piping around apron, neck of dress, eyelashes & eyebrows, blue dots sparsely spread over dress & large blue apron bow in back. Marked & incised "DeLee Art," copyright symbol, "1938" & girl's name, "Irene"......................**26.00**

HOENIG, LOU

To my knowledge there has not been any information printed for collectors about this person. Evidently, based on pieces I have seen, Lou Hoenig was a studio potter operating in California during the 1940s and 1950s. All the Hoenig items I have noted have been marked and either have a heavily mottled high gloss, an Art Deco appearance or a satin matte finish. Those interested in the items marked Lou Hoenig should consider purchasing what is available as the values are low now but will no doubt go up rapidly when more is discovered about this artist.

Lou HOENIG
CALIF USA

Hoenig of California

Lou Hoenig Marks

Ashtray/pipeholder, model of a duck; ashtray is open duck's back, pipeholder is top of duck's head, three cigarette rests form tail, light & dark grey mottled satin matte, marked "Lou Hoenig, Calif. USA 918," 5¼" h. (ILLUS. next page) **$37.00**

Model of Duck Ashtray/Pipeholder

Figure of a Woman

Dish, cov., oblong, Art Deco style, spruce green w/oblong white knob, marked "Hoenig of California 501," 5" w., 7¼" l., 2¼" h. (ILLUS.).......................... **24.00**

Figurine, woman w/featureless face, holding a flower pot in each hand, heavily mottled light & dark grey at base & flower pots blending w/a mottled yellow & orange body & hair. The base is a high gloss chartreuse & marked "Lou Hoenig Calif. U.S.A.," 10½" h. (ILLUS.) **70.00**

LEPERE POTTERY

© MOYER

Le Pere

POTTERY

LePere Marks

The LePere Pottery Company came by its name in a haphazare manner. Albert Leeper, well-known Zanesville, Ohio ceramic engineer, who had been helping the founders of the business, Otto and Paul Herold, with the glazes and formulas, was responsible for its name. Leeper was on a selling trip in New York and visited Macys, Wanamakers and others. One of the buyers asked Leeper what was the name of his firm. It was not until then that Albert Leeper realized the Herolds had not considered a name. Quickly Leeper told the buyer "LePere" which was a variation of Leeper's name. The company became a huge success and orders could not be filled fast enough. In the mid 1940s copper lustre was developed. It was considered the best in the country and advertised as original

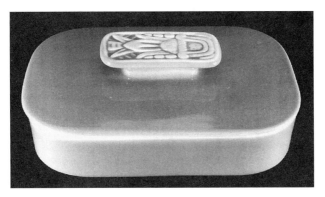

Oblong Art Deco Dish

copper luster from England. Therefore, it was not marked. Animals and birds, including horses, parakeets, rabbits, lions, dogs and cats, were produced as were many vases, pitchers, ewers, lamps and bowls. LePere operated from circa 1936 until about 1961. Occasionally a mark will be found with a copyright symbol and the name "Moyer." Harry P. Moyer was a talented modeler, mold and die maker who worked at LePere.

Creamer & cov. sugar bowl,
copper lustre w/stick spatter-type design wide band, creamer 3 ¾" h., sugar 4" h., pr. (ILLUS. bottom)...................................... **$95.00**

LePere Zanesville Paperweight

Paperweight, advertising, figure of a lion on base, caramel high gloss, incised just below lion's body, "LePere Zanesville, O." on one side of base, "1951 Ohio Lions Atlantic City" on other side, 3" l., 2 ¾" h. (ILLUS.) **28.00**

References: LePere Pottery Company by Ruth Axline, former Art Director for LePere Pottery, American Clay Exchange, April 1982; Gift Potteries-LePere Potery pamphlet by Ruth Axline; LePere Pottery catalog from China, Glass and Decorative Accessories, December 1947; Gift Pottery Business Booms Here; LePere Plant Builds New Addition, The Zanesville Signal 1947.

PADRE POTTERIES

This company was in business in Los Angeles, California from the early 1940s until the early 1950s. It is sad that more is not known about this operation as they made nice art pottery, novelties, kitchen and ovenware. Every piece I can attribute to Padre has been marked. Some of the better pieces have marks that cause additional confusion. For example, they have the normal "Padre" mark but also include "Regal Painted by Jardine" in script underglaze. Some companies produced items, had them decorated elsewhere and both companies signed the ware. This could be the case with Padre. The decorated ware is valued higher than their solid glazed kitchen and dinnerware.

PADRE

Padre Potteries Mark

Bowl, 6½" d., 2½" h., tab handles, wide horizontal rings (ILLUS. next page) **$12.00**

Copper Lustre Creamer & Covered Sugar Bowl

Bowl with Tab Handles

Padre 299 Ewer

Figure of Padre Woman

Ewer, beige high gloss ground w/underglaze purple grapes, green & brown leaves, incised mark, "Padre 299 Calif" & underglaze script, "Regal Painted by Jardine," (ILLUS.) **85.00**

Figure of a woman, h.p. bisque, yellow dress w/brown waist sash & hair, round high gloss brown base, marked underglaze in black script, "Padre California Hand painted by Maxine," 10½" h. (ILLUS.) **110.00**

Flowerpot, beige w/narrow horizontal rings, 4¼" d., 3 ¾" h. **8.00**

Vase, 6¼" h., small squared handles from shoulder to rim, light blue satin matte, marked underglaze "Padre" in an oval, (ILLUS. below) **20.00**

Padre Vase

SANTA ANITA POTTERY

Santa Anita Pottery was located in Los Angeles, California from about 1939 until the mid 1950s. Shortly after going into business, they became a division of the National Silver Company. California Modern is believed to be Sant Anita's first dinnerware line. It was textured in satin pink and matte charcoal glazes. Designers Annette Honeywell and Vreni created many lines for Santa Anita.

While not many products for this company have been seen yet, the Vreniware line which includes such patterns as Provincial Apple, Provincial Spiral, Provincial Mallard and Spiral Grape, seem to be the most plentiful. Other patterns are Countryside, Bali-Hai, Califonia Festival, Turnabout, April Showers, California Carmel, and a dinnerware series of the Flowers of Hawaii. The latter is on a plain white ground with bright colored flowers and leaves.

Santa Anita Ware

Los Angeles Ca

Vreni

Santa Anita Ware
Copyright 1951

Santa Anita Pottery Marks

Cup & saucer, Stylized Spirals patt., Vreniware, cup 4 ¾" d., saucer, 6" d. **$9.00**

Plate, 8" d., Provincial Apple patt., Vreniware (ILLUS.) **7.00**

Tray, leaf-shaped, three section, high gloss cobalt & light blue interior, rubbed bisque rim, leaf stem handle & bottom, incised, "R-144 A Santa Anita Ware Made In Calif.," 13" l., 8¼" w., 2" h. (ILLUS.) **22.00**

Provincial Apple Pattern Plate

Leaf Shaped Tray

References: Santa Anita Ware by Susan N. Cox, Collector, Column—Susan On California Pottery, November 1995; Santa Anita Company catalog, 1952

VALLONA STARR CERAMICS

Three people, Valeria Dopyera de Marsa and Everett and Leona Frost formed Triangle Studios in the early 1930s. Business boomed during World War II but after the war was over importation hurt their operation. In 1953 the company went out of business. During the years of operation varied items in numerous colors were produced.

Vallona Starr
©

Vallona Starr

Vallona Starr Marks

Corn Line Pitcher

Aladdin Salt Shaker

Gold Miner Salt Shaker

Cylindrical Tree Vase

Pitcher, 7½" h., Corn line, light green & yellow high gloss, marked "Vallona Starr Califonia." (ILLUS.) **$57.00**

Salt shaker, figural Aladdin, chartreuse w/gold trim, marked "Vallona Starr California 11," sold w/Aladdin's lamp pepper shaker. 5" h., Aladdin alone (ILLUS.) **48.00**

Salt shaker, figural prospector, mining for gold, holding silver pan w/gold nuggets in it, marked "Vallona Starr California," sold᛫ w/a whiskey jug pepper shaker, 3½" h., prospector alone (ILLUS.) **55.00**

Vase, 7¼" h., cylindrical tree trunk form pierced w/a hole, molded owl peeking out, grey, marked "Vallona Starr California 87" & copyright symbol "50" (ILLUS.) ... **37.00**

VEE JACKSON CERAMIC STUDIO

Vee Jackson Ceramic Marks

Vee Jackson started her ceramics business in 1941 in Pasadena, California. Originally she and her husband, J. Harry Jackson, supplied pins and earrings made of small clay flowers to William Hobe for his jewelry company. Jackson had a special knack for hiring talented people such as Virginia Rogers who had been head interior decorator at Marshall Field Company in Chicago, Illinois and also had retired from the Denver school system where she was art supervisor. A well-known name is that of Earl

Porter who, having learned his trade at Gladding, McBean Company, became a mold maker at the Jackson studio. Dorothy Chatham, a commercial artist who previously worked for the Bird Pottery Company, came to work for Jackson in 1947 and later became the art department's supervisor. Frank Hunt, who had worked for Brad Keeler as a ceramic engineer, was hired by the Jacksons. Their expertise in their chosen fields enabled Vee Jackson Studio to become the success that it did. In 1957 the operation was moved to San Gabriel, California.

Footed Ashtray

Ashtray, footed, purple & blue bands & gold decorations, marked in gold on bottom w/"San Gabriel California" in a circle & "Vee Jackson" in the center of the circle, 8" d. (ILLUS.).................. **$30.00**

Jar, cov., decorated w/gold bands & white grapes on orange high gloss ground, 4¼" d., 19" h. **25.00**

Jardiniere, footed, decorated w/brown & yellow flowers & stylized bird, white ground w/yellow trim at base & rim, artist-signed "Vee Jackson" & underglaze mark "Calif." (ILLUS.) **50.00**

Vee Jackson Jardiniere

WILL-GEORGE

Will and George Climes started their business in Will's garage in 1934. George made the molds and formulated glazes while Will designed, modeled and decorated the pieces. They owed much to the entertainer Edgar Bergen who collected ceramics. In fact, Bergen invested in their business as he was so impressed by what the brothers were trying to achieve. By 1940 Will and George moved the business to a new location in Pasadena. The bird line was produced during the war by Will Climes and George created his flamingo line during this time. After the war the business was renamed The Claysmiths and was also moved to San Gabriel, California. At this time, a split also occurred with Edgar Bergen. A late line, just before the company was liquidated in 1956, featured Oriental figures and flower holders with matching bowls. Lamps were also produced during this time.

Will~George
PASADENA

Will George Marks

Figure of a girl standing on a brown round base, head turned slightly to the right, left arm at side, right arm resting below waist, blond hair, black shoes, orange skirt w/blue apron, white blouse w/yellow front, yellow plate-shaped hat w/applied orange flowers & green leaves, bisque hands & face, marked "Will George" in script on unglazed white bottom, 5½" h. (ILLUS. left, next page) **$65.00**

Figure of a boy on a brown round base, head turned slightly, left arm at waist, right arm bent w/hand to collar, black boots, light blue & bisque striped pants, black & orange vest w/blue shirt, black & orange hat, blond hair, bisque hands & face, marked "Will George" in script on unglazed white bottom, 5 ¾" h. (ILLUS. right, next page) **65.00**

Will George Figures of Boy & Girl

Models of Flamingoes

Figure of a girl standing on a
round unglazed white base,
bisque overall except black
shoes, brown striped at bottom of
dress, pale green trim & brown
panel on apron & white scarf on
head, marked "Will George" in
script, 5½" h. **55.00**

Models of flamingoes, pink &
white standing on round green
base; one flamingo w/head up &
turned over back, the other
flamingo w/head down, 8" h. &
6¼" h., each (ILLUS.) **100.00**

ZANE POTTERY

*This company, operating as Zane Pottery,
has not found its niche among collectors yet.
The company was organized in 1897 in
Zanesville, Ohio when a partnership was*

*formed between John Peters and Adam Reed.
The name of the company was **Peters & Reed.**
They begin producing flowerpots but
gradually the business grew to include art
pottery. "Moss Aztec," developed by former
Weller Pottery designer, Frank Ferrell, was one
of their most popular lines. From 1921 until
1941, when the company was sold to Lawton
Gonder, Peters and Reed was known as Zane
Pottery. Early brownware with sprigged-on
decorations of flowers, garlands, grapes and so
on was unmarked but, armed with a little
knowledge, collectors have no trouble with
identification. But, because pieces were not
marked, collectors tend to purchase the items
from the last twenty years of production.*

Zane Pottery Mark

Footed Flower Frog

Corset-shaped Vase

Flower frog, footed, red clay,
irregular mushroom shape, eight
holes around outer edge, marked,
3¾" d., 1¾" h. (ILLUS.) **$30.00**

Vase, 4" h., corset-shaped,
mottled high gloss blue, marked
(ILLUS.) **48.00**

BIBLIOGRAPHY

Anderson, Timothy J., and Moore, Eudorah M., and Winter, Robert W., Editors. *California Design 1910.* California Design Publications, Pasadena, California, 1974 and 1980.

Bougie, Stanley J. and David A. Newkirk. *Red Wing Dinnerware.* Privately printed, 1980.

Bray, Hazel V. *The Potter's Art in California 1885-1955.* The Oakland Museum Art Department, 1980.

Buxton, Virginia Hillway. *Roseville Pottery for Love or Money.* Tymbre Hill Publishing, Nashville, Tennessee, 1977.

Carlton, Carol & Jim. *Collector's Encyclopedia of Colorado Pottery.* Collector Books, Paducah, Kentucky, 1994.

Colbert, Neva W. *The Collector's Guide to Harker Pottery U.S.A.* Collector Books, Paducah, Kentucky, 1993.

Conti, Steve and Bethany, A. DeWayne, and Seay, Bill. *Collector's Encyclopedia of Sascha Brastoff.* Collector Books, Paducah, Kentucky, 1995.

Cox, Susan N. *The Collectors Guide to Frankoma Pottery.* Page One Publications, El Cajon, California, 1979.

_____. *The Collectors Guide to Frankoma Pottery, Book Two.* Page One Publications, El Cajon, California, 1982.

_____. *Frankoma Pottery Value Guide & More 1933 To Present.* Page One Publications, El Cajon, California, 1993.

Cunningham, Jo. *The Collector's Encyclopedia of American Dinnerware.* Collector Books, Paducah, Kentucky, 1982.

_____. *The Best of Collectible Dinnerware.* Schiffer Publishing, Atglen, Pennsylvania, 1995.

Derwich, Jenny B., and Latos, Dr. Mary. *Dictionary Guide to United States Pottery & Porcelain (19th and 20th Century).* Jenstan Publishing, Franklin, Michigan, 1984.

Enge, Delleen. *Franciscan Ware.* Collector Books, Paducah, Kentucky, 1981.

_____. *Franciscan, Embossed Hand Painted.* Privately printed, 1992.

Fridley, A. W. *Catalina Pottery, The Early Years 1927-1937.* Privately Published, 1977.

Gibbs, Jr., Carl. *Collector's Encyclopedia of Metlox Pottery.* Collector Books, Paducah, Kentucky, 1995

Gick-Burke, Barbara Loveless. *Collector's Guide to Hull Pottery, The Dinnerware Lines.* Collector Books, Paducah, Kentucky, 1993.

Harris, Dee and Whitaker, Jim & Kaye. *Josef Originals.* Schiffer Publishing, Atglen, Pennsylvania, 1994.

Held, Wilbur. *Collectable Caliente Pottery Made by The Haldeman Potteries, Burbank, California.* Privately printed, 1987.

Henzke, Lucile. *Art Pottery of America.* Schiffer Publishing, Exton, Pennsylvania, 1982.

_____. *Pennsbury Pottery.* Schiffer Publishing, West Chester, Pennsylvania, 1990.

Hoopes, Ron. *The Collector's Guide and History of Gonder Pottery.* L. W. Books, 1992.

Huxford, Sharon and Bob. *The Collectors Encyclopedia of Fiesta with Harlequin and Riviera, Sixth*

Edition. Collector Books, Paducah, Kentucky, 1987.

_____. *The Collectors Encyclopedia of Roseville Pottery*. Collector Books, Paducah, Kentucky, 1976.

_____. *The Collectors Encyclopedia of Roseville Pottery, Second Series*. Collector Books, Paducah, Kentucky, 1980.

_____. *The Collectors Encyclopedia of Weller Pottery*. Collector Books, Paducah, Kentucky, 1979.

Jasper, Joanne. *The Collector's Encyclopedia of Homer Laughlin China*. Collector Books, Paducah, Kentucky, 1993.

Joseph, Mary and Harbin, Edith. *Blue and White Pottery*. Privately printed, 1973.

Lehner, Lois, *Lehner's Encyclopedia of U.S. Marks on Pottery, Porcelain & Clay*. Collector Books, Paducah, Kentucky, 1988.

_____. *Complete Book of American Kitchen and Dinner Wares*. Wallace Homestead, Des Moines, Iowa, 1980.

McNerney, Kathryn. *Blue & White Stoneware*. Collector Books, Paducah, Kentucky, 1981.

Miller, C. L. *The Jewel Tea Company Its History and Products*. Schiffer Publishing, Atglen, Pennsylvania, 1994.

Newbound, Betty and Bill. *Southern Potteries, Inc. Blue Ridge Dinnerware*. Collector Books, Paducah, Kentucky, 1980.

Piña, Leslie. *Pottery Modern Wares 1920-1960*. Schiffer Publishing, Atglen, Pennsylvania, 1994.

Roberts, Brenda. *The Collectors Encyclopedia of Hull Pottery*. Collector Books, Paducah, Kentucky, 1981.

Roerig, Fred & Joyce. *The Collector's Encyclopedia of Cookie Jars*. Collector Books, Paducah, Kentucky, 1991.

Saloff, Tim and Jamie. *The Collector's Encyclopedia of Cowan Pottery*. Collector Books, Paducah, Kentucky, 1994.

Schneider, Mike. *California Potteries, The Complete Book*. Schiffer Publishing, Atglen, Pennsylvania, 1995.

_____. *The Complete Cookie Jar Book*. Schiffer Publishing, Atglen, Pennsylvania, 1991.

Stamper, Bernice. *Vallona Starr Ceramics*. Schiffer Publishing, Atglen, Pennsylvania, 1995.

Tefft, Gary and Bonnie. *Red Wing Potters & Their Wares*. Locust Enterprises, Menomonee Falls, Wisconsin, 1981.

Whitmyer, Margaret & Kenn. *The Collector's Encyclopedia of Hall China*. Collector Books, Paducah, Kentucky, 1994.

Also see individual categories for additional bibliographical information.

GLOSSARY OF SELECTED CHINA & POTTERY TERMS

Baker – an open vegetable dish usually with an oval shape; a covered, large dish used for oven cooking.

Biscuit – same as bisque.

Bisque – a porous pottery or porcelain which has not been glazed and generally not useful unglazed in its unglazed state; occasionally not decorated but may have a color trim.

Blank – a plain item most often awaiting a decoration and generally found when dinnerware was manufactured by one company and sold to another company to be decorated.

Crackled glaze – deliberate spider-web effect created by erratic contraction of the glaze coating after firing.

Crazing – numerous unintentional glaze cracks of assymetrical patterns generally caused by heat from normal usage and more often found in dinner and earthenwares.

Embossed – a raised design incorporated into the body rather than applied afterwards.

Flatware – any flat piece of dinnerware such as plates and platters.

Foot – the bottom extension or extensions of a dinnerware dish or a vase, planter, and so on in pottery.

Gadroon – an embossed and sometimes decorative motif or pattern on the rim edge of dinnerware items.

Glaze – a glass-like coating applied to seal a porous body, rendering it non-porous and serving as a protective agent for underglaze decorations.

Ground – the basic body of an item, sometimes on which decorations are applied.

Hollowware – dinnerware having raised sides to hold liquids or other similar foods such as sugar, cream, milk, tea, water and casserole-type foods.

Marmite – a large earthenware soup kettle with a cover.

Matte – a dull glaze.

Overglaze – the application of a glaze over the decoration.

Petite marmite – a small individual casserole with a cover used especially for soups.

Pottery – fired at a lower temperature than porcelain and used as a catch-all term for various clays such as earthenware, redware, stoneware and yellowware.

Relief – a raised design projecting from the body.

Restaurant ware – strong, durable items designed for use in commercial establishments with the decorations (most often names and logos of the businesses) between the glaze and the body that is designed to protect the advertising due to heavy usage.

Rim – the extreme outer part of a dish particularly a plate, platter or bowl.

Sgrafitto – patterns scratched into a layer of slip before firing. An Italian term that was particularly popular with the Pennsylvania-German potters.

Slip – a liquid form of clay with a creamy texture.

Stoneware – a high-fired pottery usually resulting in a durable, non-porous body.

Tab – either a vertical or horizontal ear-type projection (usually solid) used as a handle and generally void of any opening.

Terra cotta – an unglazed earthenware most often used on vases and planters but, with inside glazing, pieces can be used as dinnerware.

Underglaze – a finish applied over a design or decoration which has been put directly onto an unglazed body.

Vellum glaze – a satiny matte finish which gives a softly rich and warm appearance.

Verge – the upward sides of a dish rising from the well.

Vitreous – the glossy surface caused by the fusion of materials at a high temperature.

Well – the bottom of a dish which is usually flat.

APPENDIX A

GENERAL POTTERY, ART POTTERY AND DINNERWARE SHOWS

American Art Pottery Association
Convention and Show
Jean Oberkirsch
125 E. Rose Avenue
St. Louis, Missouri 63119
(314) 842–9119

Pottery Lovers Reunion Pottery Show
Marvin & Jen Stofft, Managers
45 12th Street
Tell City, Indiana 47586
(812) 547-5707
Zanesville, Ohio, July

Pottery Show-Calif.
Al Nobel, Manager
Glendale Civic Auditorium
1401 N. Verdugo Road
Glendale, California 91208
(213) 380-2626
October each year

Bay Area Pottery Show
Martha & Steve Sanford, Managers
Italian Gardens
1500 Almaden Road
San Jose, California
Information: (408) 978-8408
February each year

Roseville's of the Past
American Art Pottery Show
P.O. Box 656
Clarcona, Florida 32710-0656
January each year

APPENDIX B
NEWSLETTERS

American Art Pottery Association
125 East Rose
St. Louis, Missouri 63119

Arts & Crafts Quarterly
9 South Main Street
Lambertville, NJ 08530

Pottery Lovers Newsletter
4969 Hundson Drive
Stow, Ohio 44224

Tile Heritage Foundation
Flashpoint
P.O. Box 1850
Healdsburg, California 95448

Pottery Collectors Express
P.O. Box 221
Mayview, Missouri 64071

APPENDIX C
AUCTION HOUSES

Butterfield & Butterfield
220 San Bruno Avenue
San Francisco, California 91043
(415) 861-7500

Cincinnati Art Gallery
635 Main Street
Cincinnati, Ohio 45202
(513) 381-2128

David Rago
9 S. Main St.
Lambertville, NJ 08530
(609) 397-9374

Treadway Gallery, Inc.
2029 Madison Road
Cincinnati, Ohio 45208
(513) 321-6742

ABOUT THE EDITOR

For nearly twelve years Susan N. Cox has shared her expertise in the field of 20th century American ceramics and glassware through her regular *Antique Trader Weekly* column, "American Pottery, Glass and China." Now she has brought together her years of knowledge and experience to produce a new pricing guide to all types of 20th century American ceramic wares. Susan was a Contributing Editor for Antique Trader Books *Pottery & Porcelain—Ceramics Price Guide,* which appeared in 1994, and now she focuses her attention on the topic of collectible American pottery and porcelain wares produced since the turn of the century, a field of study dear to her heart.

In addition to being a columnist, Susan also edited her own newsletter featuring American ceramics, *American Clay Exchange,* for a number of years while also authoring three books on Frankoma Pottery of Oklahoma.

With this outstanding background, Susan was a natural choice to prepare Antique Trader Books' *20th Century American Ceramics Price Guide*, a truly comprehensive guide to one of the fastest areas of collecting in today's market.

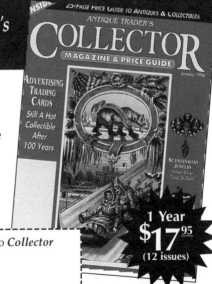

ANTIQUE TRADER WEEKLY

BUSINESS REPLY MAIL
FIRST CLASS MAIL   PERMIT NO.50   DUBUQUE, IA

POSTAGE WILL BE PAID BY ADDRESSEE

ANTIQUE TRADER WEEKLY
PO BOX 1050
DUBUQUE   IA 52004-9969

COLLECTOR MAGAZINE & PRICE GUIDE

BUSINESS REPLY MAIL
FIRST CLASS MAIL   PERMIT NO.50   DUBUQUE, IA

POSTAGE WILL BE PAID BY ADDRESSEE

COLLECTOR MAGAZINE & PRICE GUIDE
PO BOX 1050
DUBUQUE   IA 52004-9969